# Criminal Law in Context

## Sensational Cases and Controversies

*First Edition*

Lindsey L. Runell, J.D., Ph.D.
*Kutztown University*

cognella®
SAN DIEGO

Bassim Hamadeh, CEO and Publisher
John Remington, Managing Executive Editor
Gem Rabanera, Senior Project Editor
Abbey Hastings, Production Editor
Asfa Arshi, Graphic Design Assistant
Kylie Bartolome, Licensing Associate
Natalie Piccotti, Director of Marketing
Kassie Graves, Senior Vice President, Editorial
Jamie Giganti, Director of Academic Publishing

Cover image: Copyright © 2016 iStockphoto LP/gremlin.

Printed in the United States of America.

3970 Sorrento Valley Blvd., Ste. 500, San Diego, CA 92121

# Brief Contents

# Detailed Contents

# Chapter 1

# Foundational Elements of Crime

## Introduction to the Chapter

Crime is generally defined as immoral acts that cause harm to persons and/or property and can range in severity depending on various attendant circumstances, such as personal characteristics of the victim and offender and the type of force used, along with the perpetrator's level of culpability. This chapter provides an overview and discussion of two categories of crime that are central to American jurisprudence, *mala in se* and *mala prohibita* crimes, along with how criminal laws outline the classification of such offenses as either felony or misdemeanor-level crimes. These are basic components of criminal law, so understanding them in the context of actual cases is a crucial part of studying crime. A related concept is that criminal actions are offensive to society as a whole, even though not all individuals within a community are directly impacted by such conduct in a particularized way, because it is the combination of the threatened, perceptual, and actual harms associated with a crime event that justifies the imposition of punitive sanctions on law violators. These objective conceptions aside, not all bad acts are criminalized; some are but less than others in accordance with criminal laws, which create boundaries between immoral or unethical behaviors that are legitimate in some instances and illicit conduct that is deemed more serious and therefore punishable through incarceration or even death. That distinction between *mala prohibita* and *mala in se* crimes will be examined in this chapter through the lens of cases and controversies surrounding JonBenét Ramsey's death, O. J. Simpson's trial, and Joe Exotic's rise to and fall from fame, which reflect those foundational elements of crime.

## *Mala In Se* Crimes

Crimes that are *mala in se*, or "bad in fact," are in direct violation of the Ten Commandments and the layered web of policies and statutes that reflect those directives and are part of the fabric of the U.S. legal system. Living within this society comes with a tacit agreement to uphold those standards, which among others include "thou shalt not kill; thou shalt not steal" (ESV Economy Bible, 2017, Exodus 20:2–17; U.S. Const. amend. V). It is unlawful to take another person's life or property by theft or fraudulent means, and therefore crimes involving that

FIGURE 1.1 *Mala in se* crimes

conduct—such as murder, manslaughter, robbery, and burglary—are classified as felonies, and the punitive treatment of individuals who commit those acts seems logical and perhaps even essential to advancing public safety and crime control interests. Because felony crime occurrences shock the figurative moral compass that grounds society, they are also likely to garner extensive media attention, academic research, and discourse. This sensationalism effect of those crimes that are *mala in se*, or inherently evil, often corresponds to the heinousness of the underlying offense(s) and reflects a general consensus about rule compliance and expectations for people to resolve conflict respectfully through nonviolent means. Homicidal acts that fall within the category of parenticide or pedicide, which are crimes that involve the killing of a parent or child respectively, exemplify this point and when committed become featured news stories that transcend the offender's arrest, trial, and conviction. Persons sentenced for those types of crimes—such Erik and Lyle Menendez, Gypsy Rose Blanchard, and Andrea Yates—are infamous, and the circumstances surrounding their offenses are a mainstay of American popular culture. These, along with other widely publicized cases, will be discussed in detail in later chapters but are mentioned now to elicit critical thinking about how conceptions of serious crimes are formed, perpetuated, and reinforced by criminals and noncriminals alike.

**PAUSE AND REFLECT**

Why do you think certain crimes are so consistently viewed as being especially shocking? For example, why are we more shocked by parenticide than by a murder that results from a robbery in progress? Why are we often more shocked and fascinated by a specific, single instance of murder, like the O. J. Simpson case, than by a mass shooting, such as the recent case in San Jose in which an employee killed nine coworkers?

## Crimes Against Persons

Victim:
JonBenét Ramsey

Defendant:
Unknown

Case in point: What happened to JonBenét Ramsey? That is a lingering question that continues to haunt the American public over 2 decades since her murder, which literally shocked the nation for a host of reasons, but primarily because she was only 6 years old at the time she was killed, and her parents were initially the prime suspects. People also found intriguing that JonBenét was a beauty queen at that young age, having won countless pageants under the tutelage of her mother, Patricia (Patsy) Ramsey, a former beauty queen herself who held the title of Miss West Virginia in 1997. JonBenét was named after her father, John Bennett Ramsey, an entrepreneur and multimillionaire. JonBenét, the child beauty queen, lived with her parents and older brother Rusty in Boulder, Colorado, in a nice neighborhood and comfortable home, a picturesque life with the trappings of the

American Dream. That all changed on the morning of December 26, 1996, when JonBenét went missing literally overnight. Details of JonBenét's death and the ensuing investigation can help further understanding about some fundamental challenges that come with proving the elements of *mala in se* crimes such as kidnapping, (sexual) assault, burglary, and murder through circumstantial evidence and in real-life situations where collected crime scene data might become compromised through the investigative process. From the beginning, it was believed that JonBenét had been kidnapped from her own home on Christmas night in 1996. The next morning her mother awoke to find a three-page ransom note threatening to kill Jon-Benét unless she and her husband paid the author of the note $118,000—coincidentally, the amount of John's recent holiday bonus. The note read: "You will withdraw $118,000.00 from your account. $100,000 will be in $100 bills and the remaining $18,000 in $20 bills" (Sylte, 2016). It also had instructions not to call the police, which Patsy disregarded. Suspicions about the Ramseys' involvement continued to escalate, with the discovery that the ransom note was written on Patsy's notepad with her pen.

Although investigators remained uncertain about who perpetrated the kidnapping, the note seemed to present clear and direct evidence that a kidnapping did in fact occur. The general elements of that crime include the forcible taking or moving of an individual through fraudulent or coercive means (C.R.S. § 18-3-302, 2016). In this case Patsy called the police to report that JonBenét went to sleep in her bed but was not there the next morning and that the ransom note left behind suggested a nefarious reason behind her unexplained disappearance. Law enforcement officers responded to the call that same morning and conducted an initial search of the home but did not find any additional clues as to JonBenét's whereabouts. It was not until the second search, completed later that afternoon, that a detective discovered JonBenét's deceased body in a spare room in the basement that had not been previously checked. The child succumbed to a violent death, which was inflicted through strangulation and blunt force trauma to the head. Clearly, JonBenét was the victim of a murder, which is defined as the unlawful taking of human life. But whether it was a murder of the first or second degree—that is, premeditated, deliberate, or instead malice driven—remained a mystery. Or perhaps the person who took JonBenét's life acted with a lesser intent, like recklessness or negligence, and thereby committed a manslaughter (C.R.S. §§ 18-3-102, 104, 2016).

Either way, JonBenét's killer did assault her, a crime that involves the intentional infliction of fear of harm or unwanted touching, as there were bruises found on her body that were likely caused by the release of a stun gun laser. There was also evidence that a broken brush was used to forcibly penetrate JonBenét's body in a sexual manner, and the use of foreign objects in that way constitutes sexual assault or rape under contemporary laws (C.R.S. § 18-3-402, 2016). Investigators had reason to believe that JonBenét was kidnapped, assaulted, and then murdered. But the lingering and pertinent question was: Who was responsible for these horrific *mala in se* crimes? JonBenét's parents claimed that she was in bed when they went to sleep, and there were no signs of forced entry into the home. The windowpane in one of the basement windows was broken, but John admitted to doing that to gain entry into his home after getting locked out of it at some point prior to the murder. These developments fed speculation about the possibility that JonBenét's killer was an intruder who, by unlawfully entering the basement through the broken window with the intent to commit a felony inside, committed a burglary (C.R.S. § 18-4-202, 2016). It was unknown exactly how long the window had been broken before the murder happened; however, crime scene investigators found spider webs outside of it, a discovery that largely discredited the intruder theory.

Patsy and John Ramsey remained primary suspects for over a decade after the tragedy, until 2008, when the advent of DNA testing revealed no match between their DNA and the biological evidence found in JonBenét's underwear and under her fingernails, which has since been linked to an unidentified male. Later that year, the Ramseys were officially cleared as suspects in the investigation (McKinley, 2016). What happened to JonBenét Ramsey was a tragedy, in that she was kidnapped, assaulted, and murdered in her family home, which was possibly burglarized in the process. The fact that the perpetrator of these *mala in se*, inherently evil crimes has not been identified fuels America's fascination with this case. The 2020 release of the documentary *JonBenét Ramsey: What Really Happened?* was expected to breathe new life into this cold case, with fresh perspectives provided by Lou Smit, a well-known private instigator, who before his death worked tirelessly to uncover what really happened to JonBenét, but to no avail (Schnuur, 2021). The JonBenét Ramsey case and continuing mystery surrounding it illustrate how *mala in se* crimes are harmful both in substance and to the fabric of society (Chang, 2020).

## *Mala Prohibita* Crimes

Conduct that is defined by law as bad, or *mala prohibita*, does not pose a prima facie threat to personal safety or property but could potentially interfere with overarching societal interests in order maintenance, public health, welfare, and safety, depending on the time, manner, and place in which it is carried out. Such actions can legally be performed in situations outside of those proscribed under the law, and that is an important distinction from *mala in se* crimes, which are never permissible under the law per se but can be justified or excused as part of an affirmative defense. Some examples of *mala prohibita* offenses that are recognized in some variation in every U.S. jurisdiction are drug possession, public intoxication, and speeding. One rationale behind criminalizing such actions is to deter more-serious-level offenses—*mala in se* crimes like robbery, assault, or murder—that could conceivably evolve from those activities. Individuals who engage in these and other behaviors that are statutorily categorized as dangerous in context but not in nature generally face less harsh punishments than *mala in se* offenders. However, one important caveat is that *mala prohibita* offenders can face strict liability or punishment for committing such acts, even if done unintentionally. The following excerpt from the Pennsylvania public intoxication statute illustrates both the deterrent purpose and strict liability effect of statutes like this one, which prohibit conduct that is legal in certain circumstances but not others:

A person is guilty of [public intoxication] if he appears in any public place manifestly under the influence of alcohol or a controlled substance … to the degree that he may endanger himself or other persons or property, or annoy persons in his vicinity. (18 Pa. C.S. § 5505, 2014)

Someone who is intoxicated from drugs or alcohol in a public place and while under that influence presents a threat to property, others, or themselves violates the law and does not have to possess any specific level of intent in doing so; therefore, any corresponding punishments are imposed through strict liability—that is, without any regard for that person's culpability or lack thereof. Threatened but not actual harm must be caused by the public intoxication, which reflects how these types of statutes that impose contextual prohibitions on conduct that is otherwise legal are intended to reduce public fear of crime and criminal victimizations.

Those restrictions aside, it is legal in all states for individuals who are over age 21 to consume alcohol in private residences, bars, or other establishments that are licensed to serve alcohol—but not to operate a vehicle after consuming an amount of alcohol that is deemed excessive under the law. Public safety and crime concerns surrounding alcohol use are further advanced by traffic safety laws, which make it illegal for persons with a valid driver's license who are at or above the legal minimum drinking age to operate a vehicle when their blood alcohol content level exceeds the applicable state-based limitation. Like how alcohol is regulated in the United States, persons who meet the applicable state minimum age requirements are eligible to obtain a license or permit to operate a motor vehicle. Driving is legal under those circumstances yet prohibited under others, like while intoxicated by drugs, alcohol or at an excessive speed, given the potential risk of serious injury or death likely to occur from such recklessness. Reckless driving is criminalized as a misdemeanor offense in all jurisdictions but can be used as evidence in a felony prosecution for manslaughter if it results in death. For instance, under Virginia Code § 46.2-852, reckless driving is defined as "driving a vehicle on any highway recklessly or at a speed or in a manner so as to endanger the life, limb or property of any person." Here the term "recklessly" is used to confer reckless intent, which is determined from actions that imply a conscious disregard for human life or safety. Under this definition, speeding is a clear form of reckless driving, which could also occur as a result of tailgating, texting, or talking on a cell phone while driving; failing to properly signal a turn; and driving in a manner that is unsafe due to inclement weather like heavy rain, snow, or ice. *Mala prohibita* crimes are constructed through legislation like the above portion of the

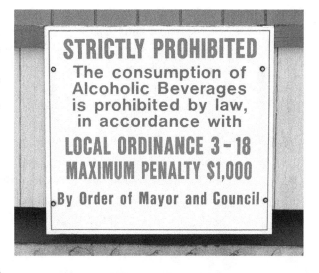

FIGURE 1.2 *Mala prohibita* crimes

Virginia Code, which provides standards for distinguishing between lawful and unlawful driving, based on the manner in which the driving is done. Such statutory prohibitions on actions that are neutral in content but imminently dangerous depending on the attendant circumstances serve important safety and crime control goals that are at the forefront of public discourse. Recent data show that a staggering 70% of serious car accidents are due to reckless driving by a driver who was speeding or under the influence of a controlled substance, and more than 13,000 of these reckless-driving incidents result in death on an annual basis (Insurance Information Institute, 2021). These are powerful reinforcements of actual and potential dangers associated with alcohol misuse and traffic violations.

## Crimes Against Nature

Victim:
Wildlife

Defendant:
Joe Exotic, the Tiger King

Other types of lawful conduct limited by statute in certain instances include hunting or killing animals for any purpose, which is a highly controversial activity but one that is not as widely disavowed as reckless driving and public intoxication. That all changed when Joe Exotic, better known as the "Tiger King," entered the public stage by way of Netflix in 2020. But before delving into that case, it is important to explore the foundations of state and local animal hunting regulations along with federal endangerment statutes and how these laws impose limits on a hobby enjoyed by many: the process of hunting animals and preparing captured prey for food, to display as a keepsake, or to sell. In the United States animal hunting is primarily governed by varying state laws that impose licensure requirements, seasonal and place limitations on when, where, and how people can shoot and kill wild animals such as deer, bear, fish, and rabbit for gaming or food purposes, depending on the type of prey. But under federal law, those very same gaming activities are deemed outright illegal when done against certain animals that are in danger of becoming extinct or whose natural habitats are threatened by human consumption or waste. Therefore, certain forms of animal hunting are *mala prohibita*; that is, deemed illegal in context, through statutory prohibitions, but not because the substance of those actions is bad. The primary sources of federal regulations on gaming and wildlife activities include the Endangered Species Act, Lacey Act, and Animal Welfare Act, which collectively criminalize the "taking" of any fish, migratory bird, plant, plant product, or other wildlife species whose survivability is threatened or endangered as defined under the law. That prohibition is construed broadly to include "harm, harass, pursue, hunt, shoot, wound, kill, trap, capture, or collect any wildlife within the United States" and also the transport through interstate or foreign commerce of any listed animal or raw material for personal gain. It applies regardless of whether the organism is living or dead. However, the taking of endangered or threatened species is permissible under the Endangered Species Act and conferring U.S. Fish and Wildlife Service agency if "incidental to a lawful activity"—that is, done to advance a public interest in wildlife conservation, exhibition, approved research, or educational purpose (7 U.S.C. § 2131, 1996; 16 U.S.C. § 1531, 1970; 16 U.S.C. §§ 3371–3378, 2003).

Tigers are among the growing list of species subject to both domestic and international protection under the Endangered Species Act and the Convention on International Trade in Endangered Species of Wild Fauna and Flora, respectively. An estimated 5,000 tigers are held in zoos, breeding facilities, animal attraction centers, and other forms of human captivity across the United States, compared to about 3,900 tigers living in the wild worldwide. A mere 6% of those places are licensed establishments, which leaves most confined tigers vulnerable to abuse, unhealthy living conditions, and illegal trafficking, which is all exacerbated by the demand for tiger parts in other countries (L. Henry, 2020). Concerns about tiger safety and protection became a household topic of conversation in 2020, with the Netflix release of *Tiger King: Murder, Mayhem and Madness*, a widely popular docuseries based on the life of Joseph Allen Maldonado-Passage (né Schreibvogel) better known as "Joe Exotic" or "Tiger King." At the time of filming, Joe Exotic, as he is aptly called, owned the Greater Wynnewood Exotic Animal Park (GW Park), which he made home to approximately 200 wild cats, including lions, tigers, and "ligers," a lion–tiger crossbreed species. There were more wild cats living at GW Park than in certain parts of Asia. Wolves, reptiles, sloths, monkeys, bears, and lemurs were among other exotic animals held there. As Joe Exotic's popularity grew, so did suspicions about the welfare and health of the animals he bred, owned, and showcased at GW. Oklahoma law enforcement authorities eventually received numerous complaints alleging that some GW lions and tigers were left in cages with, open, insect infested wounds and were severely malnourished. Joe Exotic was later convicted on 17 counts of felony charges for killing five tigers and for selling or attempting to sell endangered species, including tiger cubs, lemurs, and lions, through interstate commerce. He was also charged with filing false documents that claimed those animals would be donated for research purposes, but they were instead sold for personal profit, in violation of the Endangered Species Act and Lacey Act. Although his commission of those *mala prohibita* offenses were highly publicized, they were overshadowed by his involvement in a $3,000 murder-for-hire plot against his rival and fellow wildcat enthusiast Carole Baskin, which is a *mala in se crime*. For years Baskin had fueled through various media outlets suspicions about Joe Exotic's animal abuse and neglect. Ironically, she won a $1 million judgment against Joe Exotic for copyright and trademark infringement and was awarded ownership of GW Park in that settlement. Joe Exotic did not fare as well and is currently serving a 22-year federal prison sentence for attempted murder (*mala in se* crime) and violating the Endangered Species Act and Lacey Act (*mala prohibita* crimes), all felony violations (Borden, 2020).

| | |
|---|---|
| Marijuana possession and use is a controversial topic in criminal law, given that those activities have been legalized in most states for recreational or medicinal uses, yet they are completely criminalized under federal law. Draw from what you have learned about the distinctions between *mala in se* and *mala prohibita* crimes. How do the legalization and criminalization of marijuana fit into those crime categories? | **PAUSE AND REFLECT** |

## Felony and Misdemeanor Crime Classifications

Under the law, both *mala prohibita* and *mala in se* crimes are classified as either felonies or misdemeanor crimes; the difference between those crime categorizations depends on the specific crime, offender, and victim characteristics, such as the use and type of weapon used in furtherance of the crime, the perpetrator's level of intent, whether the victim is a member of a vulnerable group, and the extent of injuries inflicted on the victim. Criminal statutes provide a crucial source of guidance for understanding how those and other attendant circumstances are important in distinguishing when the same criminal act can be charged as a felony or misdemeanor offense. For instance, an assault is generally defined as an intentional act that causes an imminent fear of injury or actual harm to another person; however, such action is defined as a "simple" misdemeanor or "aggravated" felony depending on the context in which it was performed. In Pennsylvania a simple assault occurs when someone "negligently causes bodily injury to another with a deadly weapon" (18 Pa. C.S. § 2701) and is a second-degree misdemeanor. To negligently cause a result means to act without exercising reasonable care, or the same amount of caution that most people ordinarily would. Whereas that same underlying action is treated as an aggravated assault, a second degree felony if the perpetrator acted with a more specific, elevated level of intent and "attempts to cause or intentionally or knowingly causes bodily injury to another with a deadly weapon" (18 Pa. C.S. § 2702, 2014). An aggravated assault is further escalated to a first-degree felony if the victim is a child, officer, school employee or an agent serving on behalf of an officer or school employee. Felony convictions carry a sentence of more than 1 year in prison, while misdemeanor sentences are much less severe and typically require restitution, community service, less than 1 year spent in jail, or probation, and those distinctions carry important implications that extend far beyond incarceration. Individuals with felony criminal records are likely to encounter collateral consequences to incarceration, such as employment and housing impediments, that misdemeanor offenders will not, given the deeply rooted criminal and social stigmas attached to crimes that are defined as felonies; a term that connotes a serious threat to society. Most criminal defendants, whether charged with a felony or misdemeanor crime, plead guilty and in doing so waive their Sixth Amendment right to a jury trial and are then sentenced at a subsequent hearing. But what about those individuals who plead not guilty and choose to go to trial to prove their innocence? More importantly, how do attorneys utilize criminal law at trial to convince jurors to see their position, that the defendant is guilty or not guilty of the crime(s) charged?

### Beyond a Reasonable Doubt

Victim:
Nicole Brown
Simpson and Ronald
Goldman

Defendant:
O. J. Simpson

Criminal laws provide a framework for conduct qualifying as a felony- and/or misdemeanor-level offense, but it is how well the required substantive elements are demonstrated through evidence and coinciding applications of criminal procedures during arrest, investigation, and trial phases that will determine the disposition of criminal charges in an acquittal or conviction. On June 17, 1994, the American public witnessed this firsthand with the nationwide televised broadcast of a police caravan trailing a white Bronco that was cruising along a busy stretch of a Los Angeles highway. This was no ordinary police chase, because Orenthal James ("O. J.") Simpson, a famous former NFL player, just happened to be hiding in the back of that vehicle, which was being driven by his friend, A. C. Cowlings. These events ensued when O. J. learned that police planned to charge him with the double murder of his ex-wife, Nicole Brown Simpson, and her friend Ronald Goldman, which had occurred several days prior, on June 12, 1994. O. J. fled, and an estimated 95 million people were along for the ride, at least figuratively, for the duration of the 45-minute slow-speed chase, which ended in his arrest at his Brentwood, California, mansion. O. J. was subsequently arraigned and pled not guilty to two counts of first-degree murder, thereby invoking his Sixth Amendment right to a trial—which would turn out to be one of the most notorious ones in American jurisprudence. Marcia Clark was the lead prosecutor in the case and had the burden of proving beyond any reasonable doubt that both killings were "accomplished by means of a destructive device, weapon of mass destruction, armor-piercing ammunition, poison, lying in wait or torture or done in a way that is willful, deliberate and premeditated" (PEN § 189, 2019). First-degree murder is a *mala in se*, felony-level offense, and in California individuals convicted of this crime face anywhere from 25 years to life in prison. The stakes were certainly high for O.J. in deciding to go to trial, because in doing so he risked losing his freedom and a multitude of fans and millions of dollars in endorsements that he had accrued throughout his extensive football and entertainment career.

At first glance it seemed that the prosecution's burden of proving the requisite statutory elements of first-degree murder was straightforward, given that both victims were stabbed to death, presumably with some type of "destructive device," and as a result there were copious amounts of forensic evidence found at the primary and secondary crime scenes. Nicole's Brentwood condominium was the primary crime scene, since that is where her and Ron's bloodied bodies were found, along with a discarded left-handed black leather glove, hairs, shoeprints, fibers, and other trace evidence. O. J.'s Rockingham estate, which was located approximately 10 minutes away from there, was the secondary crime scene, and that residence was also linked to the murders through blood and fiber evidence found on O. J.'s (now infamous) white Bronco and in various places throughout the home, like in the foyer, master bedroom, and driveway and on a pair of socks and a right-handed glove that matched the one found at the primary crime scene. Forensic testing done on the collective crime scene evidence confirmed the presence of DNA from O. J., Ron, and Nicole. At trial, the prosecution relied heavily on those details in their attempt to convince the jury that O. J. was the person responsible for committing the murders. They also focused on multiple domestic abuse allegations that Nicole had previously made against him to convince the jury that the murders were driven by purposeful, deliberate, and premeditated intent; offense characteristics that are indicative of first-degree murder. There was scientific and circumstantial evidence in support of the prosecution's theory that O. J. killed his former wife and her friend, perhaps in a jealous rage, but those details did not suffice to quell reasonable doubts about what actually happened to them on the evening of June 12, 1994 (Margolick, 1995).

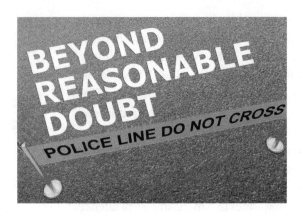

FIGURE 1.3 **Beyond a reasonable doubt**

O. J.'s team of prominent defense attorneys, better known as a "dream team," were able to present reasonable doubt about his guilt by bringing the jury's attention to glaring procedural mistakes made by crime scene investigators. The crux of their position, which also happens to be a major limitation of criminal law, was that the substantive elements of a criminal offense cannot be conclusively proved if the criminal procedures used to obtain evidence of such crime are not performed properly. At trial, the dream team argued that the investigation was flawed from start to finish and highlighted the following examples of how police officers did not maintain proper chain of custody protocols: evidence was collected, personally handled, and not submitted for forensic testing right away; blood samples were contained in plastic instead of paper bags and therefore subject to degradation; and a vial of O. J.'s blood that was taken while he was in police custody was spilled at the laboratory where crime scene samples were also tested, and that presented a serious risk of cross contamination. The defense attorneys then honed their attention on Mark Fuhrman, one of the first police detectives to arrive at O. J.'s Rockingham estate (secondary crime scene), and his racist epithets about evidence fabrication and racial profiling that he had made in a prior interview with Laura Hart McKinney, a screenwriter and professor. A total of 61 redacted interview recordings and transcripts were shared with the jury, who were then left with the question of whether Fuhrman, a White man, might have planted or tampered with evidence to incriminate O. J., who is Black (Fleeman, 1995; Robinson, 2016). The defense devoted specific attention to the now infamous set of gloves, found separately at each of the two crime scenes. O. J., who did not testify in the case, was asked by the prosecution to try on the actual gloves, which did not fit his hands. In a dramatic courtroom showing, the gloves were noticeably too small, and forensic scientists who subsequently testified in court explained that the presence of blood or other bodily fluids like sweat that the perpetrator left on or inside the gloves would not have likely caused that extent of shrinkage in the time span between the crime and trial. All of this, the dream team concluded, presented reasonable doubt that O. J. was the person responsible for murdering Nicole and Ron. As Johnnie Cochran, the lead defense attorney in the case, famously proclaimed: "If it doesn't, fit, you must acquit" (Deutsch, 2014). On October 3, 1995, the nation was still watching when the jury did just that and acquitted O. J. on both first-degree murder counts (Shapiro, 2020).

Less than 2 years later, O. J. was back in the national spotlight when a different jury found him liable, or responsible, for both deaths in a civil lawsuit brought by the victims' families. The judge in that case ordered O. J. to pay $33.5 million to the families of Nicole and Ron for wrongfully causing their deaths. The verdict was announced in a nationwide televised event that was so sensational news outlets scrambled to split resources between it and former president Bill Clinton's State of the Union address, which aired the same day. O. J.'s civil liability for the murders was also newsworthy due to the sheer fact that he had been found not guilty of the same acts in the prior criminal trial. How could that be? Prosecutors must prove the elements of the crime(s) charged beyond a reasonable doubt, which is higher than the standards of proof that are applied in civil cases and is the highest one there is in the entire American legal system. O. J.'s criminal defense team presented reasonable doubt, which led the jury to decide that the prosecution failed to meet that burden and therefore O. J. Simpson was not guilty beyond any reasonable doubt. Instead, the jury that convened in his civil trial had to decide whether the evidence showed it was more likely than not that he was responsible for the deaths; that is, by a preponderance of the evidence. The plaintiffs' attorney was able to satisfy that much lower standard of proof despite lingering questions surrounding key evidence in the case. There is no doubt that O. J. has made an indelible mark on American society, as could be seen in the documentaries *O. J. & Nicole: An American Tragedy* and *O. J.: Made in America*, which cover his criminal trial, acquittal, and more.

## Conclusion

At the core of the American legal system is the classification of crimes according to severity of harm and corresponding threats posed to public welfare and safety. Under the law, the terms "*mala in se*" and "*mala prohibita*" are used to distinguish between conduct that is so harmful that it is unlawful unless legally justified or excused and those actions that are legal but only under certain circumstances. Conceptually, these crime categorizations are helpful to society as whole in understanding the boundaries of permissible conduct with other people, in public places, and in relation to animals and nature. However, "*mala in se*" and "*mala prohibita*" crimes are not colloquial terms, which can make it challenging for some people to fully comprehend important differences between these offense types, along with the nature and impact of them in real-life contexts. Reflect on the cases discussed in this chapter to reinforce these foundational elements of criminal law both conceptually and contextually.

## THINK AND APPLY

Can you recall a true crime event that was widely covered in the news? Consider the facts surrounding it, and use any or all of the following foundational elements to classify the crime(s) involved: *mala in se* crime, *mala prohibita*, felony, and misdemeanor.

## Credits

# Chapter 2

# Sources of Criminal Law

## Introduction to the Chapter

The American criminal justice system is centered on criminal laws that are enacted by each state legislature, the District of Columbia, and the federal government and bound by the scope of the U.S. Constitution. These divergent sources of criminal law are essential to arrest and trial outcomes and are connected through roots in common law and the Model Penal Code, which promotes uniformity among the various state penal codes. This chapter includes a careful examination of the origins of criminal law, the elements of some criminal offenses and affirmative defenses that are contained within it, and also how those rules were distinctly applied in the highly influential and publicized cases surrounding Daniel McNaughten during the 19th century in England; Andrea Yates's crimes, which occurred in Texas at the turn of the 21st century; and the "Central Park Five," a group of teenagers sentenced to prison in the late 1980s for crimes they did not commit. People might be familiar with those sensationalized case details but not as much with the substance of the laws that attorneys drew from and that jurors used in deliberating guilt or innocence of the accused persons in the trials that followed. To truly understand the outcomes of these and other well-known criminal cases and controversies, it is important first to explore the various sources of criminal law on which they are based.

## The Layered Web of Criminal Laws

The United States Code (U.S. Code) is a compilation of federal laws that specify the elements of crimes against the federal government, such as treason or terrorism, or federal employees and other law violations that involve conduct across more than one state, such as drug trafficking and organized crime. Crimes against persons and property—such as burglary, robbery, assault, rape, and murder—along with the corresponding legal defenses are covered in the penal code of each state and the District of Columbia, and it is those types of offenses that typically shock society's collective conscience and become embedded into the fabric of popular culture for decades following the actual crime event. Although state legislation must at least accord with federal law, each state government retains the power and freedom to construct criminal statutes within its jurisdiction that are different from laws in other states prohibiting the same conduct.

For example, murder, which is a form of criminal homicide, is generally defined as the unlawful taking of human life, but each state and the District of Columbia has its own distinct classification system for that offense; however, all include first-degree and second-degree murder categorizations that are framed by distinct levels of intent. Both first-degree and second-degree murder are defined as intentional killings, but first-degree murder must be accompanied by a premeditated, deliberate, or some purposeful intent. In contrast, second-degree murder is not a crime of calculation but one that is inflicted through malice or ill will. Only three state penal codes contain another category of murder, third-degree murder, which is applied to unintentional killings that occur within those jurisdictions, but each one has varying qualifying criteria for that criminal charge. In Florida third-degree murder includes any killing that occurs during the commission or attempted commission of a nonviolent felony. Under the Minnesota Penal Code, prosecutors are required to show a bit more, that the unintentional killing was caused by the perpetrator's reckless conduct or conscious disregard for human life or safety. Both those situations could be covered under the Pennsylvania criminal code, which defines third-degree murder vaguely as follows: "all other kinds of murder [not qualifying as first- or second-degree murder] shall be murder of the third degree" (18 Pa. C.S. §2502). This example demonstrates that divergencies exist in state criminal penal codes even though they share a common source: state-created legislation. In 1962 the American Law Institute created the Model Penal Code to bring uniformity in criminal law across states (American Law Institute, 1985). States are encouraged but not obligated to follow these guidelines, which include robust descriptions of criminal offenses and defenses along with legal commentaries on those topics, or articles as they are referred to in the document. Nearly three quarters of all state penal codes incorporate portions of the Model Penal Code, but only a few include all components of it.

FIGURE 2.1 The layered web of criminal laws

As discussed, all state penal codes contain first-degree and second-degree murder classifications, but only in a few is murder also defined in the third degree. Those distinctions are legal and a legitimate exercise of state legislative powers. So a person who commits a reckless homicide might be charged with third-degree murder in a state where that offense is recognized but not in most states, where either second-degree murder or manslaughter would be possible options in such a case. Should that raise any concerns about justice and whether it can truly be served by the intricate, layered web of criminal laws that are inherent in the U.S. criminal justice system?

## Common Law

Criminal laws also reflect traditional common law concepts, which do not consistently align with the Model Penal Code. Common law, which originated in England, is created by judicial decisions and provides the framework for the American criminal justice system. It has stringent characteristics that do not always bode well under contemporary law; therefore, certain aspects of it have been eliminated from every state penal code, yet others remain an integral part of current law. For example, at common law the crime of burglary was strictly defined as breaking and entering a dwelling or house of another at night with the intent to commit a felony therein. Under that definition, criminal liability for burglary was limited to very specific circumstances and excluded situations in which someone enters a home or building through an unlocked or open door without permission, for the purpose of committing a felony offense inside. Aside from that and other conduct that would not qualify as common law burglary, the temporal "at night" requirement further restricted criminal prosecutions for burglary in the United States. The scope of burglary under contemporary state laws is broader and goes beyond the common law to encompass any unlawful entry into property with the intent to commit a felony inside. In similar ways the requisite elements of rape have evolved over time and depart from common law standards for that offense, which were extended only to male perpetrators and female victims who were not married and required the utmost proof of force, such as eyewitness testimony or physical injury. Rape is now categorized as a gender-neutral offense that can occur through the infliction of constructive or actual force by and against any person regardless of their gender and relationship to each other. Common law rape and burglary are among a host of other traditional legal conceptions that have no place in American jurisprudence, but the McNaughten test for legal insanity does.

### The McNaughten Rule

The McNaughten rule for determining insanity is named after Daniel McNaughten, a Scottish-born merchant who traveled to London in 1842 in preparation to commit a crime that changed the scope of the law in England and the United States. He stayed there for 16 weeks in a rented room, which he specifically chose because of its proximity to 10 Downing Street

Victim:
Edward Drummond

Defendant:
Daniel McNaughten

("Number 10"), where the English Parliament was headquartered during the 19th century. Each day, McNaughten followed a man whom he thought was Robert Peele, a former British prime minister. On January 20, 1843, he lay in wait for "Peele," who was walking back to his office after running an errand at the bank. McNaughten fired a single shot to the man's head, which eventually killed him. But it turned out that the victim was really Edward Drummond, the private secretary to Robert Peele. It was a true case of mistaken identity, but that is not the most notable fact of that case. McNaughten's revelation to police, which he made during his interrogation, was:

> The Tories in my native city have compelled me to do this. They followed me to France, into Scotland and all over to England. In fact, they follow me wherever I go. … They have accused me of crimes of which I am not guilty; they do everything in their power to harass and persecute me. In fact, they wish to murder me (Asokan, T.V., 2007, p. 223).

At trial the defense presented this as evidence that McNaughten was delusional and influenced by paranoid thoughts when he killed Drummond, and therefore his actions should be excused. His attorneys further explained that McNaughten believed that he needed to kill Drummond (whom he mistakenly believed was the British prime minister) to save his own life from being taken as part of a government-orchestrated conspiracy to halt the Chartism movement. As an active member of that group, McNaughten had been a staunch and fearless advocate for labor and political reform during widespread protests that drew national attention and controversy. In his mind, this all contributed to Peele's organized plot to kill him. The jury believed his explanation for the crime and returned a verdict of not guilty by reason of insanity. Public unrest ensued after McNaughten was acquitted and sentenced to a mental asylum for the remainder of his life, and it eventually prompted the British government to formalize a narrow standard for determining legal insanity to prevent the same outcome in future cases with facts similar to *R v. McNaughten* (1843), in which the link between the defendant's alleged mental illness and crime commission was supported by a single statement made during a police interrogation. On January 19, 1843, the McNaughten rule was announced, and according to it, a criminal defendant could only be found not guilty by reason of insanity if, at the time of the crime commission, they suffered from a mental disease or defect and because of that condition did not understand the difference between right or wrong generally or did not know their specific conduct was wrong or criminal in nature (De Fabrique, 2011).

FIGURE 2.2 **The strict McNaughten rule for insanity**

## Model Penal Code

The common law–based McNaughten rule remains the predominant standard for legal insanity in the United Kingdom but not in the United States, where state penal codes are split between using it and the other criteria for evaluating insanity pleas. Over time, the McNaughten test has been intensely scrutinized, particularly among psychiatric and legal experts, because it is so strictly written that it only accounts for specific cognitive dysfunctions to the exclusion of other traits, such as low impulse control, severe anxiety, or depression, which are also known to debilitate mental health and trigger associated deviant behaviors. For those reasons, some state legislators were drawn to the Model Penal Code, which strikes a balance between tradition and science, with an outlined cognitive–behavioral standard for state courts to use in deciding when a defendant's actions should be excused by reason of insanity (Holtzman, 1969; Letman, 1982). Under the Model Penal Code, a person should not be held criminally responsible for an action they committed while suffering from a mental defect or condition under which they lacked the substantial capacity to understand the difference between right or wrong generally or more specifically to act in accordance with the law. This substantial capacity test is much broader than the McNaughten rule, as it permits individuals who commit a crime while experiencing cognitive and/or behavioral deficits to plead not guilty by reason of insanity regardless of whether their ability to understand right from wrong or conform their conduct accordingly was completely lacking or just deficient because of those conditions (Model Penal Code § 4.01). Yet some state laws like Texas Penal Code § 8.01 retain the common law McNaughten rule, which leaves jurors to grapple with applying that stringent standard in cases like the one featuring Andrea Yates, who claimed to be insane when she drowned each of her five children separately.

### Texas Law for Insanity

Andrea Yates is a name that resonates across America and perhaps even around the world. Ironically, her notoriety was born when she was arrested and charged with multiple counts of pedicide for taking the lives of her own children. At the time, Andrea was living in her hometown of Houston, Texas, with her husband, Rusty, and their five children: Mary (6 months), Luke (2), Paul (3), John (5), and Noah (7). Rusty worked as a National Aeronautics and Space Administration engineer, while Andrea stayed at home with the kids, working hard to homeschool them, care for their basic needs, and much more. In a home-footage video that is in public circulation through YouTube, the Yates children are seen wearing costumes handmade by Andrea and acting out parts in a play performed in the family living room. From the outside, Andrea seemed to be leading a happy and fulfilled life, but that was far from the truth. In fact, Andrea experienced postpartum psychosis, overdosed on medication prescribed to treat her depression, and was repeatedly institutionalized for psychiatric treatment from 1994 to 2000, during the 6-year span that she birthed her five children. Postpartum psychosis is a rare and

Victim:
Mary Yates, Luke Yates, Paul Yates, John Yates, and Noah Yates (children)

Defendant:
Andrea Yates (mother)

severe form of postpartum depression that affects only about 10% of women who give birth. Symptoms of that condition include serious delusional thought patterns and behaviors that can hinder the ability to distinguish real from imagined experiences. By 1999 Andrea had four children and was taking the antipsychotic drug Haldol to manage her depression. That same year she attempted suicide twice by overdosing on sedatives and was placed in the hospital, where she received more closely monitored medical treatment. Andrea was treated by several doctors during that stay, one of whom was Dr. Eileen Starbranch, a psychiatrist who advised her and Rusty against having any additional children due to a strong likelihood that giving birth again would worsen her symptoms of psychosis. That advice went unheeded, and Mary, the Yates's fifth and last child, was born in November 2000, but Andrea killed her just 6 months later. Andrea first drowned Luke, then Paul and John, but then paused afterward to carry their bodies onto her bed, where she covered them with a sheet. Mary was killed next and Noah, the eldest and only living Yates child at that time, saw her lifeless body in the bathtub. Noah suspicious of his mother, unsuccessfully tried to escape her wrath. Andrea caught and submerged him underwater in the bathtub until he died, just as she had done to his siblings (Esterbrook, 2002).

Media reports of Andrea Yates, the Texan homemaker and mother who killed her children, roused questions among the public about how any rational person could do something like that. People began to wonder: Was it possible that she was insane? Those suspicions were validated on July 30, 2001, when Andrea pleaded not guilty by reason of insanity to multiple counts of capital murder (CNN, 2020). The case then proceeded to trial with every major news outlet and the public in tow, and the law was at the center of it all. Specifically, Texas Penal Code § 8.01, which reads, "It is an affirmative defense to prosecution that, at the time of the conduct charged, the actor, as a result of severe mental disease or defect, did not know that his conduct was wrong." It reflects the McNaughten rule but from a narrower lens, because in Texas the legal insanity defense can only be raised by persons who claim not to have known that their alleged conduct was in fact criminal or wrong because they suffered from a mental illness. Perhaps one might think of this as a "literal lack of knowledge" about the wrongfulness of the specific, alleged criminal conduct. But the law does not permit defendants to plead not guilty by reason of insanity if their position is instead that due to mental illness, they did not know the difference between right and wrong at all so their actions should be excused. That is like a "conceptual lack of knowledge" about what is considered wrongful conduct generally. In affirmative defense cases, the burden of proof shifts from the prosecutor to the defense. Andrea's defense attorney had to convince the jury that regardless of whether she understood that killing in general is unlawful, she thought it was right to kill her children when she drowned them due to her prolonged postpartum psychosis. Evidence shows that is not an easy task, to convince jurors that a defendant who is competent to stand trial and appears as such is the same person who, while experiencing some symptom of mental disease, committed a crime but did not know that action was wrong. Andrea took her chances even though fewer than 26% of insanity defense cases successfully end in a not guilty verdict (Chiacchia, 2000).

During the prosecution's case-in-chief, they played a recording of the 911 call that Andrea made immediately after murdering her five children. In it, the jury could hear her calm responses, through labored breaths, to the dispatcher's requests for basic information like her name, the ages of her children, whether they or someone else was in the house with her, and the nature of her emergency. Andrea never expressed the specific reason for her call but articulated a need for a police officer and ambulance. She then called her husband at work telling him to come home and that all the children were harmed. Rusty later revealed how alarming that call was, especially since Andrea seemed fine earlier that morning as she was preparing breakfast for their children when he left for work. The responding officers reported that Andrea spoke in an emotionless tone and the clothing she wore appeared to be drenched with water. She immediately admitted to officers to that she killed her children and led them to the bodies, which she had lined up on her bed under a sheet, all except for Noah's, which was still face down in the bathtub. The prosecution argued that Andrea's actions during and after the murders were methodical and intentional and therefore were indicative of capital murder, which they had charged her with. Under Texas law, any person can be found guilty of capital murder who intentionally causes the death of more than one person or any individual under 10 years of age (Tex. Penal Code § 19.03). But the defense's position was that Andrea did not deliberately kill her children but was instead driven by a psychosis-induced compulsion that made her unable to understand the nature of what she was doing. For unknown reasons, one of Andrea's former psychiatrists discontinued her prescription of Haldol, a drug used to treat postpartum psychosis, just months prior to the drownings. Individuals with postpartum psychosis who do not receive the proper medical treatment can have extreme hallucinations and other dissociations from reality. Perhaps Andrea had been experiencing similar symptoms, since she told investigators that she killed her children to save them from the devil, because they were not developing properly. The jury did not think so and returned a guilty verdict on March 12, 2002. Andrea was sentenced to life in prison, but her story did not end there (Lezon & O'Hare, 2006).

In a shocking twist of events, Andrea Yates was granted a new trial in 2005 because the judge who presided in the first one made a mistake in allowing Park Dietz, an expert witness for the prosecution, to testify that an episode of *Law & Order* featuring a mother who drowned her children aired shortly before Andrea did the same. In that trial, the prosecution followed up with evidence that Andrea regularly watched that crime drama series and further implied that she got the idea for how to murder her children from that episode. But that testimony was problematic because *Law & Order* never aired an episode involving that story line; by the time that was confirmed, the jury had already heard the testimony, deliberated, and found Andrea guilty of capital murder. Her attorney filed a motion for a new trial on the grounds that Dietz's erroneous testimony created an unfair risk of prejudice in that the jury might have overvalued it in their determination of guilt. That motion was granted, and Andrea pleaded not guilty by reason of insanity again. This time the jury verdict was in her favor, not guilty by reason of insanity, and in 2006 she was transferred from prison to a mental institution, where she remains today (McLellan, 2006). The name Andrea Yates is known to many and likely to stir vivid recollections of her, the Texan homemaker-turned-murderer—not only because she took the lives of five children, whom she had birthed, but also fascinating is that she did it out of insanity. Over a decade later, people are still watching Andrea Yates through various television shows, which among others include a featured episode on the aptly named series *The Crimes That Changed Us*. The Andrea Yates case is also a landmark in American jurisprudence because it represents a successful application of the insanity defense through the Texas Penal Code, which reflects at least in part the common law–originating McNaughten rule.

**PAUSE AND REFLECT**     Rank the legal tests for insanity covered in this chapter—McNaughten rule, Model Penal Code, and Texas Penal Code § 8.01—in order from narrowest to broadest. Andrea Yates was found not guilty by reason of insanity in accordance with that Texas law, which requires proof that at the time of the conduct charged, "the actor, as a result of severe mental disease or defect, did not know that his conduct was wrong." She was sentenced to a mental institution, where she remains decades later. Draw from the facts of the Andrea Yates case that were covered in this chapter and apply them to the above portion of the Texas statute to explain whether you believe that she was in fact not guilty by reason of insanity.

## Beyond the Law: Extralegal Factors

Criminal law is composed of intricate rules of conduct that are based in common law, amended, and reinforced through the Model Penal Code and federal, state, and constitutional laws. To many, justice is served when a criminal prosecution is conducted following a legal arrest and ends in a fair determination of guilt or innocence made by an unbiased decision maker(s) after close consideration of the law. But the reality is that there are factors outside of the written law that may influence case outcomes; these include media sensationalism, social and political pressures, and fear of crime. These are very palpable, but far less tangible and objective criteria than the formal legalities contained in the common law, statutes, and constitutions. Yet such extralegal factors can shape the trajectory of cases that are quite literally dissected in prime-time news events, plastered on the front pages of local and national newspapers, and then vetted through the court of public opinion—all before an actual criminal trial takes place. What happens when the disposition of a criminal case is driven by the public fear of crime along with concerns and expectations regarding the administration of the law, instead of how closely the evidence aligns with the letter of the law? The crime of the century happens.

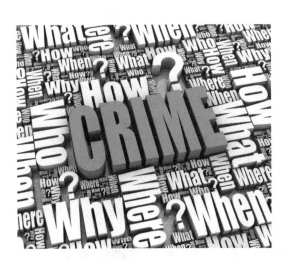

FIGURE 2.3 **Court of public opinion**

## The Crime of the Century

The Central Park Jogger incident otherwise known as the "crime of the century" took place between the late hours of April 19, 1989 and early morning of April 20, 1989. A time when New York City was depicted in the media by unprecedented violent crime rates, a crack cocaine epidemic and crime victimizations (Staples, 2012). People were captivated by the Central Park Jogger case not only because of the horrific circumstances that were involved but also due to these highly sensationalized crime data, which instilled growing tension among law enforcement and the public alike. In 1988 a record-breaking 1,986 homicides occurred in New York City, and most were attributed to the estimated 600,000 drug users who became addicted to crack cocaine during the late 1980s. Crack cocaine, which is cheaper and therefore more accessible than powder cocaine, had a particularly devastating effect among residents of low-income, urban communities of color in regard to addiction and susceptibility to disproportionate punishments imposed under laws that prioritized the criminalization of crack cocaine over powder cocaine. What lay beneath these Rockefeller Drug Laws was the socially constructed assumption that violent crimes were rampant due to a crack cocaine epidemic that was caused and perpetrated by persons of color (Drucker, 2002; Marriot, 1989).

Against that backdrop, America was ready to see what would happen to the Central Park Five, the five Black and Latino males named Antron McCray, Kevin Richardson, Yusef Salaam, Raymond Santana, and Korey Wise, who were ages 14 to 16 when they were arrested in 1989 for the vicious assault and rape of Trisha Meili, a 28-year-old White woman.

Meili had been jogging in Central Park when she was pummeled in the head with a blunt force object, tied to a tree, sexually assaulted, and then left to die. By the time she was found, over 75% of the blood had drained from her body through the extensive injuries she had suffered, which included a dislocated eye, severe skull fractures, and brain swelling. As a result, Meili remained in a coma for 2 weeks following the attack and awoke with no recollection of the events, particularly who was responsible for that horrific incident. Yet the media provided the public with answers that the victim herself could not. On April 21, 1989, just 1 day after Meili's near lifeless body was found, the front-page headline of the *Daily News* read: "Wolf pack's prey—female jogger near death after savage attack by roving gang." The featured article elaborated on more details about how this "wolf pack" was a group of about 30 teenaged gang members who were terrorizing New York City residents through an onslaught of assaults inflicted on a rising count of victims, including a man walking alone from the store, a couple riding their bike, a male jogger, and a taxi driver. This report coincided with police attributing Meili's attack to that infamous wolf pack, and specifically the Central Park Five, who they suspected were members of that gang. The media frenzy escalated once police released the identity of those suspects to the public. Pete Hamill surmised in a published *New York Post* article that they came "from a world of crack, welfare, guns, knives, indifference and ignorance … a land with no fathers … to smash, hurt, rob, stomp, rape." In other news, they were

> Victim:
> Trisha Meili
>
> Defendant:
> The Central Park Five

portrayed as "animals" who had been "wildin'" when they bludgeoned and sexually assaulted Meili (Singleton & Gentle, 2013; Sorkin, 2014).

It appeared that the Central Park Five were guilty in the court of public opinion, but what about under the law? There were no eyewitnesses, and the only scientific evidence collected from the crime scene was DNA found on the victim which did not match any of the suspects. Police just had circumstantial evidence that the Central Park Five had attacked Meili, which meant they, along with the prosecutor, had to present a clear connection between those inferences and the elements of the crimes charged. What sources of law did police draw from in doing so? The starting point is New York Penal Law § 240.10 (2014), which prohibits assembly

> with four or more other persons for the purpose of engaging or preparing to engage with them in tumultuous and violent conduct likely to cause public alarm, or when, being present at an assembly which either has or develops such purpose, he remains there with intent to advance that purpose.

On April 19, 1989, police arrested Kevin Richardson and Raymond Santana for committing this Class B misdemeanor offense, and the two remained in police custody for hours into the next morning, when Meili's body was discovered in Central Park. When police learned what had happened to her, they began to suspect that Richardson and Santana might have been involved, given the proximate time between their alleged unlawful assembly and Meili's victimization. They also called other suspected wolf pack gang members—Antron McCray, Yusef Salaam, and Korey Wise—to the station as part of their investigation. Some say "timing is everything," but criminal laws cannot be enforced against persons based on mere coincidences, so law enforcement attempted to gather more information from all five underaged suspects in what are now considered some of the most infamous police interrogations in American legal history (History.com Editors, 2019).

The Central Park Five confessed to the crimes in separate videotaped recordings, which decades later can be accessed by the public and continuously replayed through various video streaming applications like YouTube. America remains intrigued not only by the graphic nature and specificity of those admissions but more importantly the fact that they were recanted. All five teenagers claimed that police coerced them into making those confessions, after they had spent 24 hours under intense police scrutiny, without food, water, sleep, or contact with their parents or legal guardians. They all pleaded not guilty to charges ranging from rape, robbery, assault, attempted murder, to inciting a riot and thereby exercised their Sixth Amendment right to a trial, where their defense attorneys argued that the circumstances of the police questioning constituted a violation of their Fifth Amendment protection against self-incrimination (Nesterak, 2014). Under the exclusionary rule, created by the U.S. Supreme Court in the landmark *Mapp v. Ohio* (1961) case, any evidence that is obtained through illegal means cannot be used in court, and that limitation extends to violations of rights that are protected under the Fourth, Fifth, and Sixth Amendments to the U.S. Constitution. This rule is also reflected in the fruit of the poisonous tree doctrine, under which the poisonous tree is the unconstitutional act and the fruit is any information that is produced or obtained as a result of that illegality. However, the defense attorneys who represented the Central Park Five case were not able to successfully convince the trial court judge to exclude the confessions, or from their standpoint the "fruit of the poisonous tree." Just the confessions were recorded and not the alleged police misconduct (poisonous tree) that prompted them. For instance, Santana claimed that police told him he would be released if he simply admitted to being present at the scene of the crime. He obliged even though he was never really there, only because he wanted to go home. Police can legitimately use deceitful tactics during an interrogation to elicit crime-related information, but it is well established that juveniles are more likely to make false confessions as a result. Those procedural and constitutional protections aside, the videotaped confessions were played in court, and the jury returned guilty verdicts as follows: Anton McCray, Yusef Salaam, and Raymond Santana were convicted of rape, assault, robbery, and riot. Kevin Richardson was found guilty of attempted murder, rape, assault, and robbery. Korey Wise, who was 16 years old at time, was tried as an adult and convicted of assault, sexual abuse, and inciting a riot. All five defendants were sentenced to 6 to 13 years in prison and remained incarcerated until 2002, when they were exonerated through DNA testing. A semen sample found on the Meili's body was matched to Matias Reyes, who also confessed to the crimes. On December 19, 2002, after years of wrongful imprisonment, the Central Park Five were released and became a national symbol of an egregious miscarriage of criminal law; a situation wherein the law is miscarried or executed without proper fairness and justice (Suddler, 2019). In 2014 they reached a $41 million settlement in a civil lawsuit against New York City for malicious prosecution, racial discrimination, and emotional distress. Five years later, Netflix released *When They See Us*, a four-part series based on the Central Park Five case (Harris, 2019).

## Conclusion

The well-known crimes and controversies surrounding Daniel McNaughten, Andrea Yates, and the Central Park Five represent distinct applications of criminal law and the various sources from which it originates. The McNaughten rule is part of the common law and was created after McNaughten was found not guilty of murder by reason of insanity. That verdict reverberated from England to the United States, where 21 state penal codes include elements of the McNaughten test, which requires defendants who plead insanity to prove their criminal acts resulted from a complete or partial cognitive impairment. But in other states, like Texas, the law regarding insanity reflects standards that depart from common law. That particular distinction was brought to light when Andrea Yates drowned her five children and then claimed she was insane when she did it, having imagined that she was acting as a savior and not a killer. Under Texas law, her defense attorney had a higher burden than what is required under the common law McNaughten test, to prove that Yates did not know that her specific actions were wrong. The common law provides more leeway, allowing defendants the option to also prove insanity by showing an inability to differentiate between right and wrong, conceptually. But the Model Penal Code substantial capacity test for insanity is more comprehensive in that it excuses criminal acts that a perpetrator commits while experiencing cognitive or behavioral deficits. Unlike McNaughten and Yates, the Central Park Five were wrongfully convicted of crimes that the public believed they were responsible for, but the evidence showed otherwise. The cases discussed in this chapter are staples in American criminal culture because of how the law was applied, or not, throughout the trial processes that followed.

## THINK AND APPLY

Different sources of law were used in the cases involving Andrea Yates and Daniel McNaughten, but both applications led to not guilty by reason of insanity verdicts and the subsequent institutionalization of the defendants involved. In contrast, the improper administration of criminal law and procedure resulted in the wrongful convictions of the Central Park Five, who were incarcerated for decades before being exonerated and released from prison. These case outcomes represent clear discrepancies in the law. But what could be done to ensure more consistent and fair applications of the law? Would you recommend any changes to the sources of law (and criminal procedure) discussed in this chapter—common law, the Model Penal Code, Texas Penal Code § 8.01, and fruit of the poisonous tree doctrine—to enhance fairness and justice goals?

*Credits*

Fig. 2.1: Copyright © 2013 Depositphotos/mybaitshop.
Fig. 2.2: Copyright © 2015 Depositphotos/ivelin.
Fig. 2.3: Copyright © 2011 Depositphotos/OutStyle.

# Chapter 3

# The Criminal Mind

## Introduction to the Chapter

Every crime, whether it is committed against persons or property, is defined by an illegal action, the actus reus, and corresponding level of culpability, the mens rea. Both elements are outlined by criminal laws. Statutory clarity requires legislators to enact laws that clearly specify these core components of crime to ensure that people are sufficiently aware of the types of conduct that are subject to criminalization when performed with the requisite mental state, and laws that lack those characteristics could be considered void for vagueness and invalidated.

In the American criminal justice system, persons facing criminal charges are presumed innocent until proved guilty, and prosecutors must prove guilt by showing concurrence between the actus reus and mens rea elements of the crime charged—that the defendant, acting with a certain level of intent, violated, or attempted to violate the law. Concurrence relates to the crime occurrence and the simultaneous connection between the criminal action and criminal intent that constitute it. But a person can only be held criminally liable for voluntary and intentional actions that are both the actual and foreseeable causes of the victimization. What constitutes a crime is spelled out under various sources of federal, state, and common laws; those elements, while distinct, are interwoven and dependent on each other, much like a linked chain. In this chapter, students will learn about the various layers to the criminal mind through in-depth descriptions and contextual examples of purposeful, knowing, reckless, and negligent intent. The infamous homicides committed by Derek Chauvin and Chris Watts are also covered to provide insight into how prosecutors use direct and circumstantial evidence to prove the mens rea components of the crime(s) charged. This material is summarized through an examination of the transferred intent doctrine, which originates from common tort law and continues to breathe life into how criminal liability is constructed under contemporary criminal laws.

## Concurrence

What if someone commits a crime but claims they did not mean to do it? Absent some affirmative defense such as a legal excuse or justification for such behavior, is it not generally unacceptable under the law for someone who is of sound mind to simply say, "I did not mean to do it"? Accidents can and do happen in all aspects of life among children and adults alike, who certainly do not intend for their behaviors to cause harm to other persons or property. But there must be some level of accountability for the performance of conduct that is prohibited under laws that are written with statutory clarity. For example, a vehicular homicide may be treated as involuntary manslaughter if the person responsible for the incident failed to exercise reasonable care while driving by texting or being under the influence of drugs or alcohol. Or that same act might be deemed an accidental killing if the actor was instead sober and attentive to the road but was nonetheless unable to avoid the harm because the proximate cause of it was something outside of their control, like a person running onto a busy highway. Although it is a crime to unlawfully take another person's life, that conduct in itself does not suffice to support criminal charges, because it must be accompanied by a showing of concurrence between it and a corresponding mental state that is defined in the applicable statute. That same principle applies to all unlawful acts and is a core basis for punishment in the U.S. criminal justice system. Both direct and circumstantial evidence are useful in proving that a crime was perpetrated with a specific purposeful or knowing intent or a more generalized mental state such reckless or negligent intent. Direct evidence of criminal intent can be obtained from confessions, video footage of the incident, the defendant, eyewitnesses, victim testimonies, and other case-related information that provides a clear indication of what the offender was trying to accomplish by committing the crime: to harm, kill, or scare the victim? Or perhaps someone else? Less precise is circumstantial evidence, which—just as the term suggests—includes case circumstances that are possible but not conclusive proof of intent, such as a murder suspect who is overheard threatening to kill or seen fighting with the victim prior to the victim's death. Under those circumstances, it can be inferred that the alleged perpetrator planned the homicide or alternatively acted in a heat of passion, and the difference could literally be life or death. Crimes that are done on purpose such as premeditated murder are subject to the harshest punishments, such as life imprisonment and potentially capital punishment, when there are aggravating factors involved, such as a victim who is a child or law enforcement officer.

**PAUSE AND REFLECT**

Have you ever heard the phrase "ignorance is bliss"? Perhaps you might recall someone saying those words who was trying to avoid taking responsibility for conduct that they knew was morally wrong or illegal, by claiming to be ignorant about the wrongfulness of their actions. Adults who are not mentally impaired cannot avoid criminal punishment for illicit conduct by making such declarations. In other words, ignorance is not bliss, at least under the law. However, there are some crimes that are committed unintentionally, by accident, and therefore with no criminal mind. What factors should prosecutors use to distinguish those harms done with no criminal culpability from actions that are driven by some level of culpable intent?

## Categories of Mens Rea

Criminal conduct must be intended in order to be punishable under the law. The four basic categories of criminal culpability that are recognized in the Model Penal Code and reinforced in federal and state-based criminal codes are in descending order: purposely, knowingly, recklessly, and negligently. These categories of mens rea are distinctly defined by statute, yet the differences between them can seem subtle when applied to real-life situations; this gives prosecutors considerable discretion in making charging decisions and jurors ample opportunity to evaluate how well the evidence presented at trial aligns with the elements of the crime(s) charged. Consider the following scenario involving Sam, the shooter, to enhance understanding of these points. Sam picks up his gun, aims it at Jess, and pulls the trigger while exclaiming, "You are going to die!" Jess suffers fatal gun-

FIGURE 3.1 Categories of mens rea

shot wounds as a result. The actus reus is a homicide, or the unlawful taking of a person's life, but the prosecutor must also prove intent. Under these circumstances, Sam acted with a purposeful intent, the highest level of culpability, and the statement he made when firing the gun could be used to prove that he did the shooting on purpose, with a specific intent to kill. Now, consider a situation in which some challenges arise with respect to that evidence. Perhaps the eyewitness who allegedly overheard Sam tell Jess she was going to die has now recanted that statement and refuses to testify. Without that testimony, the prosecutor might decide that the remaining evidence best reflects that Sam acted knowingly, which is also a specific level of intent. In accordance with the Model Penal Code and state law variations of it, a person acts knowingly if they commit an unlawful act knowing that it will almost certainly bring harm to another person or property. Purposeful and knowing intent are distinct categories of mens rea, but both are characterized by a demonstration of the offender's subjective mental state. To prove that Sam acted knowingly, the prosecutor might admit evidence that he is a licensed gun owner and because of that possesses a superior understanding of how guns operate, including that there is a strong possibility that firing a gun at somebody will result in serious injury or death. Other circumstances regarding Sam's experience with guns can also be used to show his awareness about the risks associated with firearms. Since purposeful and knowing intent are the two highest forms of mens rea, any criminal act done with one or both of these levels of intent will be punished more severely. Applying that to the scenario, if Sam killed Jess on purpose or shot at her knowing that her death would likely result, he could face murder charges in accordance with language contained in the applicable statute; for example, in New Jersey, where "criminal homicide constitutes murder when: the actor purposely causes death or serious bodily injury resulting in death; or the actor knowingly causes death or serious bodily injury resulting in death" (NJ Rev. Stat. § 2C:11-3, 2013).

## Establishing Specific Culpability

Victim:
Shannan Watts, Bella Watts, and Celeste Watts (mother/children)

Defendant:
Chris Watts (husband/father)

A criminal act that is done purposely and driven by a specific intent goes beyond a mere desire to inflict harm and is aimed to further achieve a particular injurious outcome. Purposeful crimes are defined by statute and vary by type and nature but share in common some level of deliberation. Such planning and preparation can be seen in the case of Chris Watts, whose methodical murder of his wife, Shannan, their two daughters, Bella and Celeste ("CeCe"), and unborn son sent shock waves across the nation. Chris executed this murderous plot during the early morning hours of August 13, 2018, and then went to work, which was all part of a grand scheme to kill his family, hide their bodies, and act as if they were missing. He hoped that with his family gone, he would be one step closer to starting a new life with Nichol Kessinger, a coworker with whom he was having an affair. On the day of the killings, a friend drove Shanann home from the airport upon their return from a weekend business trip in Arizona, and that was the last time she was seen alive or heard from again. Over the next 24 hours, countless phone calls and text messages to Shannan remained unanswered, and her friends shared their concerns about her whereabouts with police. During that time, police notified her husband Chris who promptly returned home from work to assist them in conducting a protective sweep of the home, in search of clues about where Shannan and their daughters might have gone. One of the responding officers captured on his body camera Chris picking up Shanann's phone from a kitchen counter and in a panicked tone making the ironic revelation that it was her "lifeline" for conducting sales transactions through her consulting business and that she would have never left home without it. The video also shows Chris expressing feigned astonishment as he pretended to discover that Bella's and CeCe's blankets, which he said they always slept with, were missing from their bedrooms. Chris, still in character, playing the role of the vigilant and distraught husband, offered to take the rest of the day off from work to drive the routes that Shannan would usually take to and from the girls' schools or when visiting their friends. He was literally acting for the cameras and continued that performance in live news events, pleading for the safe return of his family, whom he had killed. That charade finally ended when Chris boldly agreed to take a polygraph test and failed it. When investigators confronted him with results, he admitted to strangling Shanann, but claimed to have done that as a reaction to her killing their daughters, Bella and CeCe. Despite those lies, prosecutors had enough evidence to charge Chris with three counts of first-degree murder and tampering with a deceased human body. He was sentenced to life in prison without the possibility of parole. But it was not until several months after spending time in federal prison that Chris finally admitted the whole truth, that he had murdered his entire family on purpose (Collman, 2020).

Chris Watts committed multiple counts of first-degree murder since he acted with "deliberation and intent" in causing those deaths. Colo. Rev. Stat. § 18-3-102 (2021). He told investigators that even though his marriage to Shannan had been troubled for months prior to the murders, the tension between them erupted in a heated argument after her return home from a business convention in Arizona. During that confrontation, Chris told her their marriage was over, and in response Shannan threatened to never let him see their girls and unborn son. Chris became enraged and set his deadly plan into motion by drugging Shannan with oxycodone, which he hoped would incapacitate her and potentially kill the baby; from his perspective either outcome would help facilitate the murders. Next, he strangled Shannan to death by intentionally squeezing on her jugular vein to stop the flow of oxygen to her brain, a purposeful act that reflected his deliberate and premeditated intent to end their marriage and family in order to pursue a more serious relationship his girlfriend. Pursuant to Colorado law and in most jurisdictions, deliberation and premeditation can form within seconds or minutes, as the emphasis is not on quantifying how long the criminal reflection took but rather on the quality and nature of that process; that is, whether a particularized criminal plan was formed. Chris possessed that requisite intent when he firmly pressed onto Shannan's jugular vein until she stopped breathing, which he said he knew had to be done in order to ensure her death and his planned freedom from their life together (O'Leary, 2020). After killing Shannan, he loaded her deceased body into his truck, along with his sleeping daughters, and then drove 45 minutes to an oil field. As Chris shared with police, he knew that drive would take a considerable amount of time, which provided an opportunity to make a different choice and perhaps even turn around, but he chose not to. He drove with a specific purpose, to dispose of his wife's body and murder his children in a place that was familiar to him but not known to law enforcement as a likely crime area. Chris arrived at the oil field, which he had been to on many prior occasions through his work as an operator for an oil company. He knew there were two 20-foot oil tanks on that property, and he used both of them to separately dispose of his daughters. He suffocated CeCe first, which prompted Bella to ask if she would face the same fate. Once again, Chris had a chance to stop when his daughter literally asked him to, yet he continued with his plan, his purpose. He smothered Bella too and then squeezed each girl through a slight 8-inch opening that was at the top of each tank. After that, he made a call to Nichol, his then girlfriend, and his daughters' school to unenroll them. Chris then went to work, where he was conducting business as usual—that is, until police notified him about his wife's possible disappearance. Equally astounding is the fact that Chris Watts murdered his entire family with a specific intention to start a new life without them and also took deliberate steps to transform that plan into reality immediately after killing them. These horrific events are on replay for whoever is watching the Netflix documentary *American Murder: The Family Next Door*.

## Establishing General Culpability

Criminal homicide that is committed recklessly, in the heat of passion, or with negligence may constitute voluntary or involuntary manslaughter, subject to variations in the applicable law. The corresponding maximum penalties can range from 30 to 40 years of imprisonment to potential life and death sentences that convicted murderers face. The basis for that punishment distinction lies in the fact that conduct that is reckless or negligent is less blameworthy than actions committed with a purposeful or knowing intent. Recall the shooting death that Sam perpetrated against Jess, but with the following change in facts. Imagine that at the time of the shooting it was dark and foggy outside, which made visibility extremely limited. Under these conditions, Sam does not see anyone standing within his vicinity, but he thought he might have heard some voices off in the distance. He ignores that inkling and playfully fires his gun into the darkness, and the bullet strikes and kills Jess, who was camping in a nearby, unseen location. Sam could be charged with manslaughter in New Jersey and other states where culpability for that crime is based on a showing of recklessness, which is generally defined as a conscious disregard of a substantial and unjustifiable risk. Recklessness is a general type of intent and is characterized by both subjective and objective elements of proof. If Sam were charged with manslaughter, the prosecutor would have to first show that he was aware of the possibility of injury associated with firing the gun into the darkness yet proceeded with that action anyway. It is important to note that this level of awareness is one of mere probability and therefore not the requisite certainty that is needed to demonstrate a knowing intent. What is considered probable or not probable is judged according to the objective component of the recklessness standard; that is, conduct that a reasonable person would view as posing a substantial (but not certain) and unjustifiable risk. Going back to the scenario, although Sam did not know that Jess was lurking in the darkness when he fired the gun, he did hear some muffled voices; even that aside, most people would assume that there is a substantial risk that some unseen person could be shot by the stray bullet. In addition, there was no justification for Sam's behavior, as it was not driven by necessity, such as in defense of self or others. Based on those facts, Sam could be found guilty of manslaughter for recklessly causing Jess's death due to his conscious disregard for the substantial and unjustifiable risk of bodily injury or death that arose from shooting a gun into a dark public place (see NJ Rev. Stat. § 2C:11-4, 2013; A.R.S § 13-1103, 2018).

This is the essence of a general intent crime, which is executed with recklessness or negligence and therefore not done in order to achieve a felonious outcome or with certainty that one will occur. Although both reckless and negligent intent are general forms of mens rea, they are distinct in that negligence covers the lowest level of culpability and is akin to unintended mistakes. Negligent conduct falls outside of how a figurative "reasonable person" is expected to behave under ordinary circumstances. In theory, it is easy to imagine this reasonable person as the ever-prudent driver who never drives above the posted speed limit or as the diligent business owner who, when a customer spills a beverage on the floor, promptly posts a warning sign so customers know to avoid the slippery surface and also notifies them through the intercom system before cleaning it up. However, in reality things can go awry in the sense that even reasonable people might get distracted or misjudge a situation and in doing so perform conduct that falls below the standard of care that this imagined, legally constructed "reasonable person" would use in a certain situation. If unintended yet unreasonable conduct results in harm to persons or property, the individual responsible for it can face criminal punishment and/or civil liability for being negligent. Applying this to the scenario of Sam the shooter, Sam could be found negligent for shooting Jess if he had no prior experience with firearms and was simply admiring the gun while touching the different parts on it when he accidentally tugged too hard on the trigger, which emitted the fatal bullet. A jury could find that an ordinary reasonable person in that situation who was unfamiliar with guns would have been more careful and perhaps not have touched it. If the defendant in a negligence case has a specialized skill, knowledge, or expertise, then the trier of fact will be instructed to adapt the reasonable person standard in consideration of those particular qualities. For instance, a central inquiry to allegations of police misuse of force against citizens is discretion and whether the accused officer misapplied the considerable power that gives them the freedom to determine when force is necessary to protect the public and maintain order, based on the totality of circumstances. That was the question on the forefront of everyone's mind when George Floyd stopped breathing and died after Derek Chauvin, a police officer at the time, kneeled on his neck for 9 minutes and 29 seconds.

## Criminal Recklessness and Negligence

Since May 25, 2020, most Americans have grown familiar with the phrase "I can't breathe," which George Floyd repeated approximately 20 times while Derek Chauvin knelt on his neck, and it lives on in a presidential speech, popular song lyrics, signs, clothing, murals, statutes, and so much more (Biden, 2021; K. Henry, 2020; Peter, 2020). There is no doubt that Floyd's death ignited a spark through protests across the nation and even around the world, which garnered the attention of major news outlets, politicians, social justice activists, law enforcement advocates, and others.

Victim:
George Floyd (civilian)

Defendant:
Derek Chauvin
(former police officer)

The manner of Floyd's death was shocking in itself, but another sensational element of this case was that he was Black male, and Chauvin is White and was a police officer; a racial/power differential that some believed motivated Chauvin to use deadly force. Chauvin has openly denied that race was a motivating factor in his decision to use a knee hold to subdue Floyd on that fateful day in 2020; however, that remains a subject of debate in public discourse and media coverage. But what is not debatable is the law and the applicable portions of the Minnesota Criminal Code. On May 29, 2020, Chauvin was arrested, along with other responding officers, for his actions in connection with Floyd's death. He was arraigned; pleaded not guilty to charges of second-degree unintentional murder, third-degree murder, and second-degree manslaughter; and with that set into motion what would become the first criminal

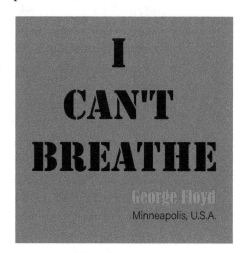

FIGURE 3.2 I can't breathe

trial held in a Minnesota state court to be televised and broadcast (nationally) live. People were tuned in to see Chauvin in real time and more importantly whether a jury would find that he was criminally responsible for Floyd's death or instead that he was innocent, having exercised ordinary care and discretion such as a reasonable police officer in his shoes would have done. On, April 20, 2021, a jury found him guilty on all counts charged, which was seen as a victory to many but an aberration of justice to some. Minnesota laws on second-degree unintentional murder, third-degree murder, and second-degree manslaughter provide an anchor in this sea of opinions and thereby common ground for understanding why jurors decided that Chauvin recklessly and negligently caused Floyd's death (Levenson, 2021; Sepic, 2021).

Under Minnesota law, third-degree murder is defined as an unlawful killing (actus reus) that is done with a reckless intent (mens rea). Recall that recklessness is generally described as a conscious disregard for a substantial and unjustifiable risk of bodily harm or death. Section 169.195 MN (2021) similarly stipulates that

> whoever, without intent to effect the death of any person, causes the death of another by perpetrating an act eminently dangerous to others and evincing a depraved mind, without regard for human life is guilty of murder in the third degree.

This seems applicable to the case, as there is no indication that Chauvin had a set plan or purpose to end Floyd's life by kneeling on his neck. Instead, he claimed to have used that tactic to detain and arrest Floyd for attempting to use counterfeit money. But the issue was whether he was so careless in doing so that he disregarded Floyd's safety and well-being. The jurors decided that he was, based on uncontested evidence that Chauvin continuously pressed his knee into Floyd's neck while Floyd expressed that he could not breathe over and over again; a crowd of onlookers, including an off-duty firefighter, pleaded with him to release that hold and check for a pulse; and Floyd's body moved uncontrollably from resultant seizures. This illustrates how a perpetrator can be made aware of imminent risks associated with their actions based on the totality of circumstances and that consciously ignoring such circumstantial awareness can have both fatal and criminal consequences. Jurors also found that Chauvin's negligence was a contributing factor in Floyd's death and that he was therefore guilty of second-degree manslaughter pursuant to Section 609.205 MN (2021). Specifically, he exhibited "culpable negligence" in using his knee to block Floyd's airflow for approximately 9 minutes and thereby created an "unreasonable risk" of "death or great bodily harm," which occurred as a result (Section 609.205(1) MN, 2021). Culpable negligence requires a level of intention that is more defined than the mental state of someone who accidently brings harm or even death upon another person.

Criminal liability for negligent conduct—in other words, culpable negligence—is based on the reasonable person standard, which as you may recall is the obligation that people have to be as careful and diligent as this figurative reasonable person, who makes sound choices in every situation. There are instances in which the reasonable person standard is customized to account for specialized knowledge or expertise that is attributed to certain individuals like lawyers, doctors, and police officers and that they are expected to utilize in their respective profession. Chauvin was a law enforcement officer on duty when he killed Floyd, and so in order to prove negligence, the prosecutor had to show that Chauvin's conduct fell below the ordinary standard of care that police officers exercise when deciding whether to use force, and particularly deadly force. At trial, Minneapolis Police lieutenant Johnny Mercil, a use-of-force trainer who testified for the prosecution, revealed that officers in the jurisdiction where Chauvin worked are trained to only apply pressure holds when needed to subdue a resistant suspect, to the shoulder or back areas and not on the neck. Mercil confirmed records indicating that Chauvin participated in use-of-force training in 2018, at which time he learned that and other best practices for de-escalating interactions with citizens to minimize the potential need for use of deadly force. Applying these standards to the facts, Mercil conceded that it was reasonable for Chauvin to initially use force against Floyd, who communicated his resistance to being in placed in the squad car. But Mercil added that such use of force was no longer justified after Floyd was handcuffed, on the ground, and compliant. The defense countered by arguing that even then Floyd remained a threat, given the presence of fentanyl and methamphetamine in his system at the time of his death. That aside, the jury found that it was unreasonable for Chauvin to hold Floyd down with his knee since he was trained to do otherwise, and such culpable negligence and conscious disregard for Floyd's life were the primary causes of his death, according the chief medical examiner assigned to the case. Chauvin was also convicted of unintentional second-degree murder for killing Floyd through the infliction of substantial bodily harm, which is considered a third-degree assault and felony offense in Minnesota (Associated Press, 2021a; Neuman, 2020; MINN STAT §§ 609.19, 609.223, 2020). At Chauvin's trial, his defense attorney claimed that he never intended to kill Floyd and instead was performing his law enforcement duties to serve and protect. Yet a jury found him guilty of three counts of homicide based on circumstantial evidence of his recklessness and negligence, which illustrates how general intent can be conceptualized and proved under the law.

## Transferred and Constructive Intent

A core principle of the American legal system is that criminal convictions must be supported by a voluntary admission of guilt or proof beyond a reasonable doubt that the defendant committed the crime, with the corresponding level of specific or general intent. However, real-life situations are more complex in that there may be concurrence between the actus reus and mens rea, but the outcome of that intentional criminal action may not be what the perpetrator actually planned for or expected to happen. The common law tort doctrine of transferred intent provides guidance for when criminal punishment is imposed in cases in which things go wrong in the sense that the offender intentionally commits a criminal act, but that intention is misdirected, which results in harm to someone or something other than the intended crime target. Based on that principle, once a defendant formulates a criminal plan to carry out an intentional tort and, with it in mind, perpetrates an assault, battery, false imprisonment, kidnapping, or infliction of emotional distress, that criminal mindset is constructed by the attendant circumstances of that accompanying criminal act. Under the transferred intent rule, the specific intent behind those intentional torts is constructed as a fluid concept that, once established, can be linked to whatever person or thing is injured as a result of the unlawful conduct. There are variations in how this doctrine is applied under contemporary state laws, but generally the underlying intentional conduct must be complete, the harm must be reasonably foreseeable, and there must be sufficient proximity between it and the harm caused to the unintended victim. It is important to note that in tort law, civil liability for transferred intent is limited to the commission of intentional torts, such as the ones listed earlier; these are characterized by a higher level of culpability, such as purposeful or knowing intent, making such tortfeasors responsible for punitive damages that exceed the monetary amount needed to compensate a plaintiff for their harm suffered. The transferred intent doctrine is rooted in common and tort laws, and there is a well-established framework for applying it in intentional torts cases. But reliance on it as a basis for criminal punishment stirs concerns about fairness and justice, since individuals convicted of specific intent crimes can face life imprisonment or death, which is unequivocally more than just having to pay punitive damages to their victims.

**PAUSE AND REFLECT**

As discussed, prosecutors have discretion to decide when someone who has broken the law and claims to have done so by accident is criminally culpable because they should have known better or were careless in their actions. The point is that not all accidents are criminalized, but some are, depending on the totality of circumstances surrounding a particular case. Should that same principle be applied to transferred intent cases, thereby absolving some criminal actors of any responsibility for actions that they committed on purpose but with the intent to harm someone other than the affected victim? After all, unintentional conduct is what accidents are made of, right?

In most jurisdictions, criminal punishments may be imposed pursuant to the transferred intent rule if the illicit action was purposeful or driven by knowing intent, the action is completed, there is sufficient proximity between it and the harm caused to the unintended victim, and the resultant injury is reasonably foreseeable. For crimes that require a showing of recklessness or negligence, courts are not so inclined to transfer the offender's general intent to harm to an unexpected victim in order to satisfy the mens rea element of the crime charged. Recall that recklessness and negligence are prescribed the lowest levels of blameworthiness for careless actions and unreasonable behaviors, respectively. So the transferred intent doctrine is rarely applied to cases in which the requisite mens rea for the crime charged is recklessness or negligence, since in those instances, the defendant faces criminal punishment for making a miscalculated judgment and because of that not foreseeing the injurious consequences of their actions. Although, in accordance with the law, the fictitious reasonable person would have possessed such foresight and avoided engaging in the reckless or negligent behavior that the offender carried out. In that regard, someone who acts recklessly or negligently engages in risky behaviors because they are not careful and considerate of how their actions might threaten public safety, but they lack any specific intent to bring harm. It seems futile to also punish such individuals for harm that is further attenuated from their reckless or negligent action through some interference, when they do not even calculate the dangers that are directly connected to their initial action that set the chain of events into motion.

In contrast, potential criminal liability for specific intent crimes is widened under the transferred intent rule, which is used to punish offenders who perform an unlawful act with the specific goal of causing injury or expecting that particular result. Such criminal conduct is driven by purposeful or knowing intent, the highest levels of culpability, which denote foreseeability and also the intentional infliction of harm; therefore, criminal liability is imposed for the harm caused, regardless of who or what actually suffered such harm. This rationale is illustrated in the following hypothetical situation. Suppose that Cathy wants to stab her friend Jane, who has betrayed her. Cathy reaches for a knife with the intent to use it for that very purpose. She raises the knife above her head in preparation for what she knows will be an effective stabbing motion. Jane's husband, Joe, who is standing next to her, sees what is about to happen and suddenly intervenes by stepping in front of his wife to protect her. Cathy brings the knife down at the exact same time, stabbing Joe to death. She is shocked by the unexpected turn of events and defends herself against first-degree murder charges for Joe's death on the grounds that she never planned to kill him. In most jurisdictions, Cathy would nonetheless be charged with first-degree murder, as there is sufficient evidence that she had formulated and possessed a deliberate and premeditated intent to kill Jane, which is constructively transferred to Joe. Based on these facts, prosecutors would also have the discretion to charge Cathy with the attempted murder of Jane. In sum, the transferred intent rule acknowledges the seriousness of conduct driven by a purposeful or knowing intent by constructing a figurative connection between it and any foreseeable injury that results from it.

## Conclusion

The criminal mind is multidimensional and can be described using the categories of mens rea, which include purposeful, knowing, reckless, or negligent intent in accordance with the statutory language. Criminal laws hold the key to understanding a person's level of culpability, if any, for the commission of an unlawful act, as such rules provide a baseline for distinguishing between actions that are specifically done to inflict pain or death and those that might be equally harmful in effect but not in intent. Draw from the divergent events leading up to the arrests, convictions, and incarceration of Chris Watts and Derek Chauvin to conceptualize the criminal mind, and more importantly how it varies by offender and is so closely tied to the offense charged and supporting evidence of it. The criminal mind is not an abstract concept, but instead made up of one or more categories of mens rea, which must be carefully applied through corresponding laws and based on evidence of intent directly obtained from the offender, implied through their actions, and in some cases measured against the ever-prudent reasonable person who does no harm.

## THINK AND APPLY

In this chapter, you read about two fictitious legal concepts, the reasonable person and transferred intent, and how both require a judge or jury to stretch their imaginations in considering whether, based on the evidence, a defendant should be found guilty of a crime and if justice would be served by that outcome. The reasonable person standard and transferred intent doctrine are intangible yet inherent components of the American legal system. Taking that into consideration, do the reasonable person and transferred intent rules help facilitate or complicate understanding of the criminal mind?

### Credits

# Chapter 4

# Criminal Acts

## Introduction to the Chapter

For many it is easy to envision criminal acts, especially ones that are sensationalized in print, televised, and social media forums that offer instant and continuous access to cases and controversies surrounding Chris Watts, Andrea Yates, Nicole Brown Simpson, George Floyd, and so many more. You should be familiar with these names of victims and offenders whose lives ended or forever changed with the commission of a homicide, the most serious and egregious harm against persons and society in general. Those illegal acts are commonly represented in the media and also a popular topic in public discussions, but there are countless other violent and nonviolent crimes—such as burglary, robbery, assault, kidnapping, identity theft, and credit card fraud—that constitute felony- and misdemeanor-level offenses. But before these classifications can even be made, there must be some inquiry into whether a particular bad act is one that can be punished under the criminal laws or is merely just offensive to humanity. These two concepts do not necessarily accompany one another, since not every immoral act is against the law, even though all crimes, by their very nature, are deemed wrongful as *mala prohibita* or *mala in se*. This chapter will take readers back to the basics, first with a careful look into what constitutes criminal acts—volitional movements and culpable omissions, including the difference between preparatory and complete actions—and then an in-depth examination of the elements of inchoate or incomplete crimes of solicitation, conspiracy, and attempt. It draws from the infamous cases involving Gabriel Fernandez and Amy Fisher (the "Long Island Lolita") to provide readers with an enhanced and comprehensive understanding of criminal actions in both content and context.

## Criminal Omissions

Criminal acts can be performed through either conscious movements or inaction when there is an imposed duty under the law to do something. Much like how physical movements are prompted by signals that are initiated from the brain, the "physiology of crime" includes a voluntary criminal action or inaction that is triggered by some level of intention, whether purposeful, knowing, reckless, or negligent. From this perspective, both criminal acts of volition and omission can be analogized to the human body, which under ideal circumstances functions in a way similar to the operation of a well-oiled machine that has all working parts moving synchronously but is also susceptible to dysfunctions that can occur when one or more parts breaks down or there is a disconnect between them. For instance, there are certain expectations that come with purchasing a car, which at the most basic level includes a warranty that it will work and provide a reliable form of transportation. What if shortly after the car is purchased, it no longer starts and simply stops doing what it is supposed to? The buyer will most likely feel frustrated over the broken promise made by the car retailer, that they were making a sound investment in an operable and reliable vehicle, and may be entitled to just compensation or a new vehicle depending on the terms of that agreement. Similar to a purchase warranty, the law promises protections from harm afforded by individuals who have a duty to act with care and in consideration of others. These legal duties to act are distinct, based on the context of the relationship from which they arise, and are imposed on help-giving professionals such as doctors, educators, social workers, emergency aid volunteers, parties to a contract, social hosts, and parents. The obligor, or person who is obligated to protect others due to their status in one or more of those positions, can face criminal liability for failing to uphold any of the corresponding duties imposed under the law. For instance, medical doctors take an oath to continuously learn and apply the best practices when administering health care services, and any failure to do so could result in a malpractice suit and even criminal punishment for negligence. Even persons who do not work in the medical field have a duty to do no harm if they voluntarily assume the risks of injury that can occur from helping another person in need of emergency aid and are obligated to take reasonable actions to avoid worsening their situation. Contractual duties also arise from the formation of an underlying promise, whether implicit or explicit, to give another party what they bargained for or expected. Those are distinct from parental duties, which in American culture inherently require more from mothers, fathers, and legal guardians, who must provide their children with basic necessities, protect them from any foreseeable dangers, and otherwise avoid neglecting or imposing harms on them. This societal expectation is reinforced through a host of state and federal laws that make it

FIGURE 4.1 **Child abuse and misuse of care**

a misdemeanor or felony crime for any person who bears one of those relationships to a child biologically or through guardianship, foster, or adoption to intentionally disregard such responsibilities. Recall from Chapter 3 that there are four basic levels of criminal culpability that exist under the law and span from willful to negligent conduct, so parents who do not purposely act to hurt their children could still be held accountable for omissions of care that are the direct and proximate cause of such an outcome. That is what happened to Pearl Fernandez, who committed criminal acts against her son Gabriel Fernandez through neglect (omission of care) and abuse (volitional act).

## Omissions of Parental Care

On May 22, 2013, Pearl Fernandez called police to report that her son Gabriel Fernandez was not breathing and unresponsive, which set into motion the unraveling of one of the most horrific cases of child abuse and systematic neglect in the history of American justice. Pearl failed to nurture and protect her son as any reasonable mother is expected to do for an 8-year-old child, and so did the child welfare system. Many people were deeply disturbed by news reports that painstakingly detailed what Gabriel had endured over the course of his short life: prolonged starvation, confinement to a box for 8 months and then to a dresser with handcuffs, persistent beatings and BB gun shootings, forceful feedings of cat feces, and no medical attention. He was officially declared brain dead just 2 days after first responders removed him from the home that he shared with his mother and her boyfriend, Isauro Aguirre. There was no doubt that Gabriel was literally tortured to death, given what the medical examiner discovered on his deceased body, which among other injuries bore skull fractures, missing teeth, lung lacerations, deep bruising, brain swelling, contusions, and burn scars. But investigators still needed to interview Pearl to determine whether she committed any criminal acts or inactions that led to her son's untimely death. During those conversations and later at trial, Pearl remained firm in her stance that she had never acted with any ill will toward Gabriel or had any other intention to hurt him. Nonetheless, there was sufficient circumstantial evidence to show that Pearl had planned his death, through the infliction of severe and relentless acts of abuse and neglect upon him. She and her boyfriend were both charged with first-degree murder for the "unlawful killing" of Gabriel "with malice aforethought" and premeditation (Penal Code 187 PC, 1996). Blood spatter marks collected from the crime scene were substantial and linked to Gabriel through DNA evidence and testimony from his siblings, who recalled countless instances of him being strangled, beaten, and pepper sprayed by Pearl and Isauro. The autopsy test results substantiated this and also that Gabriel's body was significantly malnourished due to prolonged starvation and having consumed items such as cat fecal matter that have no nutritional value. With the release of this information came questions about how a mother could do something like this to her own child. Equally concerning was that Gabriel showed visible signs of physical and emotional abuse, which his teacher at school, along with a security guard who worked at a public welfare office, diligently reported to social workers and police, who failed to properly investigate those allegations or remove him from the home, instead believing the boy's fabricated explanations for those injuries.

The American bystander rule relieves people of any blanket duty to help another person in need, but there are exceptions to it that apply to situations in which a duty of care arises from contractual, professional, parental, or voluntary obligations. Pursuant to most state laws—including California, where Gabriel lived—it is considered a misdemeanor for social workers, law enforcement officers, and teachers not to report suspicions of child abuse or neglect (Cal. Penal Code § 11164, 2001). In the face of mounting public pressure, prosecutors had to decide whether the inactions on the part of the social workers and police officers who

> Victim:
> Gabriel Fernandez, son
>
> Defendant:
> Pearl Fernandez, mother

had reason to believe that Gabriel was being abused constituted crimes of omission under the applicable Child Abuse and Neglect Reporting Act (CANRA). This was breaking news, which threatened to overshadow Gabriel's death itself, since nationwide there are scarce cases of social workers charged with criminal negligence due to omissions of care and none in California. The prosecution had to start by delving into the relevant case-related information that was known to those mandatory reporters, since under the law their obligation to report is triggered by actual or perceived knowledge of child abuse or neglect even if such suspicions are unconfirmed at the time. On April 23, 2013, just about a month prior to Gabriel's death, Arturo Martinez was working as a security guard at the Department of Public Services when he observed the boy, his mom, and siblings enter that building to apply for public assistance. Martinez later testified at trial that he called 911 immediately after seeing them to report that Gabriel was "sad, full of bruises, with (17 to 23) cigarette burns on the back of his head, neck, lacerations" (Stuelp, 2017). He also noted that Gabriel kept rubbing noticeable bruises on his wrists, which he surmised were from being tied up. After hearing all of this, the 911 dispatcher informed Martinez that he should instead call the nonemergency line, which he did, also providing his and Gabriel's home addresses. Eventually, an officer did visit Gabriel at home and saw his bruises but concluded they were from falling off a bike and not a sign of parental maltreatment. Coincidentally, by that time in late April 2013, officials at the elementary school that Gabriel attended were increasingly alarmed by the open wounds on his head, surrounding chunks of missing hair, and statements he made with others. Jennifer Garcia, his teacher at the time, revealed that in her trial testimony and specifically how Gabriel had asked her if it was normal for a mom to hit a child with the metal part of a belt and to bleed afterward. During those talks, Gabriel also said his mom punched him in the mouth and repeatedly shot him with a BB gun. Following protocol, she communicated that information to the school principal, who then directed her to notify the Department of Children and Family Services (DCFS). This seemed the logical next step and aligned with the applicable Penal Code § 273d PC (2011), which makes child abuse a crime and defines it as the willful infliction of cruel or inhuman physical punishment or injury that is traumatic and considered an unreasonable disciplinary action against a child. Stefanie Rodriguez, the social worker assigned to the case, went to Gabriel's home and noted that he was bruised but concluded that was the result of an accident, as he suggested, and not any parental abuse (Pocklington, 2020; Stuelp, 2017).

The story of Gabriel Fernandez's short 8-year life is overshadowed by the horrendous abuse, neglect, and torturous death that he suffered at the hands of his own mother and her boyfriend, and those details have been broadcast nationwide and sensationalized in the Netflix original documentary *Trials of Gabriel Fernandez*. Of particular interest is what happened to the individuals whose criminal actions, both volitional and indifferent, were the cause of those horrific events. Both his mother, Pearl Fernandez, and her boyfriend, Isauro Aguirre, were convicted of first-degree murder with the special (aggravated) circumstance of torture. Since Pearl pleaded guilty, she received a life sentence without the possibility of parole, but Isauro did not and was sentenced to death. There were also four caseworkers from DCFS who were informed of the child abuse allegations and saw that Gabriel was physically harmed yet failed to remove him from the home. The prosecutor also charged each of them with one felony count of child abuse but not for violating CANRA, which obligates them as social workers to report such suspicions to administrators within their department or law enforcement and makes it a misdemeanor offense not to. Shortly after, a judge dismissed those charges on the grounds that the caseworkers never had custody or control over Gabriel and therefore could not be held responsible for perpetrating, even if indirectly, any acts of force against him (Burke, 2020). What happened to Gabriel is unthinkable, but even more tragic is how it happened—through his mother omitting her primal responsibility to care and protect him from harm and her boyfriend, who allegedly got satisfaction from hurting him, along with the structural inequities in the California child welfare system (at the time). Since Gabriel's 2013 death, the California DCFS has been revamped to reduce caseworker loads and enhance training and mentorship for employees. But perhaps people wonder as they watch the trials of Gabriel Fernandez on the news and in documentaries if more should have been done. Do you?

As discussed in this chapter, criminal charges and prosecutions were filed against individuals whose conduct contributed to the torture and death of Gabriel Fernandez, a process that has been publicized through the media. A much-less-discussed aspect of that case is how criminal laws were applied in that case and specifically the prosecutor's decision to charge the social workers involved with felony counts of child abuse and not for violating their mandatory duty to report suspicions of child abuse and neglect, which arises under the Child Abuse and Neglect Reporting Act (CANRA). What do you think was the rationale behind that charging decision? Would you have done things differently? Explain.

**PAUSE AND REFLECT**

## Volitional Acts

A volitional act is a voluntary movement that is triggered by some level of intention and may constitute an *actus reus,* or criminal act, if done in violation if an applicable criminal law, even if the performed action falls short of what the actor actually intended to do. Inherent in the American legal system is the idea that adults should be held accountable for any harms or potential harms that arise from their engagement in illicit or risky behaviors, as such conduct is presumptively intentional, whether driven by purposeful, knowing, reckless, or negligent intent. This is a rebuttable presumption that can be countered through showing that even though the defendant performed an overt act such as an aggravated assault, it was motivated by some factor outside of their control and not volition. For instance, a defendant's medical history may be relevant to showing that their criminal conduct was not volitional and was outside of their control because they were experiencing unanticipated effects from prescribed medication or symptoms related to a dysfunctional health condition such as epilepsy. Courts are split as to whether that type of information will suffice to disprove actus reus, and much depends on the facts of a case, particularly whether the defendant knew or had reason to believe they were prone to having uncontrollable bodily movements. Determining whether a criminal act is volitional is sometimes easier said than done, as complications can arise in cases wherein the defendant claims their actions were prompted by an unconscious thought. But once the actus reus of crime is established, the focus of the law then turns to what the criminal actor did: just preparing to commit a crime, taking some steps in furtherance of their intended criminal plan, or completing everything they intended to do. Such conduct is distinguishable as preparatory, inchoate, and complete crimes, yet all are punishable under criminal laws, which aim to protect against both actual and threatened harms.

## Preparatory and Inchoate Offenses

The topic of criminal punishment garners quick, steadfast public attention and disagreement over how it should be imposed, especially when it comes to incarceration, which is viewed by some as the key to unlocking crime control and others as just a cog in a cycle of crime, imprisonment, and reoffending. It is debatable which method of criminal punishment is best for the collective good of society, but one thing for certain is that people generally expect criminal punishment to effectively serve some crime-reduction goal, such as deterrence, retribution, rehabilitation, incapacitation, or reentry. That is the rationale behind the criminalization of criminal conduct that does not go beyond the planning stages or consists only of a preliminary attempt, solicitation, or conspiracy that never comes to fruition. Preparing to commit a crime is like preparing to cook a meal, a process that typically begins with deciding what to cook and evolves with choices about which ingredients are needed and a plan for how those items will be made into a meal. Most people will fail in their attempts to cook a meal without taking some time to plan. The same holds true for overt, criminal acts, which are in essence the product of conscious thought or lack thereof about how to obtain the desired outcome of the crime, whether it is money, fame, respect, fun, or something else. Just like preparing to cook a meal, a motivated offender who is considering dealing drugs might start by purchasing that product and carrying it with them as they continue to identify potential clients and formulate a plan for making sales. Even if those acts do not culminate in any actual drug sales, they would still constitute illegal drug possession. The elements of that preparatory offense are actual possession of a controlled substance and actual knowledge of the character and nature of the item. Under the doctrine of constructive possession, individuals who lack physical control over drugs can still be charged with "possessing" them if such substances are located within their reach or proximity, such as the closeness of a glove compartment to a passenger in a car. Actual intent to use or distribute is not a required element of drug possession, which is criminalized in order to deter individuals from taking any steps closer to selling drugs, because just like cooking an unplanned meal, selling drugs without possessing the right product is likely to be a recipe for disaster.

As you learned in this chapter, drug possession charges must be supported by evidence that the defendant had actual or constructive control over the controlled substance, which they knew were illicit drugs. Outside of someone confessing to having such items on their person or within reach, those elements must be proved by circumstantial evidence, which means the prosecution has the burden of fitting all case-related information into a puzzle for jury members to make logical inferences about what the defendant knew or had reason to know (see *United States v. Torres*, 2010; *United States v. Tran*, 2009). In cases like these, what factors do you think should be relevant to the consideration of whether the alleged drug possessor had actual knowledge about what they were carrying?

## Attempt

Inchoate offenses cover incomplete criminal actions, yet unlike preparatory offenses, such conduct brings the perpetrator even closer to the crime commission through an attempt, solicitation, or conspiracy. All crimes present a threat to society, but inchoate crimes do so especially, since such acts are unfinished—which leaves people to speculate: What if the perpetrator had successfully executed their criminal mission to hurt, steal, kill, or rape? What harms would have been inflicted on the victim and possibly others? Attempt crimes can be classified as a misdemeanor or felony offense in correspondence

FIGURE 4.2 **Drug possession, a crime of preparation**

with the seriousness of the crime that was attempted and the applicable statute(s). The requisite elements are that the perpetrator possessed some level of intent to commit a crime and took simultaneous actions in furtherance of it, which for some reason did not achieve the intended crime. In accordance with federal law and most state penal codes, actions that constitute a criminal attempt must be driven by a "specific intent" to cause a particular harm or injury. Attempt charges merge with charges for the targeted crime if achieved, which means a person cannot be charged with both offenses. Complete attempts occur when the criminal actor performs every element of the intended offense, but because of some factor or influence outside of their control, the crime is not actually executed. But an attempt is incomplete if the actor instead fails to take all steps needed to perform the crime due to intervening circumstances.

The following scenario between Albert and Bob will help illustrate the difference between complete and incomplete attempts. Assume that Albert wants to shoot and kill Bob. In preparation for that crime, Albert purchases a firearm and learns how to use it. His actions go beyond that planning stage when he lies in wait to pull the trigger once Bob arrives home from work. Not only does Albert possess a gun that he intends to use to shoot and kill Bob, but he follows through with that plan by firing a single bullet toward Bob when Bob exits his vehicle. Bob is startled by the sound of the gun and quickly darts away from the approaching bullet, which just misses his head. Albert attempted to kill Bob, but whether it was a complete or incomplete attempt is dependent on the facts, how closely his actions came to the unlawful taking of human life; the actus reus of homicide and his intended purpose. Albert's attempt to kill Bob was complete when he fired the gun toward that intended victim because there was nothing left for him to do except hope for the anticipated outcome. The fact that Bob was not struck and possibly killed by the bullet was wholly due to him moving and not any inaction on Albert's part. However, if instead Albert never pulled the trigger because a police car drove past or a neighbor walked by, that would be an incomplete attempt because his intention to kill remained steadfast even though his efforts toward achieving that goal did not. Incomplete attempts include those and other situations in which the actor renunciates or gives up on the planned criminal action before finishing it due to some external interference and not by their own will or volition.

Both incomplete and complete attempts are punishable under the law, and the available defenses to those crimes are limited in both number and scope. For instance, a renunciation or abandonment of the criminal objective is only a defense if it is both voluntary and complete. A voluntary and complete renunciation occurs when an offender changes their mind about committing a crime and also reinforces that retraction by stopping the crime from progressing any further (18 Pa. C.S. § 901, 2014; Tex. Penal Code Ann. § 15.01, 1994). Another possible defense to attempted crimes is impossibility, whereby an offender tries to avoid punishment for their criminal attempt by claiming that the crime could never have been fully performed due to facts unknown to them (factual impossibility) or because the intended illicit actions were not illegal at the time (legal impossibility). In the United States factual impossibility is not recognized as a viable defense, since regardless of whether the crime could have possibly been achieved, the defendant still possessed the intent to break the law. Accordingly, "it shall not be a defense to a charge of attempt that because of a misapprehension of the circumstances it would have been impossible for the accused to commit the crime attempted" (18 Pa. C.S. § 901(b), 2014). In context, a factual impossibility could be applied to an instance in which a shooter points a gun at their intended victim and pulls the trigger only to discover that there are no bullets in the gun. What that person intended to do, which is commit an aggravated assault or homicide by unlawfully shooting another person, remains illegal even though the absence of bullets in the gun made that outcome impossible; therefore, such actions constitute a punishable criminal attempt. A different situation arises when the unfinished criminal act would not be considered illegal had it actually been performed. In that case of legal impossibility, the actor engages in conduct with the mistaken belief that it is illegal, but it really is not, so it would have been impossible for them to violate the law had they successfully completed the act that they misperceived as a crime. Legal impossibility is a viable defense to a criminal attempt charge because what the defendant did is not punishable under the law, and it could be applied to scenarios such as this: Betty, who just turned 21, lives in a state where recreational marijuana use is legal. She never bothered to read the applicable law, and relying on what a friend tells her, thinks that 25 is the minimum age to purchase recreational marijuana. Betty goes to a licensed dispensary, selects some edible products that are on sale, and approaches the cashier. She sees the customers in line before her showing their IDs and becomes nervous that she will get in trouble for what she thinks will be an underage purchase of marijuana. Betty puts down the edibles and quickly leaves the store. Although Betty walked into the dispensary with the specific purpose to conduct an underage purchase of marijuana and took steps to achieve that goal, it was legally impossible for her to do, since she met the statutory age requirements for the purchase of recreational marijuana. Legally, she could not be charged with any criminal attempt.

Renunciation (abandonment) and legal impossibility are affirmative defenses that can be raised by persons charged with a criminal attempt who admit to performing some conduct in furtherance of an unlawful offense yet argue that their actions were not the nature and type of behaviors that the law was designed to criminalize. Criminal laws provide defendants with such opportunities to raise affirmative defenses, since there is no deterrent value served by punishing them for conduct that they voluntarily and completely stopped or that was never against the law to begin with. Both renunciation and legal impossibility excuses are limited in scope, but defendants are likely to face particular challenges to asserting a renunciation defense. Recall the elements of the renunciation defense, which is a voluntary and complete abandonment of the criminal objective, as evidenced by some action that thwarts the crime in progress. But at what point do actions done in progress toward a crime become so close to that planned offense that even if stopped, the renunciation could not be considered complete? The answer depends on which of the following four tests is used in a particular jurisdiction—probable desistance, res ipsa loquitor, proximity, and substantial steps—to determine whether a complete or incomplete attempt could be punishable. These legal standards are distinctly focused on certain aspects of the defendant's conduct and designed to measure the sufficiency of such behaviors toward advancing the criminal goal. In doing so, these tests expand opportunities for individuals to contest criminal attempt charges, beyond the limited renunciation and legal impossibility defenses, which is also an incentive for crime avoidance.

The probable desistance and res ipsa loquitor tests are centered on what actions the offender has left to do in order to complete the crime, whereas the proximity and substantial steps tests measure what they have already done in efforts to facilitate the crime. Each of these standards is aptly named after the specific aspect of the attempted criminal behavior that it is intended to measure. In applying the probable desistance test, courts will look at how much was done, beyond mere preparation, to perform a criminal act, and the key inquiry is: Based on those circumstances, is it probable that the defendant would have desisted or stopped had it not been for something or someone getting in their way of finishing what they had started? We will draw from a hypothetical situation, involving Jeff the attempted arsonist, to further enhance understanding of this and the other standards. Jeff wants to set his neighbor's house on fire as revenge for cutting down his beloved tree, and he purchases a container of gasoline, matches, and lighter fluid to do it. With these materials in hand, he walks over to his neighbor's home and pours the lighter fluid and gasoline onto the structure but is unable to light the match due to extremely strong wind conditions. At that moment, Jeff changes his mind and decides not to follow through with his original plan. Based on everything that he had already set up for the arson, it is probable that he would not have desisted from it had he been able to light the match on his first try. Similarly, that evidence supports attempted arson charges under the res ipsa loquitor or unequivocal test. The Latin term "res ipsa loquitor" translates to "the thing speaks for itself," and as applied to inchoate offenses, it provides a basis for criminal liability when the conduct in question plainly shows an attempt to commit a crime. So, a court could find that since Jeff intended to set his neighbor's house on fire, purchased inflammatory materials, poured them onto the home, and then unsuccessfully lit a match while standing near the structure, there is no doubt that he would have completed the arson had the wind been on his side. In other words, by both the probable desistance and res ipsa loquitor standards, there was nothing left for Jeff to do except light the match, which he had already attempted to do.

The proximate and substantial steps tests are based on what the offender has already done to progress toward completing the intended crime, rather than what they have left do. Jeff would need to do more than douse the property with lighter fluid and gas and unsuccessfully light a match for his conduct to be considered substantial or close enough to the arson. So, now assume that he lights the match and reaches down to activate the fluid and gas but has

a change of heart before starting the fire. Although Jeff did not follow through with his plan, he came so close to it that arson would be a reasonably foreseeable consequence of the actions he had already taken to achieve that result. The substantial steps test is a part of the Model Penal Code and was created to bring consistency across the various processes that courts use to evaluate whether a crime was attempted, or rather the conduct was more attenuated to the offense and therefore preparatory. Under it, the criminal attempt must be proved by an overt act or omission that constitutes a substantial step in a planned crime that is corroborated by additional evidence of the offender:

FIGURE 4.3 Criminal attempts: pieces of a crime

lying in wait; enticing the victim to go to the scene of the crime; investigating the potential scene of the crime; unlawfully entering a structure or vehicle where the crime is to be committed; possessing materials that are specially designed for unlawful use; possessing, collecting, or fabricating materials to be used in the crime's commission; and soliciting an innocent agent to commit the crime. (Model Penal Code § 5.01(2), 1962)

In May 1992 the nation was reeling from vivid news reports about how 16-year-old Amy Fisher had infamously taken a substantial, proximate step toward killing the wife of her adult boyfriend.

## Attempted Murder

The name Amy Fisher certainly resonates with many people who can recall back to May 1992 when it was plastered across television screens, newspaper articles, and tabloid magazines. She was only in high school, but the media dubbed her the "Long Island Lolita" with the emergence of details about her work as an escort, which she later claimed her 38-year-old boyfriend, Joey Buttafuoco, encouraged her to do for extra cash. Their ages and intimate relationship together made Amy a victim of statutory rape, but that sensational story was overshadowed by her criminal attempt to kill 37-year-old Mary Jo Buttafuoco, who was married to Joey Buttafuoco at the time. Amy obtained a .25 caliber handgun and with it approached the Buttafuoco residence and rang the doorbell. She waited patiently at the front door until Mary Jo appeared and then shot her directly in the face. Shockingly, Mary Jo survived the bullet wound but was left with facial paralysis and severe hearing loss. There was no homicide, but did Amy attempt to commit one? The prosecutor alongside the American public audience believed she did, and Amy Fisher was promptly charged with attempted murder. News reports revealed that Amy had been enraged by Joey's refusal to end his marriage to Mary Jo and wanted to take her life as revenge. With that, the prosecutor found probable cause that she intended to kill Mary Jo and "also engaged in conduct which tends to effect the commission of such crime" (N.Y. Penal Law § 110.0, 2014) by purchasing a firearm and using it to shoot her intended victim. In accordance with that law, Amy had completed an attempt to murder Mary Jo, and the nonfatal outcome of her consequences did not diminish her culpability. But she was offered a plea deal, which allowed her to plead guilty to reckless assault rather than face a trial for attempted murder. Amy took it and received a 5-to-15-year sentence but was released from prison after just 7 years. In true sensational fashion, Amy Fisher's saga continued even through her imprisonment when Joey Buttafuoco was indicted on 19 counts of statutory rape, sodomy, and child endangerment for his alleged sexual affair with her. He also received a plea deal, pursuant to which all those charges were dropped except for a single count of statutory rape, which he pleaded guilty to and was subsequently sentenced to 6 months in jail. Even though Amy Fisher served a reduced sentence as part of a plea deal, what cannot be diminished is what she did, which constitutes a criminal attempt under any of the four standards discussed in this chapter (Killelea, 2017; Schemo, 1992).

| Victim: Mary Jo Buttafuoco |
| Defendant: Amy Fisher |

## Solicitation

Solicitation is another inchoate offense, and just like attempted crimes, it involves the performance of an illicit act done with an intention to achieve a certain criminal result. An important distinction between those inchoate crimes is that solicitation requires involvement from more than one person, whereas criminal attempts can be done by a single individual. Prostitution and murder for hire are examples of solicitation that have been popularized through television and media culture. Perhaps you can recall one of the countless *Dateline* NBC News episodes in which a husband or wife solicits someone, usually an undercover police officer, to kill their spouse. In the recorded conversation played during those airings, the solicitor can be heard saying how they want the murder to happen, how much they are willing to pay, and other relevant details that can later be used as evidence of solicitation. Under federal law, a person can be found guilty of solicitation who intends to have another person commit a violent felony and with that mindset makes some expression of that intent in a way that "strongly corroborates" their intended goal, such as through commands, inducement, or other "endeavors to persuade such other person to engage in such conduct" (18 U.S. Code § 373, 1984). Statutory definitions of solicitation vary but similarly contain broad language for describing the various types of conduct that might qualify as an act of solicitation. In addition, the actus reus component of solicitation is minimal compared to the other inchoate crimes of attempt and conspiracy. The crime of solicitation is complete once the criminal actor expresses in some way their desire to have another person do something in violation of the law, and no additional steps need to be taken satisfy the elements of proof. This is in contrast to how attempted crimes are construed under the law, on the basis of whether the defendant took enough actions in furtherance of the planned offense. In solicitation cases, the key inquiry is whether there is sufficient evidence to corroborate the criminal request; no matter how it was made and factual impossibility, that the request could not have actually been carried out, is irrelevant. Factual impossibility is never a valid defense to inchoate offenses, since the purpose of criminalizing such incomplete actions is to deter more serious illicit conduct, such as completed crimes. That is particularly relevant to solicitation cases, due to the circumstantial nature of the offense and the inherent possibility that the person who is solicited to commit the criminal act, whether it is a police decoy or private citizen, might in fact lack any intention of bringing that criminal plan to fruition. As per the federal government, "it is not a defense to a prosecution under this section that the person solicited could not be convicted of the crime because he lacked the state of mind required for its commission" (18 U.S. Code § 373, 1984). Persons charged with solicitation may raise the affirmative defense of renunciation by showing that they abandoned the criminal plan and thwarted the desired crime. Such abandonment must be voluntary and complete, and therefore a product of the criminal actor's own volition and not influenced by any factor outside of their control, such as a fear of getting detected or apprehended by police. But if the solicited crime is actually carried out, the defendant can be charged as an accessory for aiding and abetting it but not for solicitation, because that inchoate offense merges into the completed, solicited offense.

## Conspiracy

A commonly used expression in American culture is "two heads are better than one," which people might say to exemplify the power of collaborative thought, teamwork, and success. In colloquial terms, that mantra is used to highlight the distinct value in efficient critical thinking and decision making that often occurs when people combine their energy and resources rather than work independently. But there lies the core danger of conspiracies, or agreements that are formed between two or more persons to commit an unlawful act. When multiple individuals are united by a specific criminal objective and formulate a plan to carry it out, their desired crime is furthered by joint efforts that could make it more impactful than it would be if there were just one perpetrator. Conspiracy is a specific intent crime, and that mens rea element is reflected by evidence that one or more conspirators purposely entered into an agreement to commit a crime with the intention to facilitate it (Model Penal Code § 5.03(1) (a), 1962). Under this unilateral rule, only one party to the conspiracy must possess that specific intent, which in turn could be established even in cases wherein one of the conspirators is an undercover police agent or someone else who participates in the agreement but has no intention of ever following through with it. The more stringent bilateral rule bars conspiracy convictions in those situations because it requires evidence that each conspirator intended to form the criminal plan on purpose, to achieve that illicit outcome. In most U.S. jurisdictions, the unilateral rule is used to evaluate criminal intent in conspiracy cases, and proof of the underlying criminal agreement must be substantiated by an overt act. A conspiratorial agreement can be created through words or actions or can be formalized in writing and is typically demonstrated through circumstantial evidence. The overt act in furtherance of it could be minimal, such as conduct done in preparation for a crime commission, but not quite enough to constitute a criminal attempt. For instance, assume that Abe and Lincoln plan to rob George at gunpoint and then purchase the firearm that they intend to use for the crime. Both actus reus elements of conspiracy are satisfied: The criminal agreement was made, and the firearm purchase is an overt action in furtherance of it. However, that transaction would not suffice for a criminal attempt charge, because that action would not bring them close enough to completing the crime.

Once the criminal act and intent elements of conspiracy are proved, the parties to that purposeful agreement can be held liable for crimes committed by a coconspirator in further-ance of it and any foreseeable consequences of such actions pursuant to the Pinkerton rule. Courts will consider the nature and type of role that each conspirator had and weigh close involvement in preparing to commit the crime toward finding it reasonable to hold a party accountable for actions taken by their crime partner due to their collaborative facilitation of a criminal plan (*Pinkerton v. United States*, 1946). The Pinkerton rule applies even if a coconspirator does not know every other party to the agreement, so long as they are aware that there are others involved in it and committed to the criminal objective, such as in chain conspiracies and wheel conspiracies. A chain conspiracy operates like an assembly line, if you could envision one that starts with the machine conductor turning on the equipment and placing the product on it, and then each worker standing in place ready to perform a distinct function in the manufacturing process. Similarly, a drug manufacturer gets the product ready and then releases it down a line of drug workers, from a kingpin, to large- and small-scale drug dealers, and finally the costumer. Each person has a different role or criminal objective, yet they all share in common the same agreement—to move drugs. In contrast, a wheel conspiracy features a single ringleader who is at the hub of this wheel or criminal agreement, such as in a gang. From that central position, the gang leader directs members to commit various crimes for the purpose of obtaining money, respect, or power for the gang. Each person who joins the gang understands their purpose and agrees to facilitate it. These examples illustrate that in both wheel and chain conspiracies, the involved coconspirators can still be held liable for agreeing to commit a crime in concert with others and purposely facilitating it and any foreseeable actions done in furtherance of it, even though they may not personally know every other person who is connected to it. Punishment for conspiracy varies according to state penal codes, which impose sentences that correspond to or are lower than the most serious crime targeted by the agreement, or equivalent to a misdemeanor sanction. States also retain the discretion to punish a conspiracy more harshly than the underlying crime. After all, conspiracy is the only inchoate offense that does not merge into the completed, agreed-upon crime. Conspirators are also uniquely subject to expansive criminal and civil sanctions under the federal Racketeer Influenced and Corrupt Organizations Act (RICO), which applies to both state and federal law violations. But renunciation is an affirmative defense to conspiracy and requires a defendant to show that they decided not to follow through with the criminal plan and also stopped it from being executed. That abandonment must be voluntary and complete, so not motivated by any influences external to the defendant's free choice.

## Conclusion

Criminal acts or the actus reus of crime include omissions and volitional acts, and both are multidimensional concepts. The law only criminalizes culpable omissions or inactions if the criminal actor was supposed to do something but did not because of their professional or personal relationship to the person harmed, a contractual agreement, or voluntary choice to assist. What happened to Gabriel Fernandez represents a harsh reminder of the importance of parental and systematic care systems and the harms that can result when people who have a duty to administer such care fail to do so. Criminal acts can also be performed through volitional movements, which must be voluntary but not necessarily complete. Incomplete crimes, better known as inchoate offenses, consist of illicit behaviors that fall short of an actual crime commission and are instead an attempt, solicitation, or conspiracy to violate the law. They are distinguishable by separate mens rea and actus reus elements, but all can be disproved upon a showing of renunciation that is both voluntary and complete. Decades after Amy Fisher attempted to kill Mary Jo Buttafuoco, her story lives on as an example of why inchoate crimes are punished under the law.

### THINK AND APPLY

Draw from what you have learned in this chapter and rank the inchoate offenses of attempt, solicitation, and conspiracy in order from least to most serious, and explain your reasoning.

# Chapter 5

# Parties to Crime

## Introduction to the Chapter

This chapter covers crimes of complicity, which involve more than one person working in concert to break the law through the performance of specific and distinct behaviors that are done with intention to achieve an illicit outcome. It provides an overview of the common law definitions of complicity, which designate principals in the first and second degrees, accessories before the fact, and accessories after the fact and accompanying behaviors that distinguish them. In most state laws and federally, those standards have been consumed into two general categories: principals and accessories (or accomplices), which describe the main criminal actor and their assistants respectively. These classifications are reflected in contemporary criminal laws and are more expansive than the common law to encompass situations that involve collaborated criminal efforts among individuals whose participation is evident but not so strictly quantified by one category or another. As a result, accomplice liability covers an array of actions that are performed with the intent to aid and abet a crime commission, and whether such conduct is done before, during, or after the actual crime is not dispositive. Similarly, there is uniformity in corresponding punishments imposed under criminal laws that hold all accomplices equally responsible for any law violation that the principal committed and both the principal and accomplice(s) desired to happen. That derivative punishment principle is examined in this chapter through discussions of the crimes involving Patty Hearst and Jaycee Dugard, which occurred in different decades but stunned the nation just the same. Both cases also raise some important policy considerations related to how accomplice intent and acts are substantiated under the law. The natural and probable consequences doctrine further extends accomplice liability to any crimes that are considered a

FIGURE 5.1 **Complicity**

foreseen outcome of the aided and abetted offense, but it is rarely invoked given the harshness of it. The case of Lilo Brancato Jr. is a highlighted example of how the probable consequences doctrine is limited in application. In this chapter readers will learn about the mens rea and actus reus elements of complicit criminal behaviors, legal standards used to punish such crimes, and important ways that accomplice liability can be distinguished from and overlaps with inchoate offenses and vicarious liability.

## What Is Complicity?

What is complicity? Better yet, how do complicit crimes compare to conspiracy, which is distinctly an inchoate offense but one that also involves multiple participants? Recall from Chapter 4 that crimes of attempt, solicitation, and conspiracy are classified as inchoate because they make up some parts of a crime but not all parts that complete it. Conspiracy is distinguishable from those other inchoate crimes in that it requires a complicit agreement formed between at least two people and some action done by one of those parties in furtherance of that criminal objective. It also does not merge into the completed crime, which means that persons can face criminal charges both for conspiring to commit a crime and committing that planned offense. This is where criminal laws that govern accomplice and conspiracy liability converge. An individual who aids and abets a crime through words, overt acts, or other supporting conduct might have also conspired to commit that offense and taken other preliminary steps to achieve it. If so, they can be charged with both conspiracy and aiding and abetting a crime in accordance with contemporary accomplice liability standards, which qualify minimum assistance such as mere words of encouragement as sufficient evidence of complicity. For instance, assume that Abby and Lucy decide to rob a bank at gunpoint and have an agreed-upon day and time to execute their plan. Before then, Abby obtains a firearm to use during the robbery, which is an act done in furtherance of the conspiracy and in some jurisdictions can be enough to subject both her and Lucy to punishment for that crime. As the date of their planned robbery quickly approaches, Abby hands over the gun to Lucy and reminds her to display it to the bank teller before demanding the money. Lucy does just that on the day of the robbery, which prompts the frightened bank teller to hand over $20,000, all while Abby waits in the getaway car. Although Lucy was the principal who committed the crime, Abby aided and abetted it by providing Lucy with the gun that was used during the crime, telling her to use it, and providing an escape vehicle. In most jurisdictions, there would be no need to decipher whether she was an accessory before or after the fact, such as what was required at common law. In simple terms, Abby was an accessory to a bank robbery that Lucy committed, and therefore both could face liability for that crime and the conspiracy from which it was born.

Generally, contemporary criminal laws depart from the stringent common law categorizations of accomplice liability, which included principal in the first degree, principal in the second degree, accessory before the fact, and accessory after the fact. A principal in the first degree was the main criminal actor, the person who committed the offense, and the principal in the second degree was someone also present at the crime scene who assisted with the crime but did not directly perpetrate it. Under common law there was another designation for helpers who assisted before or after the crime but did not actually witness the crime event. An accessory before the fact could be someone who assists in the crime planning, such as by finding a location for it or luring a victim to that scene. Although an accessory after the fact provides similar assistance, such help is rendered once the crime has already been committed and is typically done to avoid police detection, evade apprehension, or minimize potential punishment. Common law accomplice liability was contingent on showing that each party to the crime, whether acting as a principal in the first or second degree or an accessory before or after the fact, knew that a crime was underway and acted with a specific intent to achieve it through their contributing efforts. Those elements of accomplice intent and acts remain an integral part of current state and federal laws, but in accordance with most modern legal standards, crimes of complicity are simplified as offenses collaborated by principals and accessories. However, a perpetrator whose role in the crime is limited to after it happens and is aimed at thwarting police detection or prosecution might face lesser punishment for obstruction of justice.

## Accomplice Intent

The commonly used expression "teamwork makes the dream work" can be used to illustrate how accomplice intent is evaluated under the criminal laws in most U.S. jurisdictions, which require a showing that each team player or accomplice acted with a specific purpose to execute a criminal plan. Just as that expression denotes, when multiple people work together through a common motivation to achieve a particular goal, those combined efforts help facilitate that goal attainment. However, there are some potential challenges that arise among team members, who might not all possess the same desire and work ethic. Perhaps you can relate if you have ever been assigned to a work group for a class or as part of your employment endeavors. A team member in one of those contexts might argue that it is unfair for a colleague or classmate to receive the same credit for a group project to which they contributed little or nothing. The same concerns may arise regarding determining the scope of accomplice liability, but the stakes are much higher, given that criminal punishment, and not just a mere class grade or job credential, is derived from the conduct of the principal actor. For that reason, under most criminal laws, accomplice intent is measured by evidence of purposeful intent; that is, each member of the team or accessory to the principal actor desired for that person to commit a crime, which was reflected in some action on their part. Such is outlined in the Model Penal Code § 2.06(3), 1962, which extends complicit liability to actions done "with the purpose of promoting or facilitating the commission of the offense." Other criminal codes contain a lesser, general intent standard for establishing accomplice liability, since when it comes to teamwork, some group members are bound to perform more or less than others—but that does not necessarily diminish everyone's shared desire to earn a certain grade, credential, or criminal outcome. Awareness is key to that determination, insofar as each accomplice must have possessed actual or constructive knowledge that a crime was planned and with that mindset had reason to believe that their actions would likely help facilitate it (18 Pa. C.S. § 306(c), 2014; RCW 9A.08.020, 2011).

PAUSE AND REFLECT

Under Pennsylvania law, a person can be charged as an accomplice even if they did not act with a specific purpose to achieve the criminal result if they possessed a level of intent that corresponds to the requisite mens rea element of the crime committed. That means

> when causing a particular result is an element of an offense, an accomplice in the conduct causing such result is an accomplice in the commission of that offense, if he acts with the kind of culpability, if any, with respect to that result that is sufficient for the commission of the offense. (18 Pa. C.S. § 306(c), 2014).

Explain whether you perceive this as a narrow or broad application of accomplice liability. Also, does that seem fair, given the analogy of complicity crimes to group-based projects?

## Constructive Intent

Victim:
United States

Defendant:
Patricia Campbell
Hearst

Criminal laws require that accomplice intent be demonstrated by evidence that individuals who assisted the principal actor also desired to facilitate the crime, just as people use accessories to enhance their appearance. The problem lies in the fact that people are much less willing to express their intention to be an accessory to a crime than they are to want to look their best, which can leave criminal prosecutions in accomplice liability cases reliant on circumstantial evidence. In true crime fashion, the circumstances surrounding the Patty Hearst case, both her kidnapping and bank robbery participation, were the subject of scrutiny as America grappled with understanding her role as a victim turned accomplice. The name Patty Hearst literally struck a nerve across the nation on February 4, 1974, when she, the granddaughter of one of the most prominent and wealthiest American business owners, was violently kidnapped by members of the Symbionese Liberation Army (SLA) right from her home. Emotions heightened along with the ever-growing media frenzy over the dramatic details of how the SLA members perpetrated the kidnapping, which began with a violent attack on Hearst's fiancé and continued with gun-wielding threats to onlooking neighbors. But the worst or most sensational aspect of her story was still to come and started to unfold just 2 months after the kidnapping with the release of a recording to the public. In it, Hearst was overheard denouncing her family and pledging allegiance to the SLA. People, not least her family, were shocked at how a 19-year-old UC Berkeley college student from such a privileged background could literally join forces with her kidnappers, SLA members who espoused political insurgence and shared a goal of inciting an anti-capitalist revolution. There was nothing in Hearst's past to indicate her alignment with those viewpoints. The public was perplexed and still reeling over those developments when less than 2 weeks later Hearst was seen among other SLA members on a bank surveillance video pointing an assault weapon at bank employees during what appeared to be a bank robbery. There was no doubt that those actions helped "encourage, facilitate or aid" in "the felonious taking of personal property in the possession of another ... accomplished by means of force or fear" (Penal Code 211 PC, 1993; Penal Code 31 PC, 2008). That incident occurred in California, and under the law in that state, any person who aids or abets a crime commission is considered a principal criminal actor.

The prosecution relied on the audio recording of Hearst committing herself to the SLA mission, along with the video footage of her seen carrying out that criminal plan—circumstances that they believed showed she had perpetrated a bank robbery beyond, any reasonable doubt. But before the jury could decide whether that evidence would suffice, there was yet another twist in the Patty Hearst saga. At trial, Hearst's attorneys conceded that she performed conduct that she knew would aid in the bank robbery but asserted that those actions were unintentional, and therefore she should not be punished for that crime. The specific claim was that Hearst was not acting on her own volition when she walked into a bank armed with an assault rifle to perpetrate a robbery. Instead, her defense team argued that she had suffered from Stockholm syndrome, a psychological condition they attributed to her 19-month captivity with the SLA, during which she was allegedly abused and brainwashed. Hearst claimed to have experienced associated trauma, which influenced her to make that infamous recording and assist in the bank robbery—not because she wanted to but rather because she had grown sympathetic toward her captors and learned to identify with them, and that included joining in their criminal routines and behaviors. Nonetheless, the jury found Hearst guilty of willfully aiding and abetting her captors, and she was sentenced to 7 years in federal prison. But the court of public opinion had the final say, and former president Jimmy Carter commuted her sentence to time served after just 2 years of imprisonment. Still, 27 years after that notorious bank robbery, people were watching as former president Bill Clinton granted Hearst a full pardon on the last day of his presidency. The story of Patty Hearst, the college student heiress who went from kidnapped victim to bank robber, has been retold in countless documentaries, books, and classrooms over the decades since those events transpired. An important theme in that story is accomplice intent and how that element can be constructed by the facts and despite a defendant's claims to the contrary.

## Accomplice Acts

Accomplice acts can be construed from a broad array of conduct, in accordance with any applicable statutory criteria that sets forth the actus reus elements of complicity crimes and the behaviors that constitute such concerted actions. For instance, Model Penal Code § 2.06(3), 1962 defines accomplice acts as conduct that "aids ... or attempts to aid such other person in planning or committing the offense." Many state statutes contain action words such as solicit, encourage, request, direct, or demand to illustrate some examples of how a person can aid and abet a crime (18 Pa. C.S. § 306(c), 2014; RCW § 9A.08.020, 2011; Tex. Penal Code Ann. § 7.02(a)(2), 1994). However, such statutory language is not exhaustive and only provides a basis for courts to determine whether assistance in a crime amounts to an act of complicity.

Case precedent is also useful in that inquiry. Accordingly, mere words communicated can suffice as overt actions intended to encourage, request, solicit, or demand, and that captures the broad scope of accomplice acts and how they can be performed through either verbal or physical expressions. Accomplice acts must be displayed by some overt act or failure to act, which means that simply being present at the crime scene and doing nothing or fleeing once the crime ensues does not constitute conduct that qualifies as such. There is an exception in that persons who are under a legal duty to protect another person from harm and know of an illicit danger to that person but fail to intervene or take some other action to prevent it are considered an accomplice to the crime committed (Model Penal Code § 2.06(3)). Recall from Chapter 4 the specific legal duties of care that are imposed on parents, through contract formation, by professional status, or via the provision of voluntary aid and how criminal liability may be imposed for inactions for failures to execute those obligations. Those responsibilities remain and must always be fulfilled, even against other persons whose conduct poses a threat to the individual whom they are supposed to protect, and a failure to do so could be considered an inaction that aided and abetted a crime and therefore the subject of accomplice liability. Case precedent is rich with examples of how that derivative punishment principle is applied to omissions of care. Accordingly, a parent who stood by watching her child be assaulted by another person and failed to take any reasonable steps to stop it contributed to that assault and was charged with aiding and abetting it (*State v. Walden*, 1982). Citing that rule, a court in a different jurisdiction held that a mother acted as an accomplice to her boyfriend when he inflicted numerous sexual assaults upon her daughter, which she knew about and did nothing to stop (*People v. Swanson-Birabent*, 2003).

**PAUSE AND REFLECT**

As you have read, crimes of solicitation and complicity are composed of similar actus reus elements that involve one person encouraging, requesting, directing, or otherwise trying to get another person to commit a crime. Nonetheless, they are distinct offenses. List the key differences between solicitation and complicity. Discuss whether you think potential punishments for solicitation should be higher to deter crimes of complicity.

## Constructive Actions

Victim:
Jaycee Dugard

Defendant:
Nancy Garrido

Jaycee Dugard is a best-selling author and well-known advocate for victim's rights, but that success was ironically triggered by her own victimization that was replete with kidnapping, captivity, rape, horrific acts of sexual abuse, and maltreatment, all aided and abetted by Nancy Garrido. Most people first heard the name Jaycee Dugard on June 10, 1991, when she was 11 years old and taken by Nancy and Phillip Garrido in front of her home, as her classmates in an awaiting school bus watched in horror and news stations across the nation scrambled to get the story out. It was all too little too late for a prompt return home, as it would be 18 years until Jaycee, or "Alissa" as her captors called her, would be found. The Jaycee Dugard story should certainly be commemorated as one of survival, but it also presents a valuable illustration of when accomplice acts are constructed by both overt actions and omissions that cross over in a series of horrifying criminal events. Married couple Phillip and Nancy Garrido conspired to kidnap and enslave Jaycee indefinitely. By all accounts Phillip, a convicted sex offender who had served time in federal prison for rape, was the criminal mastermind and principal actor. He confined Jaycee to a ramshackle shelter of tents and sheds, which stood adjacent to the home that he shared with his wife. It was there that Phillip first raped her and continued to do so for nearly 2 decades, which resulted in Jaycee birthing two of his daughters as a teenager. But where was Nancy during all of this? More importantly, what role did she play?

It was established that on August 24, 2009, Nancy had accompanied Phillip, Jaycee, and their daughters to the University of California, Berkley, campus to inquire about hosting a religious event when school officials alerted police about them and their alleged suspicious behaviors. A police investigation ensued, during which Jaycee first tried to protect Phillip, who had not reported any children to his parole officer, by pretending that their daughters were relatives instead. Both Nancy and Phillip were arrested and charged with 29 counts of felony crimes, which included kidnapping, rape, false imprisonment, and committing a forcible lewd act against a child, among other offenses. America witnessed in real time the tables turn with the release and return of Jaycee and her daughters and the institutional confinement of Phillip and Nancy Garrido. Both are currently incarcerated, Phillip for 431 years to life and Nancy for 36 years to life. At the same time, reports began to emerge about how Nancy, who her brother-in-law described as a "robot," might have also been victimized by her husband, Phillip. Nancy's attorney manifested those allegations into a battered person's type of defense, by claiming that any actions she did in furtherance of the crimes charged were not voluntary but rather influenced by Phillip's exertion of control over her and the fear inside her. At trial, the prosecution weakened that theory by presenting evidence that Nancy was the sole captor for an approximate 5-month period when Phillip was reincarcerated for a parole violation. The prosecution further argued that during that time, Phillip was literally out of sight and should have been out of mind—that is, unless Nancy shared in his criminal intention to continually inflict acts of abuse and deprivation against Jaycee and her daughters. Evidence showed that she did just that in Phillip's absence from the home and when he was there would disrupt visitations from parole officers to prevent them from detecting what was happening inside. What Nancy failed to do was just as telling of her role as an accomplice, because never once over the course of 18 years did, she or Phillip allow for Jaycee and her daughters to receive professional medical or dental care services (Goldman, 2009).

PAUSE AND
REFLECT
Recall that people may voluntarily assume a legal duty of care by bringing another person into their custody or control and by doing so become obligated to take reasonable measures to ensure that individual's health, welfare, and safety, and any failure to do so could be considered an omission of care. With that in mind, do you think that Nancy Garrido's failure to provide Jaycee and her daughters with professional health care constitutes a culpable omission and one for which she should be punished as an accomplice? Explain.

What is clear is the systematic breach of care on the part of the California community correctional system, which employed the state officers who were assigned to monitor Phillip while he was on parole for most of Jaycee's nearly 2-decade captivity.

In 2009, as part of the investigation into her kidnapping, rape, abuse, and impregnation, the California Office of the Inspector General determined that those parole agents failed to properly manage Phillip, and because of that omission of care, he and Nancy were able to continually hold their victims in captivity. Jaycee was awarded slightly more than $20 million by the state of California as compensation for the resultant damages that she and her children suffered. That decision was based on the fact that the parole officers who handled Phillip's case visited his home multiple times but only inspected the interior and not the backyard areas. The state found that had their efforts been more diligent, they would have likely discovered Jaycee and her daughters, who were shackled right outside of where they stood. Jaycee Dugard spent her entire adolescence and early adult years in confinement, being sexually assaulted, raped, and forced to bear the children of her abuser, but she survived it all, and it is for those reasons people from all over the country will remember who she is for years to come. The substantial victimization that she faced is also a reflection of the deep-rooted and extensive harms that could come from crimes of complicity, which involve more than one person acting together to achieve a common criminal outcome. Nancy and Phillip Garrido committed severe acts of violence against Jaycee and her children for many years, he serving as the principal actor and she as his accomplice, but those roles aside, they were complicit in their intention to inflict harms against her body, mind, and spirit (Dearen, 2011).

## Accomplice Liability

Accomplice liability is set forth by statute and derived from any crimes committed by the principal actor, which means that someone who serves as an accomplice to a crime should face the same punishments as the person who is found guilty of perpetrating it. This derivative punishment principle aims to punish individuals who intend for a crime to be completed and in furtherance of that mindset perform acts that are done to aid and abet the facilitation of it. However, sentencing outcomes in cases involving complicit crimes may depart from that standard, based on certain offender and offense characteristics such as a perpetrator's prior criminal record or demonstrated efforts to abandon the criminal plan, circumstances that can potentially aggravate or mitigate punishments, respectively. But in accordance with the Model Penal Code and most criminal laws, accomplice liability can still be imposed even if the principal criminal actor is not prosecuted or is prosecuted but for a lesser charge than what the other parties to the crime faced, so long as there is sufficient evidence of their intent to commit the crime and conduct contributing to it. For instance, under Pennsylvania law,

> an accomplice may be convicted on proof of the commission of the offense and of his complicity therein, though the person claimed to have committed the offense has not been prosecuted or convicted or has been convicted of a different offense or degree of offense or has an immunity to prosecution or conviction or has been acquitted. (18 Pa. C.S. § 306(g), 2014)

In context, such a situation may arise due to the commission of procedural error, like a coerced confession or illegal search and seizure, that results in a violation of the principal actor's constitutional rights and the exclusion of evidence leading to an acquittal or charge reduction. Under the law, such procedural mistakes do not diminish the substantive elements of the complicit crime; that two or more persons desired to violate the law and achieved that goal through collaborative efforts. In theory, the natural and probable consequences doctrine extends accomplice liability to crimes committed by the main perpetrator that were an unintended but foreseen result of the original criminal plan. But in practice, many jurisdictions do not enforce it in the interest of fairness and justice.

FIGURE 5.2 Natural and probable consequences doctrine

## Natural and Probable Consequences Doctrine

Lilo Brancato Jr. is well known for his 1993 role in *A Bronx Tale*, but some people are also likely to remember him as a cast member in the hit series *The Sopranos* over 20 years ago. Either way, those accomplishments are overshadowed, at least in popular culture, by Brancato's 2005 involvement in a burglary gone wrong, which was highly sensationalized in part because of his celebrity status. That aside, the details surrounding the incident were unnerving and a stark reminder of the natural and probable dangers that flow from crimes that are perpetrated by individuals who work as a team and are driven by a common criminal goal. On December 10, 2005, Brancato, along with Steven Armento, executed their plan to break into a house to steal prescription drugs, which they desired to fuel their addictions at the time. They were well on their way to achieving it after breaking

Victim:
Daniel Enchautegui

Defendant:
Lilo Brancato Jr.

a glass window to gain entrance into the home when they were suddenly interrupted by Daniel Enchautegui, a police officer who lived nearby and was alerted by the sounds from the shattered glass. Officer Enchautegui approached them, and Armento immediately fired a fatal shot to his chest. Both Brancato and Armento were subsequently arrested and charged with burglary and murder. Even though both men committed acts that led to the murder, it was not a part of their criminal objective. News of the crime also sparked curiosity and legal discourse about the scope of accomplice liability, particularly whether Brancato should have to face punishment for the murder, which he did not specifically intend to commit. He could have under the natural and probable consequences doctrine, which holds accomplices criminally responsible for crimes committed by someone else that were a foreseeable consequence of a different crime that they aided and abetted. In Brancato's case he planned to commit a burglary with Armento, who unexpectedly killed someone in the process. Naturally, homicide is a foreseeable consequence of burglary, an offense that involves an unlawful entry and an intent to take property, and both elements can involve the use of force. But the natural and probable consequences rule is not a part of N.Y. Penal Law § 20.10, which holds that "a person is not criminally liable for conduct of another person constituting an offense when his own conduct, though causing or aiding the commission of such offense, is of a kind that is necessarily incidental thereto." The jury in applying that law to the case facts found Brancato guilty of attempted burglary but not murder, and he was sentenced to 10 years in prison. Armento, his accomplice who killed officer Enchautegui, was found guilty of murder and sentenced to life imprisonment without the possibility of parole (Assefa, 2013; Nolasco, 2018).

The distinct punishments they faced reflects a dominant trend in accomplice law, to relieve accomplices of liability for offenses committed by their crime partner that they did not intentionally facilitate but which were a natural and probable consequence of their illicit conduct that was aimed at achieving a different but related crime. Lilo Brancato Jr. and Steven Armento together planned to burglarize someone's home and unlawfully entered it with the specific intent to steal items inside, but Armento acted beyond the scope of that criminal agenda when he shot and killed Enchautegui, who unexpectedly arrived at the scene. Those crime details—particularly the separate acts of complicity each offender performed, along with the prison sentences they received—reflect an important limitation on how far courts are willing to extend credit, or more aptly criminal punishment, in situations wherein one criminal team member does way more work than what the agreed-upon assignment called for and what the other group members intended.

## Vicarious Liability

Both accomplice liability and vicarious liability are based on derivative punishment principles; however, through criminal laws those concepts are distinctly characterized by how the underlying criminal act and third-party responsibility are linked together. We know that complicit crimes occur when multiple individuals collaborate and work as a team to commit a crime, and liability for any resultant law violation can be imposed on accomplices who aided and abetted the principal actor through an overt act or culpable omission. In those situations, the individuals involved have coordinated their illicit efforts to achieve a common goal, and even if such actions are done separately, they present a tangible justification for how accomplice liability derives from the principal actor's conduct. Vicarious liability requires a different, more figurative understanding of how one person's crime can be imputed to another individual who did not partake in any of the illegal conduct directly, yet through their connection to the criminal actor as a parent or employer, they must take responsibility for any resultant harm in accordance with the law.

FIGURE 5.3 Vicarious liability

Under the law, corporations along with corporate managers are considered individual entities and can therefore be subject to criminal sanctions and civil liability, such as for the illegal conduct of corporate employees, based on the common law doctrine respondeat superior, which translates to "let the master answer." Most states and the federal government have statutes in place that require the superior, or employer, to respond to crimes committed by their employees but more carefully define the circumstances of when such vicarious punishments can be imposed (32 CFR § 750.21). The Model Penal Code provides some guidance and limits criminal corporate liability to instances in which the "criminal conduct [committed by an employee] is authorized, requested, commanded, performed, or recklessly tolerated by the board of directors or by a high managerial official acting on behalf of the corporation within the scope of his or her office or employment" (Model Penal Code § 2.07). Under it, criminal punishment can only be derived from employee conduct and extended to corporate managers and perhaps even the corporation itself if the supervisors advised the employee to engage in the illegal behaviors or knew about it but failed to do anything. The employee must have also been acting within the scope of employment, which can be satisfied by a broad array of factors, including but not limited to whether the employee was working within their assigned and normal business hours, or outside of those times but as per their employer's instruction, or in accordance with what the employer directed or trained them to do. If a corporation is found liable under those or other conditions tying it to the wrongful, illegal conduct of an employee, it will typically have to pay a fine to compensate for any personal or property harm caused by it. Parents can face similar punishments for failing to properly supervise their child if such omission contributes to that minor's delinquent or criminal conduct. Laws that criminalize acts that contribute to the delinquency of a minor can be enforced against parents for furnishing their child with alcohol, controlled substances, firearms, or other items that only adults can legally possess and use. In addition, parents could be held vicariously liable for any harm caused by their child's negligent behavior if they had reason to know that child could not or would likely not exercise reasonable care.

## Conclusion

This chapter covered parties to crime, with a focus on when individuals act in concert as accomplices or accessories to the principal actor who is responsible for perpetrating the offense. If served to further a commonly shared criminal outcome, those roles, while distinct, are equally punishable under most contemporary laws, which do not retain the common law categories that separated principals by degree and from accessories before and after the fact. The cases surrounding Patty Hearst and Jaycee Dugard demonstrate that and how the elements of complicity crimes can be proved in real-life situations through both direct and circumstantial evidence. In theory, the natural and probable consequences doctrine is supposed to extend accomplice liability to unintentional but foreseeable crimes that result from the complicit conduct. But as the Lilo Brancato Jr. case shows, courts generally do not do so, which serves to limit punishment for complicit crimes only to those offenses that were inherent to the criminal plan. Vicarious liability is also based on a derivate punishment principle, but unlike accomplice liability, it is used to impose punishment on individuals who played no direct role in the crime but had some responsibility to prevent it and failed to do so. Criminal laws provide comprehensive rules to punish parties for crime, whether acting in concert as principals and accessories, through overt actions, or culpable omissions that are imputed vicariously.

## THINK AND APPLY

Refer to what you have learned in this chapter and explain whether you agree with the dominant trend to limit the application of the natural and probable consequences doctrine in accomplice liability cases. Use the Lilo Brancato Jr. case to exemplify your position.

*Credits*

# Chapter 6

# Nonfatal Crimes Against Persons

## Introduction to the Chapter

This chapter covers nonfatal crimes against persons—including battery, assault, false imprisonment, and kidnapping—which are inflicted through threatened or actual force and can result in multifaceted harm to victims and society. Each of these offenses begins with a specific intent to commit a battery, which is an unwanted, offensive, or harmful touching that is committed through direct physical contact or indirectly with an object or some other instrumentality. Either way, a battery is harmful in itself and particularly since it is a likely conduit to other nonfatal crimes against persons, unless the victim implicitly consented to it as an incidental risk of their voluntary participation in a legitimate activity, such as a sports event, concert, or medical procedure. There is only a fine line between crimes of battery and assault, which is evident in the fact that by definition and in substance, an assault includes an attempted or threatened battery. In some jurisdictions, the elements of both offenses are subsumed into a single criminal code that is enforced against a range of simple to aggravated assault crimes, including ones that are sexual in nature. Sexual assault is defined broadly to include various forms of unwanted or offensive physical contact and covers rape, which occurs by the forcible penetration of bodily orifices. Whether a battery is inflicted, attempted, or threatened, that offense is a conceivable step to false imprisonment or kidnapping, which involve unlawful restraint or movement respectively. These nonfatal crimes against persons are presented in that sequence, to help readers conceptualize the distinctions between them and how they can be performed in the same crime incident, much like the beginning, middle, and end of a true crime movie. Case in point, the murder of Ahmaud Arbery, which horrified the nation and showcased that fatality may result from the commission of nonfatal crimes such as aggravated assault, false imprisonment, and attempted kidnapping. This chapter covers that case along with the infamous sexual assault crimes committed by Bill Cosby, Jeffrey Epstein, and Ghislaine Maxwell to put nonfatal crimes against persons in context.

## Battery and Assault

### Battery

FIGURE 6.1 Battery and assault

The elements of battery are a logical starting point to understanding nonfatal crimes against persons. After all, assault crimes are classified as either a threatened or attempted battery, and false imprisonment and kidnapping coincidentally require some level of unwanted physical restraint or movement. Just like those offenses, in most states and under common law a battery must reflect a specific, purposeful intention to intrude upon the victim's personal space in a harmful or offensive manner. There are some laws that criminalize acts of battery that are done knowingly or with general intent; that is, recklessness or negligence. But acts of battery committed through reckless or negligent intent, if recognized in a particular jurisdiction, must be accompanied by evidence that such conduct resulted in actual harm, caused serious injury, or involved the use of a dangerous weapon, depending on the applicable statute. The Model Penal Code encompasses all levels of culpability for battery and punishes the infliction of consequential physical injury done with any level of intent—whether purposely, knowingly, recklessly, or negligently—but a deadly weapon must have been used to cause such harm if it resulted from negligent conduct (Model Penal Code § 211.1(1) (b) 1962). Criminal laws limit the scope of blameworthiness for acts of battery that are perpetrated through negligence or failure to exercise reasonable care, since that level of intent is either excluded entirely or must be accompanied by a specified aggravating factor of harm or weapon type. For instance, imagine that college students Brett and Ryan start throwing a soft rubber ball to each other in a public park. They are enjoying this impromptu activity when Ryan misses the ball, and a child who is in the adjacent playground gets struck by it on the arm. Brett and Ryan were so engrossed in their game that neither of them thought to first check their surroundings to ensure that it was suitable location for a football game. They certainly did not throw the soft rubber ball at the child on purpose, knowing that he would likely get injured, or consciously disregard the risk of injury to him. Rather, neither man thought about taking any precautions to avoid such an outcome, which makes them negligent since a reasonable person in that position would have exercised more care in finding a place to play football that was not directly next to a public playground. However, such negligent conduct would not be punishable under Model Penal Code § 211.1(b), which specifically prohibits negligently causing "bodily injury to another with a deadly weapon." The soft rubber ball that Brett negligently threw and that injured the child's arm is certainly not comparable to a deadly weapon. However, his actions might constitute a battery in jurisdictions where that offense can be committed through negligent acts that result in harm to the victim, regardless of whether it was caused from a deadly weapon or not.

Acts of battery may be performed with specific or general intent depending on the applicable law, but regardless of the requisite level of culpability, the criminal act element of that offense must include the attendant circumstance of nonconsent. In some states consent to physical contact is an affirmative defense to a battery or assault charge, which can be demonstrated by evidence that the alleged victim agreed to such touching through an express waiver or implicitly by choosing to participate in an activity in which those types of encounters frequently occur. Some examples include participation in contact sports such as football, attending a crowded event like a concert, or undergoing a medical procedure, which all carry an inherent risk of bodily and perhaps even offensive physical encounters. The scope of that defense is limited to interactions that are inherent to the ordinary course of activities in which people reasonably expect to touch or be touched by other individuals who are participating in the same event.

Individuals who receive medical treatment or surgery might experience some discomfort afterward, such as bruising or soreness, which are risks that are incidental to the physical contact that is involved with conducting those types of procedures. Patients who undergo any health-related intervention are typically asked to sign a consent form beforehand that details the potential risks of harm involved and to some extent protects treating physicians from punishment for any injuries caused by the operation that are reasonably related to it. However, in urgent situations individuals might not be able to provide their informed consent to medical care, including any attendant harms suffered, but such situations are generally covered under an emergency care exception and protected under the law. Of course, that exception helps reduce the potential for medical malpractice claims, but it might not necessarily serve the best interests of every patient. Consider the perspective of an individual who for religious reasons is opposed to blood transfusions but receives one as part of an emergency treatment during which they are unable to express their nonconsent. Pause and reflect about how you think such a situation should be treated under the law and why.

**PAUSE AND REFLECT**

## Attempted Battery Assault

Battery and assault are distinct crimes but treated as a single assault offense federally and in accordance with most state criminal codes in cases in which elements of both are part of the crime incident. Crimes of battery and assault both require intentional conduct that results in the infliction of threatened or actual harm against persons; however, there are key differences between them. An assault can be considered a preview to a battery, just like a commercial for a movie gives viewers a glimpse into what the film is about, such as the characters featured and basic plotline. The two categories of assault crimes are aptly called attempted battery assault and threatened battery assault, as both titles allude to the congruities between those offenses and also that an assault most often preludes a battery. Both are covered under the Model Penal Code, but many state laws reflect one or the other type of assault. An attempted battery assault is an inchoate or incomplete crime that occurs when the perpetrator takes every step needed to inflict an unwanted, offensive harm or touching upon another person but fails to make physical contact with their intended victim because something goes wrong that is beyond their control. Just like any other inchoate crime of attempt, conspiracy, or solicitation, the actus reus of attempted battery assault covers only overt actions or culpable omissions performed with a specific intent to purposely further the intended criminal goal, so mere steps taken in preparation of it will not suffice. Neither will negligent or reckless attempts, since attempted battery assault is a specific intent crime.

Assume that Mary wants to kill Abe, and in fact that is her very purpose for purchasing a firearm from a local store. But that action alone does not qualify as an attempted battery assault. Instead, under the law in most jurisdictions, she would need to take additional, substantial steps that would bring her closer to executing the shooting. Recall from Chapter 4 that states which have adopted the Model Penal Code use the substantial steps test included in that statute to distinguish attempt from preparatory offenses, and it requires the defendant's conduct to be "strongly corroborative of the actor's criminal purpose" (Model Penal Code § 5.01(2), 1962). Applying that to the example, Mary's conduct would count as an attempted battery assault if she purchased the firearm and then also used it in a way that more closely reflected her desire to shoot and kill Abe. Merely purchasing the gun does not, as people buy firearms for a multitude of reasons, many of which are legitimate in nature. But that purchase could be a substantial step in an attempted battery assault if Mary, armed with a newly bought gun, loads, aims, and fires it at Abe, whose back is to her, but nothing happens. The gun jams, which is something that Mary had no control over and did not plan for, since her criminal mindset remained consistent. Actual harm is not a requisite element of an attempted battery assault, so even though Abe is uninjured, Mary could still be punished for purposely trying to physically harm him with a gun that she had the present ability to shoot, and that in essence is an incomplete battery. Just as Mary did, the perpetrator must perform some actions that culminate in them having a present ability to make harmful or offensive physical contact with an intended victim, which is distinguishable from conduct that is only done in preparation to commit a crime and thus the inception to other future steps that need to be done for the crime to be accomplished.

In that example, Mary had possession of a gun and the present ability to shoot it, but it is important to note that both direct and indirect attempts to inflict harm or unwanted contact are punishable, and those injuries can arise from a wide array of intrusive behaviors such as spitting, throwing an object, or hitting someone with a car, among other bodily intrusions. Another point of distinction is the criminal intent element of attempted battery assault, which is satisfied by proof that the defendant purposely tried to physically harm or touch the victim in an offensive way. Negligent or reckless behaviors fall short of that standard. To illustrate that point, pretend that Mary never purchased a gun or had any intention to harm Abe. But Mary and Abe have a mutual friend who owns a gun, and while visiting her they ask to check it out. The friend assures them that the gun is unloaded. While Mary is looking at the gun, it emits a bullet that just misses the back of Abe's head. Luckily, Abe is uninjured from the accident, and Mary will likely not be charged with an attempted battery assault since the incident was caused by her negligence, or failure to exercise reasonable care in inspecting the firearm before handling it.

## Threatened Battery Assault

Threatened battery assault and attempted battery assault are similar in that neither requires the infliction of physical harm or offensive contact upon the victim; however, there are important differences between them. An attempted battery assault is complete with the performance of conduct that is intended to cause a bodily injury or disturbance even if no harm is caused. In contrast, someone who is victimized by a threatened battery assault must experience a fear of imminent harm that results from the defendant's intentional conduct, which is akin to an emotional or psychological impairment. For that to occur, the victim must have been aware of some danger connected to the perpetrator's conduct and feel afraid because of it, and that response must be an objectively reasonable one based on the circumstances. There must also be a causal link between the threatening behavior and victimization that can be established by a showing of factual and (proximate) legal causation. A threatened battery assault is a factual cause of fear of harm experienced by the victim if, but for it occurring, that person would not have been distressed. For such frightful conduct to also be considered the legal cause of that victimization, it must be proximate to it, meaning that it is a foreseeable contributing factor in the fear of harm suffered. The threatened harm or unwanted conduct must also convey a sense of immediate danger, expressed through more than just words, so that it is apparent the perpetrator possesses a present ability to follow through, or at the very least the victim and a reasonable person in their position would believe the perpetrator does. Accordingly, the hypothetical incident between Abe and Mary could only constitute a threatened battery assault if Mary aimed the gun at Abe on purpose to frighten him and he had actual or constructive awareness of that action, perhaps from seeing or hearing what she was doing. But this time, the gun is unloaded, which shows her intent only to make him afraid of getting shot but not actually shoot him. So imagine that Mary picks up the purchased firearm, aims it at Abe, who is facing her, and yells, "I am going to shoot you!" Even though Mary has no plans to pull the trigger, her purposeful actions demonstrate a present ability to do so, and reasonable persons including Abe would likely perceive that behavior as an impending threat to their personal safety or well-being. This altogether satisfies the criminal intent and act elements of threatened battery assault. Punishment for battery and assault are similarly scaled based on whether the conduct involved is classified as a misdemeanor or felony, which depends on offense characteristics such as the seriousness and type of harm caused, weapon use, and if the victim is a law enforcement officer, child, or member of another vulnerable population.

## The Fatality of Aggravated Assault, False Imprisonment, and Kidnapping

On February 23, 2020, news of Ahmaud Arbery, a 25-year-old Black man killed while jogging in a predominantly White neighborhood, rippled across the nation with shock waves that intensified as details of what happened to him leading up to the murder were released. Gregory and Travis McMichael, a White father and son pair, told police they were patrolling the neighborhood for a Black man who had reportedly committed a series

Victim:
Ahmaud Arbery

Defendants:
Gregory McMichael,
Travis McMichael,
William Bryan Jr.

FIGURE 6.2 Unlawful touching, restraint, and confinement—linking nonfatal crimes against persons

of burglaries when they spotted the person whom they believed was responsible for those crimes—Ahmaud Arbery, since he was a Black man jogging. Arbery was out on a run for exercise, but once the McMichaels joined him in their truck, it would turn out to be a run for his life. They began pursuing him in their truck, and each had a gun loaded and ready to fire as they yelled racial slurs at him, which is conduct that would likely frighten any reasonable person in Arbery's position and satisfies the criminal act element of threatened battery assault. Recall that this offense generally involves a victimization caused by conduct that is intended to intimidate and induces an imminent fear of bodily harm. In Georgia, where the incident occurred, that type of assault is considered aggravated in nature if done with a purpose to murder and the use of a deadly weapon "which, when used offensively against a person, is likely to or actually does result in serious bodily injury" (O.C.G.A. § 16-5-21, 2010). Gregory and Travis McMichael were each charged with one count of aggravated assault in accordance with that law. But that was just the opening scene in this horrific true crime story. The McMichaels continued to chase Arbery in their vehicle while displaying guns to scare him, and that scene was captured on video by William Bryan Jr., one of their neighbors, who joined the pursuit in his own truck. The three men cornered Arbery with their vehicles, and that imposed an unlawful restraint on his freedom of movement, which is considered a violation of personal liberties and false imprisonment under Georgia law (O.C.G.A. § 16-5-41, 2010). Those actions also constitute substantial steps in a kidnapping, which is an offense that involves taking a person and holding them against their will (O.C.G.A. § 16-5-40, 2010). Asportation, or movement of the victim, is also a required element in some jurisdictions, but it can be satisfied by even the slightest action. False imprisonment and kidnapping are separate offenses, yet as shown by the tragic story of Ahmaud Arbery, they can occur in tandem as part of a single crime incident and catalyze violent encounters and even fatal victimizations (Holcombe & Vera, 2021; Wiley, 2021). Travis McMichael, who followed and fatally shot Arbery, was convicted on all nine charges: malice murder, two counts of aggravated assault, four counts of felony murder, criminal attempt to commit a felony, and false imprisonment. His father, Gregory McMichael, is guilty on similar charges aside from malice murder. Their neighbor, William Bryan Jr., who joined the pursuit and filmed the crime, is guilty on all charges aside from one count of aggravated assault and one count of felony murder. All three men were sentenced to life in prison. Both the McMichael men were sentenced without the possibility of parole, while Bryan faces the possibility of parole (Andone et al., 2022).

## Sexual Assault and Rape

### State Sex Crime Prosecution

It is not hard to imagine how nonfatal crimes against persons such as battery, assault, false imprisonment, and kidnapping could contribute to conduct that constitutes a sexual assault or rape, especially given the notoriety of certain sex crimes committed by famous people. Sexual assault and rape both result in personal, intimate, bodily violations, but those offenses are defined separately under the law. Behaviors that constitute sexual assault include a broad array of conduct such as nonconsensual groping, kissing, touching, and molestation, which can but do not necessarily involve penetration, whereas the crime of rape must, as it is more narrowly defined only by acts of bodily penetration. The commonality between both sexual assault and rape is nonconsent, which under state and federal criminal codes can be proved through relevant circumstances, like the victim being unlawfully restrained, moved, threatened, or forced into submission such as what someone likely experiences through the infliction of a battery, assault, false imprisonment, or kidnapping incident. Yet it remains a challenge in some sexual assault and rape prosecutions to demonstrate that requisite element of threatened or actual force, based on testimonial evidence from the victim and the defendant—if that

Victim:
Andrea Constand

Defendant:
Bill Cosby

FIGURE 6.3 Nature and scope of sexual assault and rape

person is even available and willing to testify—as such information might be conflicting and offer only limited details of the crime event. The sexual assault crimes and controversies surrounding Bill Cosby and Jeffrey Epstein exemplify that point, the sensational fascination that the public has with celebrity crimes, and how that intrigue contributes to complexities involved with processing sexual victimizations. There remains a public spotlight on their respective sexual assault and trafficking cases, which not only served to conceptualize the perpetration of those crimes but also revealed that victim reporting and stigmatization which stem from common law perceptions of rape persists even through the application of modern criminal laws and procedures, which are distinguishable from those traditional legal standards.

Only rape was recognized at common law, which meant that other sexual violations such as assaults that did not include sexual intercourse were not criminalized. The penetration involved had to be achieved through violence and demonstrated by the utmost proof, which essentially required corroboration by eyewitnesses or some resultant physical injury suffered. The elements of common law rape were further restricted by gender and marital relationship and described as "the unlawful carnal knowledge of a female by a man not her husband through force or against her will." (U.S. Department of Justice, 2012). These stringent common law conceptions had a chilling effect on sex crime prosecutions, which is a phenomenon charac-terized by victim reluctance to report allegations of rape and participate in the case process. It became the focus of national attention during 2014–2015, when over 60 women came forward to accuse Bill Cosby of a range of sexual assault offenses and rape that dated back to the 1960s. Decades had passed since most of the alleged incidents occurred, which left people wondering what had taken so long for those women to report their victimizations. Those lingering questions aside, it was no laughing matter when Cosby, one of the most famous and successful American comedic actors of all time, escaped criminal prosecution for all but one of those offenses due to the lapse in time between when those incidents occurred and when they were reported to law enforcement. Under Pennsylvania law, there is a 12-year statute of limitations on rape and other sexual assault cases, and that procedural limitation bars the criminal prosecution of offenses committed more than 12 years prior (42 Pa. C.S. § 5552, 2014).

Andrea Constand was the only one of the Cosby's accusers whose case fell within the 12-year statute of limitations and who had standing to file a criminal complaint against him, in which she alleged that he had drugged and molested her during a 2004 business meeting. But Cosby was never charged, at least not then, because the prosecutor dropped the case, citing insufficient evidence; a decision that can be seen as reminiscent of how most rape cases were disposed of at common law. In response, Constand filed a civil suit against Cosby in which she made the same sexual assault allegations, and the case was settled for nearly $3.4 million. But that came after Cosby admitted in a deposition that he had given Constand Benadryl to help her relax, since she had been complaining of stress-related neck pain. That was incriminating, given that Constand claimed she was involuntarily intoxicated when Cosby sexually assaulted her and consequently forced to participate in that act, against her will. Once the civil suit came to an end, the prosecutor, emboldened by the burgeoning #MeToo movement and hopes for reelection, filed sexual assault charges against Cosby.

**PAUSE AND REFLECT**    Pause and reflect on what you know about the #MeToo movement and how it might have influenced the prosecutor to file aggravated indecent assault charges against Bill Cosby.

That time the criminal case did proceed to trial, where it was revealed that Cosby admitted when he was deposed in the prelitigation phase of the civil proceeding that he gave Constand that sedative to help her feel better. During the criminal trial, Constand recalled that she only agreed to take the drug because Cosby claimed it was a natural herbal supplement. Based on that testimony, her attorney argued that any subsequent sexual contact between them was fraudulently induced and resulted in Constand being incapacitated and unable to give consent. The jury decided in favor of the defense and convicted Cosby of three counts of aggravated indecent assault, which under 18 Pa. CS § 3125 (2014) is the unlawful "penetration of a per-son's genitals or anus with any part of the person's body," and it is that penetration element which sets this offense apart from indecent assault. Accordingly, that criminal act must be nonconsensual, and that can be evidenced by situations wherein the victim is unaware that such contact is happening due to being under the influence of drugs or another substance that diminishes their physical and/or mental capacity to resist. In a sworn statement, Cosby mentioned that he had obtained a prescription for quaaludes, a powerful depressant, and intended to give it to women with whom he planned to have sexual intercourse; however, he stopped short of saying that he ever followed through with that intent. That along with his admission to giving Constand Benadryl were circumstances that contributed to a jury finding him guilty beyond a reasonable doubt of aggravated indecent assault. Cosby was sentenced to serve a sentence of 3 to 10 years in prison, but some people believe that he had the last laugh because he was released after only 3 years of incarceration when his conviction was overturned on appeal. The Pennsylvania Supreme Court ruled that Cosby was denied protection of the Fifth Amendment to the U.S. Constitution because the prosecutor first dropped the criminal complaint against him for lack of sufficient evidence, then refiled it using the incriminating statements he made in the deposition to establish the elements of aggravated indecent assault. The justices specifically found that strategy interfered with Cosby's right not to self-incriminate, since it essentially compelled him to be a witness against himself in a criminal prosecution that led to his conviction; that outcome also constituted a violation of his natural right not to be deprived of life, liberty, and property without due process of law. The double jeopardy clause is also part of the Fifth Amendment, and under it, Cosby will never be retried for sexually victimizing Constand, nor will he ever face criminal punishment for the alleged acts he committed against his other accusers whose cases are barred by the Pennsylvania statute of limitations (Yan, 2015). Cosby will avoid both incarceration and having to register as a sex offender in accordance with the Sex Offender Registration and Notification Act (SORNA) due to a procedural oversight; but his audience, the American public, is left to wonder if, in the interest of justice, the show should still go on, given that there was substantive proof that he committed three counts of aggravated indecent assault beyond any reasonable doubt (Malone & Demme, 2015).

On June 30, 2021, the Pennsylvania Supreme Court overturned Bill Cosby's conviction for aggravated indecent assault despite a jury finding that he was guilty of that offense beyond a reasonable doubt. Consider that decision from both criminal control and due process perspectives. The crime control model focuses on guilt, particularly when there is ample evidence to support that finding, and advocates of that viewpoint are punishment driven regardless of whether procedural rights are contravened in the process of imposing. In contrast, the due process model is centered on procedural fairness and ensuring that constitutional protections are honored, even if the result is that someone who committed a crime is acquitted due to a procedural error. Using either the due process or crime control perspective, pause and reflect on whether you believe that justice was served in Bill Cosby's case.

**PAUSE AND REFLECT**

## Federal Sex Crime Prosecution

Victims:
Teenaged girls

Defendants:
Jeffrey Epstein and
Ghislaine Maxwell

Sexual assault and rape are *mala in se* crimes and criminalized under a host of laws at the federal and state levels, which impose corresponding punishments on individuals who violate those rules, including the rich and famous. Bill Cosby was convicted of aggravated indecent assault and accused by many other women of additional sex-related crimes that could never be prosecuted due to statutory limitations; both outcomes resulted from the application of Pennsylvania law and received widespread public attention. Most people are also familiar with Jeffrey Epstein, the successful and wealthy financial investor who was federally charged with sex trafficking of minors and conspiracy to commit sex trafficking of minors. He and Bill Cosby shared in common the fact that they both avoided criminal punishment for sexual offenses, despite being charged with such law violations. In August 2019 Epstein died in prison awaiting trial on those trafficking charges, and that came after more than a decade-long saga of suspicion over his involvement in rape, sexual assault, and abuse of teenaged girls. Reports of those crimes emerged between 2002 and 2005, when more than 50 adolescent girls and their parents told law enforcement about the illicit sexual exploits of Epstein and his girlfriend Ghislaine Maxwell. According to that information, the pair would invite victims to visit their lavish residences located in New York City and Palm Beach, Florida, where those children would unwittingly agree to give them massages that would evolve into sexual acts. Since that alleged conduct was committed across more than one state, it falls within the jurisdiction of federal law, which makes it unlawful to "knowingly recruit, entice, harbor, transport, provide, obtain, or maintain a minor (defined as someone under 18 years of age) knowing or in reckless disregard of the fact that the victim is a minor and would be caused to engage in a commercial sex act" (18 U.S.C. § 1591, 2018). The evidence in support of that charge came from the accusers, who claimed that in addition to being sexually victimized by Epstein and Maxwell themselves, the two also paid them to find other underage girls to come to their homes, where Epstein and Maxwell planned to and did have sexual contact with the other girls as well. That conduct makes up the criminal act and intent elements of conspiracy, which, as covered in Chapter 5, requires collaboration between two or more persons in formulating a plan to violate the law and some overt, intentional action done in furtherance of it, regardless of whether such conduct is completed. Furthermore, prosecutors argued that Epstein and Maxwell were both expressly told the victims' ages or otherwise had reason to know that information, but despite that evidence Epstein pleaded not guilty to the federal sex crime charges in July 2019. Less than 1 month later, he was found dead in his cell from what the medical examiner ruled a suicide, and since that happened after such a short period of imprisonment, some people believe that justice was not served. However, Epstein died as a registered sex offender, which was a punishment that resulted from a 2008 conviction on state charges. But the story of the financier, sex offense registrant did not end there, as his girlfriend Maxwell was convicted of six federal sex trafficking charges for the role she played in the sexual abuse Epstein inflicted on minors between 1994 and 2004. On December 29,

2021, after 6 days of deliberation, the jury found Maxwell guilty of the following five counts: sex trafficking of a minor, transporting a minor with the intent to engage in criminal sexual activity, and three counts of conspiracy. After hearing the verdict, Maxwell sat completely still. She faces up to 65 years in prison (Bruney, 2021; Gajanan, 2019, Winter et al., 2021).

The sexual assault cases and controversies surrounding Bill Cosby, Jeffrey Epstein, and Ghislaine Maxwell were played out in the media and in the televised documentaries *Bill Cosby: Fall of an American Icon* and *Jeffrey Epstein: Filthy Rich*, which are aptly titled to reflect general sentiments of shock and dismay that people might experience when celebrated persons are accused of such serious, bodily violations. For some, those cases ended in an anticlimactic way since Cosby and Epstein both escaped their respective punishments, but for different reasons. Their stories also illustrate that there can be a disconnect between expectations of justice and how justice is served, even under contemporary sexual assault and rape laws, which were intended to evolve from common law conceptions of those offenses and the chilling effect those traditional standards had on sex crime prosecutions.

## Conclusion

This chapter covered the elements of nonfatal crimes against persons that are perpetrated through acts of battery, assault, false imprisonment, and kidnapping along, with examples of how those offenses overlap and occur as part of the same crime incident, heightening the potential for fatality. Case in point, the shooting death of Ahmaud Arbery, which was the escalated outcome of an aggravated assault, false imprisonment, and attempted kidnapping inflicted on him in tandem during an afternoon jog. He was chased by Gregory McMichael, Travis McMichael, and William Bryan Jr., who closely followed him in their vehicles while displaying weapons, which created a reasonable fear of imminent danger that was intentional and aggravated in nature. An assault can be performed through a threatened battery, such as what Arbery experienced, or an attempted battery, which is also a specific intent crime but one that does not require victim awareness of the impending harm. That offense might also involve unwanted or offensive physical contact with intimate body parts, such as groping, kissing, molestation, and penetration; such behaviors are criminalized as sexual assault or rape in states and federally. Bill Cosby was the center of a sensational sexual assault case and controversy, which highlights inherent challenges to prosecuting sex crimes that stem from common law and persist through a combination of victim reporting reluctance and procedural rules that can both enhance constitutional protections and stymie the criminal process. Also infamous is how Jeffrey Epstein repeatedly avoided facing any serious criminal punishment for sex trafficking minors and died before that could change Ghislaine Maxwell, his coconspirator, faced the consequences of multiple sex crime convictions alone.

## THINK AND APPLY

Refer to what you have learned in this chapter and draft a statute that consolidates the crimes of battery, assault, false imprisonment, and kidnapping and reflects the overlap between them to improve efficiency in the prosecution of nonfatal crimes against persons.

*Credits*

# Chapter 7

# Fatal Crimes Against Persons

## Introduction to the Chapter

Fatal crimes against persons are homicides. They are the most serious offenses punishable under criminal laws, subject to the harshest penalties, including death if capital murder is involved. This chapter covers homicidal crimes, which are generally categorized as murder or manslaughter, depending on the specific or general intent behind the particular act(s) of fatality involved. The various types of murder are discussed, including the requisite elements of each in accordance with general definitions set forth in state and federal criminal codes, along with the corresponding punishments, which are the most severe for first-degree murder but incrementally less so for second- and third-degree murder convictions. Mens rea, or criminal culpability, is the tie that binds first- and second-degree murders, which are intentional crimes performed with malice. That element also distinguishes those types of homicides from third-degree murder and involuntary and voluntary manslaughters, which encompass distinct forms of unintentional killings. A basic assumption in American society is that there is also a tie that bonds or at the very least binds parents and their children, and that is one of the most revered connections in U.S. culture. So when news is released about a parent or child ending that relationship with an unlawful, intentional killing, respectively known as pedicide and parenticide, most people are likely to stop, listen, and watch those details emerge in what is sure to be a tragic and sensational crime story. As explained in this chapter, that was exactly the impact the Menendez brothers had on the public back in 1989 when they were arrested and charged with the deliberate murders of their parents, and that shock reverberates decades later as their story lives on in social media platforms by users who, in disbelief, avow their commitment to both men and freeing them. The complex and infamous case of Gypsy Rose Blanchard is also discussed to provide another example of parenticide, but one charged as second-degree murder; a connection is made for readers between that crime and the first-degree murder that the Menendez brothers were convicted of, since allegations of parental abuse and neglect lay at the heart of both tragedies and the public fascination with them. Readers will also learn how those intentional killings, which are classified as murders, are separated under the law from acts of manslaughter by levels of intent, which differentiate the various types of homicide. Details of the Michelle Carter case are also covered to conceptualize involuntary manslaughter, the requisite intent of criminal negligence, along with concerns about the applicability of that standard to acts that some perceived as intimating a more specific level of intention and others as a form of protected speech.

## Murder

Murder is the most serious form of homicide, since it is an unlawful killing that is done with malice, or in limited instances no specific intention. The level of that culpability determines the classification of that offense as a first-, second-, or third-degree offense. Those degree designations are linked by statutory law to corresponding punishments that descend in severity with each subsequent categorization of murder. First-degree murder convictions can result in the harshest criminal punishments, which include life imprisonment without the possibility of parole and even death if the attendant case circumstances meet the qualifying conditions for capital murder set forth by statute. Such penalty enhancement statutes exist at the federal level and in states where the death penalty remains a legal form of punishment, and list aggravating criteria for capital punishment that relate to criminal history, victim, and offense characteristics. In that regard, first-degree murder has a fatal result for the victim and potentially the perpetrator, as that person can be sentenced to death as punishment for that crime. That fatal sanction, which is reserved for first-degree murder, reinforces its distinction from other forms of homicide as the only unlawful killing that is committed on purpose through deliberate premeditation. Such requisite purposeful intent is the highest level of culpability and can be evidenced by circumstances showing that the defendant planned to execute the murder, even if such preliminary decision making transpired just moments before the killing occurred, so long as it persisted along with that criminal act.

**PAUSE AND REFLECT**

In cases of first-degree murder, deliberate and premeditated intent can be demonstrated by direct evidence such as the defendant's confession or the totality of circumstances through which such purposeful conduct is inferred. On April 15, 2015, news that Aaron Hernandez was found guilty of first-degree murder for the shooting death of Odin Lloyd rocked the nation, not just because of his professional football stardom but also given the circumstantial evidence on which that conviction was based. The murder weapon was never found, there were no eyewitnesses, and Hernandez proclaimed his innocence. At trial the prosecutor did present text messages Hernandez exchanged with the victim, nightclub surveillance from a week before the shooting, and witness testimony. None of that implicated him but was used to imply that he was present at the crime scene and that suspicious behavior after the shooting occurred (McCann, 2015). Is that enough to prove deliberation and premeditation beyond a reasonable doubt? Explain.

The criminal intent elements of second- and first-degree murder are aligned by malice since both types of homicides must be executed with such ill will or evilness, but nothing more is needed to satisfy the requisite *mens rea* for second-degree murder. Unlike first-degree murder, there is no deliberation and premeditation condition for second-degree murder, which means that offense can be proved by circumstances showing that the defendant knew their conduct would almost certainly cause death or acted with a conscious disregard of the risk of harm posed by their actions. The scope of that offense is framed by criminal laws such as Florida Statute § 782.04(2) (2021), which criminalizes a killing that is neither justified nor excused as second-degree murder "when perpetrated by any act imminently dangerous to another and evincing a depraved mind regardless of human life … without any premeditated design to effect the death of any particular individual." In that context, an unplanned death could be treated as second-degree murder if it results from the commission or attempted commission of a crime such as robbery, kidnapping, or the illegal discharge of a bomb, all of which necessitate threatened, actual force or otherwise carry an inherent risk of danger. Therefore, second-degree murder can be evidenced by a knowing intention, which makes individuals who perpetrate it less culpable than first-degree murderers, who kill on purpose, and therefore subject to a lower maximum punishment of life imprisonment but not death. (Fla. Stat. § 782.04(3), 2021). Since third-degree murder covers homicides that are performed with reckless or no intent, persons found guilty of that offense can face up to 40 years in prison, which is significant yet relatively less than the potential punishments imposed for first- and second-degree murder convictions (18 Pa. C.S. § 18.1102, 2012; Fla. Stat. § 782.04, 2021; MINN STAT § 609.195, 2020). Third-degree murder is only recognized under the laws in three states: Florida, Minnesota, and Pennsylvania, which draw a fine line between the levels of criminal intent that separate that offense from acts of manslaughter. It is described in those statutes as any murder that is not charged at the first- or second-degree level, and more specifically one that is unintentional, unlawful, and occurs during the perpetration of a nonviolent felony or other dangerous act that displays a blatant disregard for human life and safety. Recall from Chapter 3 that Derek Chauvin, a former Minnesota police officer, was convicted of third-degree murder for killing George Floyd by kneeling on his neck, which was conduct that he and his colleagues were trained not to do since it presents an imminent risk of death. Chauvin's fatal actions were unintentional yet punishable under Minnesota Statute § 609.195 as harm caused by reckless or negligent intent. As discussed in this chapter, depending on the applicable law, criminal negligence or recklessness is also an element of involuntary manslaughter, and that subtlety enhances the discretion that prosecutors have in deciding what criminal charges to file against someone who has been arrested for committing a homicidal act.

## First-Degree Murder

The trials of Lyle and Erik Menendez were the first ones featured on the groundbreaking network Court TV, and virtually everyone was tuned in to see the brothers, their courtroom attire, and more importantly what they

Victims:
Mary Louise "Kitty" and Jose Menendez

Defendants:
Lyle and Erik Menendez

FIGURE 7.1 Deliberation and premeditation

had to say in defense of killing their parents. In 1990 Erik and Lyle, who were18 and 21, were arrested in the shooting deaths of their wealthy parents. Prior to that, the Menendez family of four lived a life of luxury in Beverly Hills, truly an American Dream that began when Jose Menendez immigrated to the United States from Cuba and through hard work and determination became a highly successful and wealthy businessperson. For her part, Kitty was an elementary school teacher and then a dedicated stay-at-home mom once her sons were born. The Menendez family was privileged in more ways than one, especially Erik and Lyle, who attended the best schools and had opportunities to participate in various athletic activities, including tennis lessons with private coaches. When Kitty and Jose were found shot to death, people were literally in disbelief about the possibility that their sons were responsible, the investigating officers included, since they had initially framed the homicides as revenge killings and perhaps the result of an unhinged business deal that Jose was involved in. But that disbelief quickly turned to shock, accompanied by a media frenzy as new details of the crimes emerged that placed Erik, Lyle, and the California Penal Code into the public limelight. The sensational true crime narrative of Erik and Lyle, two wealthy brothers who coldheartedly killed their hardworking, devoted parents, was born with their arrest in March 1990, which came 6 months after the crimes took place. It seemed that people had already reached a verdict with the help of Court TV, which offered around-the-clock coverage of the crime story to feed the insatiable public appetite for it (Menza, 2017). But what about under the law—was there sufficient evidence to prove not only that the Menendez brothers murdered their parents but that they did so with purposeful intention?

Erik and Lyle Menendez were both charged with first-degree murder in California in connection with the shooting deaths of their parents, in which state that offense is defined as "the unlawful killing of a human being with malice aforethought" (Cal. Penal Code § 187(a), 2001). In that state and others, an unlawful killing is generally used in reference to any taking of human life that is neither justified nor excused under the law (Cal. Penal Code § 189.5, 2001). This means that the punishment imposed for a murder conviction can be mitigated by evidence showing that the defendant's actions were justified or excused because other reasonable persons would have reacted similarly under similar circumstances or that individual otherwise had a diminished capacity when they committed the crime. At first glance, it seemed as though Erik and Lyle had no defense, and certainly not one that would justify or excuse their murderous actions, since their eventual confessions left no doubt that they had indeed planned to kill their parents. But once again the brothers stunned onlookers by making sexual abuse allegations against their parents at trial, which they claimed should mitigate or reduce the punishments for first-degree murder they each faced. At that point, years had passed since

Kitty and Jose Menendez were killed, and the prosecutor had seemingly built a strong case for proving first-degree murder, which is an unlawful killing committed with malice aforethought. Malice aforethought originates from common law yet remains a requisite element of criminal intent for some forms of murder as defined under contemporary criminal laws, which explicate how it can be proved through direct or circumstantial evidence (Zacharin, 2020.

In the Menendez brothers' case, the prosecutor explained that in accordance with the California Penal Code, their malicious intent was implied because "the circumstances attending the killing show an abandoned and malignant heart" (§ 188(a)(2), 2001). In fact, Erik and Lyle literally did abandon their parents after fatally shooting them 15 times, not to seek medical assistance but to fabricate their alibi defense. They drove to a movie theater, discarded their bloodied clothing and shotguns along the way, and then changed into fresh outfits, all under the pretext of preparing for a night out to see the *Batman* movie, which was newly released at the time. Erik and Lyle never entered the theater and instead made a return trip to their family home, where they feigned shock over finding their parents' lifeless bodies. It certainly seemed that they had star roles in their own feature film, which opened with Erik making a call to 911 and shrieking the now notorious lie: "Someone killed our parents!" (History. com Editors, 2009). The state argued that those facts taken together show that the brothers killed their parents with evilness in their hearts or malice aforethought, and that amounts to murder in the first degree since those homicidal acts were willful, deliberate, and premeditated homicidal acts (Cal. Penal Code § 189(a), 2001). Erik and Lyle confessed to purchasing two shotguns at a store located in San Diego, more than 100 miles away from the Beverly Hills home they shared with their parents at the time. Two days later, armed with those guns, they entered the family home to find Jose and Kitty watching TV and shot them 15 times. Erik admitted to firing the fatal blows to Jose's head and Kitty's face. Their parents were left dead and unrecognizable from the impact and number of bullet wounds they suffered, all while Erik and Lyle put their acting skills to the test by pretending to be uninvolved, but that performance was hardly convincing. During the 6 months that passed between the murders and when Erik and Lyle were finally arrested for those crimes, the brothers dwindled an estimated $1 million from their parents' estate on shopping sprees that included extravagant purchases of jewelry, cars, lavish vacations, clothing, tennis lessons, a restaurant, and more (Aho, 2021).

The trials of Erik and Lyle Menendez began more than 2 years after they were arrested, when the prosecutor finally had the opportunity to present evidence that they killed their parents on purpose, through careful deliberation and premeditation. That delay was due to lengthy legal battles that ensued after they were taken into custody, over the admissibility of incriminating statements they had made to Dr. Jerome Oziel, a former therapist. Oziel recorded those confessions and shared them with his mistress, who then turned the recordings over to police, which helped establish probable cause for the arrests. For 30 months, the case stalled as courts considered the question of whether the recorded information could be revealed at trial or were instead confidential doctor–client communications and protected from disclosure. Finally, the Supreme Court of California entered a judgment declaring that some portions of the confessions could be used at trial. Erik and Lyle were indicted in 1992 and had separate trials, but both juries were deadlocked, which resulted in mistrials. These events were televised nationwide and were cause for public speculation about how the sexual abuse allegations the brothers made against their father during their respective trials might have contributed to divergence among jurors. Erik and Lyle shockingly claimed that Jose, their father and a respected businessperson, molested them from childhood through adolescence and that their mother was aware but did nothing to stop it. Their defense was an affirmative one, since they admitted to murdering their parents but claimed those actions were justified and done in self-defense to finally put an end to what they described as an onslaught of parental abuse and omissions of care. The Menendez brothers were tried together in a third trial, which was held nearly 7 years after the murders—and by that time most people had a strong opinion of them: as calculated parent murderers or battered child abuse victims. For that reason, the judge who presided in that trial prohibited video coverage and limited defense testimony about the alleged abuse. In April 1996 both men were found guilty of first-degree murder and later sentenced to life in prison without the possibility of parole pursuant to California Penal Code § 190(a). That verdict halted their freedom but not their story, which continues to live on more than 3 decades later on TikTok, a social media platform commonly used by adolescents who were not yet born to see the trials of the Menendez brothers. Ironically, those TikTok users, also called "The New Menendez Defenders," have become familiar with the case through recorded trial footage and other media artifacts and are making their own TikTok videos to explain their position that the brothers were sexually abused by their parents and that this circumstance should have been used to mitigate their punishment. Erik and Lyle Menendez were convicted of first-degree murder for killing their parents, crimes that shocked the collective conscience of a nation so deeply that they remain an embedded part of American popular culture in old Court TV footage and emergent social media outlets (Abrahamson, A., 1995; Pearson & Valiente, 2017).

**PAUSE AND REFLECT**

Pause and reflect on a sensational true crime that occurred before you were born or old enough to remember it and that you learned about through case artifacts such as news articles, recordings posted on the Internet, or other sources. How did social media play a role in your access to that information or how you processed it?

## Second-Degree Murder

Victim:
Clauddine "Dee Dee" Blanchard

Defendant:
Gypsy Rose Blanchard

Second-degree murder is a form of homicide that results from the commission of an intentional act that the perpetrator knows is almost certain to cause death, like when Gypsy Rose Blanchard convinced her boyfriend to kill her mother, gave him the murder weapon, and brought him to the residence where she lived with the victim. Those actions reflect a criminal plan to unlawfully take the life of another person and bear a strong resemblance to the elements of first-degree murder, which include deliberate, premeditated acts of homicide. There is a discrepancy between Gypsy Rose's steadfast intent to end her mother's life and the second-degree murder charge she was convicted of, and most Americans know why. Like many, the prosecutor sympathized with Gypsy for the traumatic experiences she had endured at the hands of her mother from birth through early adulthood and in consideration of those circumstances filed a lesser second-degree murder charge, despite clear evidence that Gypsy had carefully laid out the details of her mother's death and acted with a calculated purpose to accomplish that outcome. On June 15, 2005, Gypsy, along with her former

FIGURE 7.2 **Malice**

boyfriend Nicholas Godejohn, were arrested in connection with the murder of Dee Dee Blanchard, which received widespread media attention because a daughter was being accused of taking her own mother's life. Certainly, people wondered how someone could do that to their own parent. But more than that, Dee Dee was known in the community as a loving and devoted caregiver to Gypsy, who from all appearances was wheelchair bound, reliant on a feeding tube, and had a multitude of psychological impairments, making her dependent on her mother for basic necessities and medical care. After all, Dee Dee, who was a trained nurse, seamlessly articulated Gypsy's litany of chronic ailments to physicians, friends, and family, which by her accounts included among other conditions asthma, muscular degenerative diseases, and severe allergies related to a chromosomal deficiency. Dee Dee told a convincing story, drawing sympathy from near and far, which leveraged her consistent ability to obtain countless prescriptions for Gypsy from her birth until she was about 20 years old, and one noticeable side effect was weakened teeth. By adolescence, most of Gypsy's teeth had fallen out, and she also had no hair, but that was not from taking medication as her mother had led people to believe. Gypsy revealed the truth when she was arrested: Dee Dee shaved her head, kept her out of school past the second grade, and forbade her to speak in public as part of an act that involved pretending she could not walk, eat, talk, or otherwise care for herself. Follow-up medical examinations corroborated this story and prompted psychological experts to conclude that Dee Dee had Munchausen by proxy syndrome, which caused her to fabricate Gypsy's bad health and the ailments she claimed were related to it. This alarming revelation was another layer in an already sensational case, and the nation was certainly watching as more details emerged about how that abuse and victimization factored into Gypsy's ultimate decision to kill her mother (Dibdin, 2019; Kettler, 2021).

Gypsy, who was 20 years old at the time of her arrest, told investigators that after decades of being forced to be a part of her mother's act, she was ready to end the performance. She used the Internet as a way to connect with others and meet friends, which is something that she had not had the opportunity to do under her mother's control. In 2011, 3 years before the murder, Gypsy began communicating online with a man whom she had previously met at a convention, and their plans to meet in person were thwarted once Dee Dee learned of their rendezvous. Gypsy recalled a dramatic scene in which her mother allegedly destroyed her computer and cell phone, threatened to do the same to her fingers, and then chained her to a bed for 2 weeks. Fast-forward to March 2015; Gypsy was still seeking online relationships, but this time with Nicholas Godejohn, whom she even introduced to Dee Dee, but that meeting did not go well. Gypsy said it ended with her and Dee Dee in a heated argument, during which her mother threw things and called her derogatory names. It was then that Gypsy decided to kill Dee Dee in order to escape her control and relentless emotional, psychological, and physical abuse. The murderous plan was set and cultivated for 3 months, and in June 2015 it came to fruition.

Godejohn had traveled to Missouri from his home in Wisconsin prior to the murder and awaited in a motel room for Gypsy's message that her mother was sleeping, which meant it was time to kill. Once Godejohn received the message, he went to Gypsy and Dee Dee's home, where Gypsy gave him a knife and then sought refuge in a bathroom. While she was hiding, Godejohn stabbed her mother to death. Gypsy later stated that she did not actually believe he would follow through with the murder; but given her actions preceding it, she certainly knew that it was likely to happen. That constitutes a second-degree murder under Missouri law, which provides that "a person commits the offense of murder in the second degree if she knowingly causes the death of another person" (RSmo § 565.021, 2017). On July 5, 2016, Gypsy pleaded guilty to second-degree murder for her mother's death and was sentenced to 10 years in prison with the possibility of parole. The prosecutor cited the life trauma that her mother had inflicted on her as a primary factor in his decision to offer a plea deal for second-degree murder instead of seeking a first-degree murder conviction. Godejohn did not fare so well, since he was found guilty of first-degree murder and sentenced to life in prison without the possibility of parole in accordance with Missouri criminal code § 565.020, under which "a person commits the offense of murder in the first degree if she knowingly causes the death of another person after deliberation upon the matter" (Sokmensuer, 2019; Tron, 2019).

**PAUSE AND REFLECT**    Pause and reflect on the elements of first-degree murder in Missouri, which include knowingly causing the death of another person after deliberation. Based on what you have learned about Gypsy Rose Blanchard and her involvement in her mother's death, do you think justice would have been better served if she had been charged with that offense instead of second-degree murder? Explain.

## Manslaughter

Manslaughter and murder share in common homicide, which results from the commission of both offenses, but the level of criminal intent that is required to achieve that outcome is different for each of those types of death. There is no malice, deliberation, or premeditation involved with the perpetration of manslaughter, and that is what separates it from all forms of murder, whether amounting to a first-, second- or third-degree homicide. In most states and federally, an unlawful death that is not committed on purpose, with an evil intent, is considered manslaughter and classified as either voluntary or involuntary, depending on the circumstances that preceded the homicidal act. For voluntary manslaughter, what the deceased victim did to provoke the defendant and the timing and nature of that person's response are key to determining whether the evidence satisfies the elements of that offense or a more serious murder charge. In contrast, involuntary manslaughter can occur through reckless or negligent conduct that arises from the commission of a misdemeanor crime, illicit vehicular act, and other behaviors that pose an unreasonable or conscious disregard of human life and safety, such as what Michelle Carter did through text messages to encourage Conrad Henri Roy III to commit suicide (Taylor, 2019).

## Voluntary Manslaughter

Voluntary manslaughter and murder are both defined by intentional killings, but when a person who commits a homicide is experiencing a sudden heat of passion that is brought on by adequate provocation from the victim and there is concurrence between that agitated state and the resultant death, those circumstances can mitigate it from a murder to voluntary manslaughter.

FIGURE 7.3. **Heat of passion**

   To envision voluntary manslaughter in context, consider a situation wherein the killer is so enraged that they are literally blinded by their anger and so overcome by that feeling that they react in that moment by unlawfully taking the life of another person, specifically the person who did something to stir that intense emotional response within them. But people get upset every day due to the actions of others, and each person has a different temperament, with some more easily angered than others. So under the law, only provocation that is adequate or sufficient to cause a sudden heat of passion in a fictitious reasonable person with an even-keeled demeanor will satisfy the objective element of that standard. Of course, it must also be shown that the person who perpetrated the killing was adequately provoked, but that is a far easier burden to meet. This begs the question of what exactly constitutes adequate provocation. For better or worse, criminal laws do not set forth specific examples of a victim's inciteful behavior that will suffice to provoke a reasonable person and also the person who killed them. Under federal law, voluntary manslaughter is defined as "the unlawful killing of a human being without malice upon a sudden quarrel or heat of passion" (18 U.S. Code § 1112, 2008). Most states impose similar legal standards for qualifying voluntary manslaughter (18 Pa. C.S. § 2503, 2014; Cal. Penal Code § 192(a), 2001). Drawing from those same requisite elements, § 210.3 of the Model Penal Code (1962) frames voluntary manslaughter as a mitigated version of murder, and more specifically a "homicide which would otherwise be murder that is committed under the influence of extreme mental or emotional disturbance for which there is reasonable explanation or excuse." Case precedent offers context for situations that constitute adequate provocation, from objective and subjective standpoints in prosecutions for voluntary manslaughter. Generally, fighting or incendiary words alone are not considered enough to prompt a reasonable person to kill, but certain actions do typically meet that standard. In most jurisdictions, legally sufficient adequate provocation would be when the defendant observes their spouse engaged in an act of adultery and, upon seeing it, becomes so consumed by a sudden heat of passion like jealousy, anger, rage, or other intense emotion and immediately responds by killing one of both persons involved. Notice that the killing must be done through a heat of passion, which necessitates that there is no delay between the provoking event and fatal outcome. Otherwise, any evidence that the defendant took some time to cool off and calculate their actions could be used to show malice, deliberation, or other purposeful intent as a basis for escalating the charge to murder. That difference between voluntary manslaughter and murder is reflected in the maximum penalty for voluntary manslaughter, which varies by state but at the federal level is 10 years in prison, which is significantly lower than life imprisonment without the possibility of parole or a death sentence which accompany a first-degree murder conviction (18 U.S. Code §1111 (2003); 18 U.S. Code §1112, 2008). Of all the various forms of homicide, involuntary manslaughter is characterized by the lowest level of culpability and corresponding lenient punishment; as the Michelle Carter case illustrates, this can stir controversy and national discussions over whether involuntary manslaughter laws strike a fair balance between due process, crime control, and justice.

## Involuntary Manslaughter

Involuntary manslaughter involves unplanned or accidental deaths caused by deviant conduct or other behavior that falls below objective standards of reasonableness. The fictitious reasonable person has a star role in laws that criminalize involuntary manslaughter and define it by death resulting from careless conduct which that imaginary individual, acting ever so prudently, would have avoided. That criminal intent element can be construed as negligence or recklessness depending on the statute, but both levels of culpability are essential to involuntary manslaughter and reflect the unintentionality behind that type of homicide. Recall from Chapter 4 that a person who is negligent fails to exercise the amount of care that an ordinary, reasonable person would in their position, and that breach in judgment causes harm. Whereas recklessness encompasses a higher level of blameworthiness since it involves a conscious disregard of a risk to human life, and that dismissal causes the danger to escalate into a bodily injury. In accordance with federal law, a homicide that is inflicted through negligence or recklessness is criminalized as involuntary manslaughter and can include "the commission in an unlawful manner, or without due caution and circumspection, of a lawful act which might produce death" (18 U.S. Code § 1112, 2008). It also encompasses the misdemeanor-manslaughter rule, which imposes strict liability for any death that results from "the commission of any unlawful act not amounting to a felony" (18 U.S. Code § 1112, 2008); that is, during the commission or attempted commission of a misdemeanor. For example, assume that a shoplifter steals a low-priced item from a store, and the owner slips and falls while chasing them and dies from the injuries sustained as a result. If the incident occurred on federal territory, the shoplifter may be charged with involuntary manslaughter pursuant to the misdemeanor-manslaughter rule applied under that federal statute. Most jurisdictions and the Model Penal Code reject that stringent result and instead limit punishment for involuntary manslaughter to unintentional killings that are driven by reckless or negligent intent, which include vehicular deaths that are caused from driving while under the influence of drugs or alcohol.

## The Scope of Involuntary Manslaughter

The Massachusetts involuntary manslaughter statute is likely to be familiar to most people who learned of it through the infamous and first-of-its-kind suicide by text case. The statute defines involuntary manslaughter as "an unlawful killing that was unintentionally caused as the result of the defendants' wanton or reckless conduct" (Mass. Gen. Laws ch.265, § 13, 2019). On February 4, 2015, Michelle Carter was indicted for that crime in an unprecedented prosecution based on evidence that she caused the suicide death of her then boyfriend Conrad Henri Roy III through text communications. People around the world watched news of her widely covered bench trial. It featured a prosecutor who came armed with a manuscript containing lengthy text message conversations that Carter had with Roy on July 12, 2014, the day that he killed himself through carbon monoxide poisoning. The prosecutor set the scene for the judge and public audience: Roy had researched possible ways to die from carbon monoxide fumes, and as he sat in his truck contemplating which would be the most effective, Carter helped him solidify a plan through text messages describing how to attach a hose to the exhaust pipe and securely position it through the window into the truck. She continued to explain that his death would come quick, about 20 to 30 minutes later, and reassured him that his family would not be traumatized by his suicide. Carter had even offered to console his parents once he was gone. The state argued that those text communications constituted "wanton or reckless conduct" because Carter was aware that Roy had attempted suicide on more than one prior occasion and nonetheless persisted in encouraging him to succeed this time around. She repeatedly asked him when he would be ready to try again and admonished him for being indecisive, saying that doing so was only make things worse by prolonging the inevitable. At one point she even told him to get back into the truck, responding to Roy's message in which he conveyed strong reluctance over taking his own life and how that decision would impact his family. Carter was relentless, having sent Roy over 1,000 text messages consisting of similar content in the week preceding his death, which the prosecution said was a conscious disregard of his suicide ideations—which she knew about—and that such recklessness caused Roy to succeed in his suicidal plan. In 2017 Carter was found guilty of involuntary manslaughter for unintentionally causing Roy to kill himself through text messages. That landmark verdict certainly shocked the public, and particularly civil liberty advocates. But also alarming was the sentence that Michelle Carter

Victim:
Conrad Henri Roy III

Defendant:
Michelle Carter

received: a 2½-year sentence, with 15 months served and the remainder suspended (Jacobo & Smith, 2020; Shiffer, 2019).

## Conclusion

In this chapter, readers learned that homicides are generally classified as murder or manslaughter depending on the criminal intent behind it. The Menendez brothers' case was discussed to contextualize the deliberation and premeditation elements of first-degree murder, which may be construed from a criminal plan that precedes the death, accompanies it, and is continually executed thereafter. Gypsy Rose Blanchard also played a role in her parent's death but was convicted of second-degree murder as part of a plea deal, even though she too had planned that homicide. Unlike the Menendez brothers, her allegations of abuse and victimization at the hands of her mother were substantiated and sufficient to warrant that charge reduction. Despite those differences, both cases are examples of parenticide committed with malicious intent. As discussed, a few state laws also include third-degree murder, which encompass a lower culpability of reckless or negligent intent. Both voluntary and involuntary manslaughter are distinguished from all forms of murder since neither offense requires malice. In voluntary manslaughter, malicious intent is negated by evidence that the victim did something to adequately provoke the perpetrator into a heat of passion, which influenced that person to kill. In contrast, involuntary manslaughter is an unintentional killing caused by conduct which is unlawful or lawful but performed recklessly or negligently, such as cajoling someone through text messaging to commit suicide who has attempted it before.

## THINK AND APPLY

Refer to what you have learned in this chapter and think about whether Michelle Carter was appropriately charged. Specifically, consider whether, based on her persistent and arguably intentional text messaging, she should have faced a first-degree murder conviction. Or perhaps you share the viewpoint of civil liberty advocates who believe that she should not have been charged with any crime, since her actions were a form of protected speech. Which perspective do you agree with and why?

*Credits*

# Chapter 8

# Crimes Against Property

## Introduction to the Chapter

In this chapter, readers will learn about the elements of crimes against property, which are organized into two categories: nonviolent theft crimes and crimes that are perpetrated through some intrusion or damage inflicted on property and punished on a graded scale. Nonviolent theft crimes are consolidated in statutes and include offenses that involve the unlawful taking of real property, personal property, or services by larceny, larceny by trick, false pretenses, embezzlement, extortion, or receiving stolen property. The parallels between these offenses are discussed to enhance understanding of how consolidating them into a single statute contributes to more efficient criminal prosecutions. Larceny involves the taking of personal property with the intent to deprive the owner of possession of it, and that act can be achieved through the communication of a false representation of fact that prompts the owner to release the items to the perpetrator. Similarly, when property is taken by false pretenses, the individual who steals it uses deception to convince the owner to relinquish their property and the title to it, and with that the perpetrator becomes the rightful owner of the stolen items, albeit through trickery and in turn unlawfully. Deceit is also central to the crime of embezzlement, which occurs when the victim transfers their property to another person who holds a fiduciary position and through that status gains the victim's trust, which is really a facade used to conceal the nonconsensual conversion of their property. The infamous Ponzi scheme that Bernard "Bernie" Madoff orchestrated is used as an example of embezzlement and particularly to show how it involves the victim voluntarily giving up their property to someone who violates their trust by using the entrusted items for their own benefit or profit. In contrast, property obtained by extortion is acquired not with the victim's consent but under the threat of a future harm to their body, personal, or professional reputation. Robbery also involves the taking of property but through actual force or an imminent threat of such harm to the individual in possession of the items. The Abigail Catt case is highlighted in this chapter to exemplify some circumstances that can be used to aggravate punishment for robbery. The second category of crimes against property that are discussed cause some intrusion or damage to property and include criminal trespass, burglary, arson, and criminal mischief. The elements of those offenses are covered from both common law and contemporary law perspectives to provide contextual understanding of how those crimes are charged and punished, along with important differences among them.

## Consolidated Theft Crimes

Under contemporary criminal laws, nonviolent theft crimes are consolidated into single statutes, which commonly include the elements of larceny, larceny by trick, false pretenses, and embezzlement. As in Model Penal Code § 223.1 (1962) and some jurisdictions, other offenses perpetrated by receiving stolen property and extortion are also combined into those statutes, along with the corresponding penalties that are imposed on a graded scale according to factors such as the type, value of property taken, and circumstances surrounding the unlawful taking. When stolen property is worth less than a certain monetary designation that is specified under the applicable law, the underlying crime(s) is generally classified as a petty theft or second- or third-degree offense depending on the jurisdiction. Whereas grand theft or first-degree charges are imposed in situations in which the market value of the property exceeds that threshold. For instance, in Pennsylvania a theft is considered a third-degree felony if it involves the taking of a vehicle or any property exceeding $2,000, but that crime is elevated to a first-degree offense if the stolen items are valued at more than $500,000 (39 Pa. C.S. § 3903, 2007). Under the law, if multiple thefts are committed as part of a single crime incident, the aggregate price of the stolen property will be used as a baseline for determining how the offense will be graded and punished. There are divergent criminal intent and act components of larceny, larceny by trick, false pretenses, and embezzlement in accordance with varying statutes, but theft that occurs in any of those nonviolent forms results in loss of, or at the very least an interference with possession or ownership of, real property, personal property, and/or services.

Real property includes land and items that are permanently attached to it, such as buildings, and personal property covers anything else that can be owned and is movable, including but not limited to jewelry, cars, clothing, and furniture, as well as intangible items of intellectual property, such as copyrights, patents, and trademarks. In most states such deprivation in possession or ownership must be permanent and purposeful, which allows for possible affirmative defenses to be raised in cases in which assets were taken accidentally without knowledge of to whom they belonged or with the intent just to borrow the items. However, the scope of that defense is limited under laws such as this, under which

> a person commits theft if he or she knowingly obtains or uses, or endeavors to obtain or to use, the property of another with intent to, either temporarily or permanently deprive the other person of a right to the property or benefit from the property. (Fla. Stat. Ann. § 812.014, 2019)

Accordingly, in Florida theft crimes are defined broadly to even encompass situations wherein someone unlawfully took property with the intent to return it later. Also, even in other states where a fleeting property loss is considered a defense against theft charges for larceny, larceny by trick, and false pretenses, it is not for embezzlement. As discussed later in this chapter, a requisite element of embezzlement is conversion of real or personal property, and once that occurs the items taken have been consumed at least in their original form, so replacing the stolen, converted goods with alternatives does not diminish the underlying permanent deprivation of property interests.

## Larceny, Larceny by Trick, and False Pretenses

Larceny theft is generally defined as the unauthorized taking of personal property that is facilitated through the exercise of control over it and asportation, and even the slightest movement will suffice so long as it is done with an intent to deprive the owner of possession of it. The asportation element can be satisfied in either of the following ways: through some overt action on the part of the perpetrator or by the victim relinquishing control over their property upon reliance on a false representation of material fact the perpetrator communicated to them. The latter situation is considered larceny by trick, since deceit or trickery is used to gain possession of the property. Either way, the criminal act element of larceny is satisfied when someone gains possession and control over another person's personal property against the owner's free will. Closely related is theft by false pretenses, which also involves the taking of property based on an intentional misrepresentation of a fact that would likely convince any reasonable person to give up possession of something they own, whether it is real property, personal property, or services. However, larceny by trick and theft by false pretenses are distinguished by the types of items targeted and the ways they impact the victim's ownership interest in the property taken. The crime of larceny by trick must involve personal property since the exertion of control and asportation can only be achieved with items that are movable, and it is complete if those actions are done with purposeful or knowing intent to gain such possession. In contrast, real or personal property can be taken by false pretenses, as could services, since it is achieved by the victim giving up something of value that they own to another person based on that individual's false statements about a fact related to it. There is no control or asportation requirement for false pretenses. But most jurisdictions do require a transfer of possession and ownership of the property or services stolen to support a conviction for theft by false pretenses.

Draw from the following example to further compare and contrast the elements of larceny by trick and false pretenses. Pretend that Sara owns a brand-new red sports car, which her so-called friend Jane really admires. Jane has asked Sara on several occasions permission to take it for a joyride but is repeatedly turned down. One day Jane decides to take a different approach and trick Sara into letting her drive the car. Jane lies to Sara, saying that she has a family emergency and needs to use the car to get to the hospital. She does this with the specific intention of getting the car, just to drive it. Sara, believing that fabricated story, feels sorry for her friend and for that reason hands over the keys to her coveted sports car, expecting to get it back within a few hours. But Jane has other plans: to continue driving around in the car for as long as she possibly can, which will undoubtedly deprive Sara of possession in it. That exemplifies a larceny by trick, since Jane lied to Sara in order to gain access to the car, and it was only because of that false statement that Sara actually gave her the keys to it. Although Jane has no intent to take over ownership of the car, she does want to keep it and tried to accomplish that through deception, which suffices for larceny by trick. If instead Jane desired not only to drive Sara's car but also to become the rightful owner of it and took calculated steps in furtherance of that goal, she could be charged with theft by false pretenses. Assume now that Jane deceives Sara into transferring title of the car to her by offering to pay twice the amount of money it is worth. Jane is now the owner of the new red sports car, which Sara agreed to sell her based on a false representation of fact—that Jane would pay an agreed-upon price for it, which Jane neither did nor had any plans to do so. All of this constitutes a theft by false pretenses. This hypothetical illustrates some key differences between larceny by trick and false pretenses and the close similarities between them, which is a rationale behind the consolidation of nonviolent theft crimes under contemporary criminal laws.

**PAUSE AND REFLECT**

Pause and reflect on how theft crime charges may vary by degree and type based primarily on the monetary value of the stolen property and extent to which the associated loss was permanent or temporary. Corresponding punishments are also imposed on a graded scale. Less central to those outcomes is whether the stealing was achieved through trickery or deception, such as with larceny by trick or false pretenses. Do you think that using deceit to take property belonging to someone else demonstrates a higher level of culpability than overt theft acts that do not involve that element? If so, in what ways should those differences impact charging and punishment decisions in nonviolent theft cases?

## Embezzlement

Victims:
37,000 people

Defendant:
Bernard "Bernie"
Lawrence Madoff

Embezzlement is a nonviolent theft crime that is distinguishable since it involves the victim willfully transferring their real or personal property to another person, who under the law and in most jurisdictions must be someone with whom they share a fiduciary relationship. In contrast, the related offenses of larceny, larceny by trick, and false pretenses occur when the property is taken with the owner's uninformed consent or without it altogether. Another point of distinction is that a preexisting fiduciary relationship between the victim and perpetrator is an attendant circumstance of embezzlement. That connection must be one that would suffice to inspire trust from an objectively reasonable standpoint and within the victim specifically, who, feeling secure in that relationship, trusts the fiduciary to care for and manage their assets for a legitimate purpose established by contract, professional obligation, or less formally between family members, friends, and loved ones. Pursuant to federal and state laws, that entrustment element of embezzlement may be specified in general terms describing what a fiduciary relationship entails and through the specification of circumstances in which that connection and corresponding responsibilities are presumed (C.R.S. § 18-8-40718, 2016; 39 Pa. C.S. §3927, 2010; U.S.C. § 666(a)(1)(A), 2012). The criminal act of embezzlement is conversion, which occurs when the fiduciary holder misuses the property they were entrusted to manage in accordance with the owner's expectations for their own personal benefit or consumption, in violation of ethical and legal duties they were obligated to uphold by virtue of being in that position of trust. Such conduct must be performed with a specific or general intent to deprive the owner of their property interests, which results in a loss to them.

When reading that description of the criminal intent and act components of embezzlement, did you envision Bernard "Bernie" Lawrence Madoff? Or perhaps just his name came to mind. If so, you are among millions of people who recall or have learned about the 2008 fallout from the largest Ponzi scheme that ever was, orchestrated by Bernie Madoff, a highly successful and respected financier at the time. Literally every aspect of his crime was sensational, and taken together it was ripe for prime-time television and headline news. First was the fact that for decades prior to 2008, Madoff was considered nothing short of Wall Street royalty, at least in the securities world. In 1960 he established Bernard. L. Madoff Investment Securities, LLC, which he ran along with his brother and sons and amassed customers and business partnerships worldwide, until everything came to an end in 2008. That was the year that Madoff finally confessed to embezzling an estimated $65 billion from 37,000 people in various countries through a Ponzi scheme. He explained how his reputation as a savvy and successful financial investor preceded him, which initially made it easy to build a clientele. Madoff's clients were plentiful and diverse, and they included celebrities, working-class individuals, and everyone in between. Those customers, and more importantly victims, gave him their money and trusted that he would exercise due diligence and utilize legitimate market practices in deciding how to spend it on stock portfolios that rendered a profitable return on their investments. Instead, Madoff converted finances he received from new clients to pay existing ones under the facade that the distributed monies were investment returns. He continued that scheme for more than 17 years, which resulted in an exorbitant loss to thousands of investors that totaled more than $65 billion in money that they entrusted Madoff to manage in stocks, but he used it to accrue his personal wealth instead. For that, he was found guilty of 11 theft-related felonies, including embezzlement, and sentenced to 150 years in prison. Under the applicable federal law, 18 U.S.C. § 666(a)(1)(A) (2012), the requisite elements of embezzlement are as follows:

> there was a trust or fiduciary relationship between the defendant and the private organization or state or local government agency; the property came into the possession or care of the defendant by virtue of his employment; the defendant's dealings with the property constituted a fraudulent conversion or appropriation of it to his own use and the defendant acted with the intent to deprive the owner of the use of this property.

In accordance with the Securities Exchange Act of 1934, individuals who are in the business of conducting commercial securities transactions stand in a fiduciary position to the U.S. Securities and Exchange Commission, a federal agency that requires those dealings be executed with due diligence, transparency, and ethics (15 U.S.C. § 78a, 1934). Madoff breached those duties by appropriating money that he accepted from clients while acting in the capacity of brokerage chief, and in that position he was entrusted to invest those funds in the stock market on behalf of those individuals (Moyer, 2008; Yang & Kay, 2021).

## Extortion

Extortion, also known as blackmail, is consolidated in the Model Penal Code and other state laws among other nonviolent theft crimes, which include larceny, larceny by trick, false pretenses, embezzlement, and receiving stolen property. But it is distinctly charged as a felony offense, rather than on a graded scale in accordance with the value of the property taken, since that aside, a threatened harm is made to effectuate the stealing, which escalates the seriousness of extortion compared to other nonviolent theft crimes. The criminal act element of extortion is satisfied by the communication of a threat to inflict a future harm upon the property owner, which is generalized under most laws to encompass various forms of bodily injury or reputational damage on a personal or professional level. For instance, in Model Penal Code § 223.4 (1962), theft by extortion is construed broadly and, in that scope, can occur when the victim is induced into releasing their property to an extortionist who demands it by threatening to physically injure them or another person, commit a crime, accuse them of a crime, or disclose private information

> tending to subject any person to hatred, contempt, or ridicule or impair his credit and business repute, take or withhold action as an official, bring about a strike or boycott, testify with respect to another's legal claim, or inflict any other harm that would not benefit the actor.

It is important to note that under certain circumstances some threats of future harm, which may constitute extortion under state and federal laws, could otherwise be considered legal if not made with the requisite intent. In order for any threat of future harm to qualify as extortion, it must be communicated with a specific or general intent to obtain property belonging to another person and permanently deprive that individual of ownership in it. Absent such intention, hurtful threats, while unsettling, may nonetheless amount to an affirmative defense in most jurisdictions and the Model Penal Code.

Just like in prosecutions for larceny, larceny by trick, and false pretenses, punishment can be mitigated by evidence that the defendant made the menacing comment to the victim, but only with the intent to borrow the items. For example, assume that Zane tells Jack that he plans to post on social media about how Jack overcharges his customers unless he agrees to loan Zane $500. Jack is understandably upset by those comments and, feeling under pressure, gives Zane the money, which he promises to pay back to Jack. If Zane was subsequently charged with extortion, he could defend himself on the grounds that although he obtained Jack's money by threatening to harm his business reputation, he planned to repay him from the start and thus lacked the requisite intent to indefinitely take away his ownership of the property. As a result, that defense may be used when there is sufficient evidence to negate the mens rea elements of extortion. The other commonly recognized defense to extortion is that the perpetrator took another person's property under a threat of future harm but based on the honest, even if mistaken, belief that the stolen items rightfully belonged to them as compensation, restitution, or some sort of settlement. In that regard, it can be presented to show that an attendant circumstance of extortion is lacking and that the stolen property actually belonged to another person. For example, assume now that Zane is one of Jack's customers who genuinely thinks he was overcharged by $500 for a service that Jack performed in the ordinary course of his business. In an attempt to get the money that he feels Jack owes to him, Zane threatens to expose Jack's business improprieties on social media unless he receives the refund. If Zane is charged with extortion, he could defend against it by explaining that he believed the money taken from Jack was really his, and there was a legitimate basis for that belief such as a contract that existed between them.

Theft by extortion is characterized by causation and harm requirements, which must accompany the threat of future harm that is communicated with a desire to permanently deprive someone of ownership in their property. The criminal act and intent elements of the offense must both be the factual and legal cause of inducing the victim to give up their property to the extortionist. Factual causation is satisfied by a showing that absent the perpetrator's intentional conduct, the victim would not have relinquished their property, and so is legal causation if that was also an objectively foreseeable result of such behavior—meaning there is close proximity between the threatened harm and theft as substantiated by the absence of intervening factors that could have contributed to that outcome instead of the alleged extortion. Drawing from the Jack and Zane scenario, pretend that Jack is completely unaffected by Zane saying that he will post negative reviews about Jack's business unless Jack gives him $500. In fact, Zane has made similar statements in the past, which turned out to be empty threats. But Jack empathizes with Zane, and those feelings are what prompt him to give Zane the money he is asking for. The required causal relationship between the threat of future harm and release of property from the victim to the perpetrator is lacking in that situation, since Jack's desire to help Zane financially was what motivated him to pay Zane $500, thus breaking the chain of causation between the threatened future harm and payment. Finally, there is an attendant circumstance of harm, which is only met if and when the victim actually hands over the property as a result of the threatened action; anything short of that would not constitute extortion but perhaps an inchoate offense such as attempted extortion.

Pause and reflect on the elements of extortion, which generally include making a threat of future harm that is intended to and actually does result in the victim permanently releasing their property to the perpetrator. Yet extortion is included in consolidated theft crimes, among other nonviolent offenses. Also, important to consider is that extortion closely aligns with robbery, which involves property taken by the threat or actual infliction of force. What is the most appropriate way to categorize extortion under the law—as a nonviolent or violent crime? Explain.

## Robbery

FIGURE 8.1 **Robbery**

Robbery can be considered an escalated version of extortion, which involves an unlawful taking of property by a threat of future harm. An important difference is that it is necessitated by threatened imminent force or actual force against a person for the purpose of obtaining property that is within their possession or control. That requires more than mere asportation, an element of larceny that can be satisfied by the perpetrator exerting control over personal property and then moving it any distance, regardless of whether the owner facilitates the transfer or is even present when that happens. In contrast, while robbery is also in essence a crime against property, it is distinctly centered on the victim whose property is taken away by physical pressure or coercion. A point of emphasis is that such violence or impending violence must be inflicted in tandem with the unlawful taking of property to establish causation, both in fact and proximity (Model Penal Code § 222.1(1), 1962; N.J. Rev. Stat. 2C:15-1, 2013; 18 Pa. C.S. § 3701, 2014). Similar to extortion, in robbery cases the physical or threatened force must in fact cause a victim to lose their property, and there must be proximity or a close, foreseeable connection between that act and outcome. Since robbery is a specific intent crime, the forceful taking that accompanies it must typically be done for the purpose of permanently depriving the owner of possession of it. However, in some jurisdictions robbery convictions can be sustained even if the property stolen was taken with an intent to return it to the rightful owner. Robbery is a violent property crime that presents serious risks to bodily injury and public safety. For that it qualifies as a felony under criminal laws, which set it apart from other theft crimes like larceny (by trick), false pretenses, embezzlement, receiving stolen property, and extortion that are graded as a misdemeanor or felony, depending primarily on the value of the items stolen. However, it may be charged as a first-degree, second-degree, or aggravated offense, depending on factors such as the extent of injuries the victim sustained and whether a deadly weapon was used during the commission of the crime. That default standard for robbery gradation is spelled out in N.J. Rev. Stat. 2C:15-1, 2013 and other statutes under which

> robbery is a crime of the second degree, except that it is a crime of the first degree if in the course of committing the theft the actor attempts to kill anyone, or purposely inflicts or attempts to inflict serious bodily injury, or is armed with, or uses or threatens the immediate use of a deadly weapon.

Accordingly, a robbery offense can be aggravated under the applicable law to a first-degree offense if certain qualifying offense conditions are met. That is precisely what happened, in quite the public display, to Abigail "Abby" Catt, along with her father and brother in Texas back in 2013.

## Aggravated Robbery

On November 14, 2013, Abby Catt, alongside her brother and father, were found guilty under Texas Penal Code § 29.03 of aggravated robbery for driving a getaway car in the commission of two local bank robberies. In accordance with that law, her coconspirators "exhibited a deadly weapon" to facilitate the crimes, which is an aggravating attendant circumstance qualifying it as a first-degree offense. There was nothing remarkable in that, since most statutes contain similar conditions for upgrading robbery from a second- to first-degree crime and also embody the Pinkerton rule or another doctrine for imposing vicarious liability on someone for the actions of their coconspirators that they did not directly commit but nonetheless agreed to and took some action in furtherance of (*Pinkerton v. United States*, 1946).

Victims:
Comerica Bank and
First Community
Credit Union

Defendant:
Abigail "Abby" Catt

But there was one sensational detail of the Abby Catt story that stirred public interest in it from near and far: At the age of 18, Abby was recruited by her brother and father to join them in robbing banks as the getaway driver! Abby later recalled in a widely watched *20/20* episode how her brother Hayden Catt, 20 years old at the time, under their father's direction convinced her to get involved in the family crimes spree. She explained that Hayden told her that he and their father, Scott Catt, needed her to participate in the bank heists in order for them to be successful; that is, avoiding getting arrested and, more importantly, getting fast money. Abby and Hayden's mother passed away when they were young, and since then their father struggled to support them as a single parent. As planned, Hayden and Scott, disguised in construction worker vests, entered two financial institutions in 2012 just a few months apart, where Scott, armed with a pellet gun, demanded money from tellers. This constituted an aggravated robbery, as that offense is defined under Texas law as theft committed with the intent to obtain control of property by placing another in fear of imminent bodily harm or death by exhibiting a deadly weapon (Tex. Penal Code Ann. §§ 29.02, 29.03, 1994). Abby waited outside during both robberies and drove her brother and father away as they fled the scenes. In the end the Catt family obtained an estimated $170,000 from both robberies. Ironically, the construction worker vests that Hayden and Scott wore during the commission of the crimes to hide their identities were key pieces of evidence used to link them to the crimes after bank employees described those clothing items to police, who discovered they were purchased on Scott's credit card. All three members of the Catt family were arrested in November 2012 and subsequently pleaded guilty to aggravated robbery. Abby received the most lenient punishment of 5 years imprisonment, but her brother and father did not fare so well and received 10- and 24-year sentences respectively. Her crime entrée and incarceration were the subject of widespread media attention, since people were fascinated by how her connection to family is what inspired both outcomes. But beyond that, her case demonstrates in context the elements of robbery—particularly the threat of force, which can be displayed by use of a weapon during the commission of a theft, and how that aggravating factor could be used as a basis for enhancing that felony from a second- to first-degree offense (Fischer, 2019; Sederstrom, 2019).

## Receiving Stolen Property

Receiving stolen property is a nonviolent crime, that is consolidated in the Model Penal Code and in state criminal codes among other theft offenses. That offense is committed when property that is stolen such as through larceny (by trick), false pretenses, embezzlement, extortion or robbery is received by someone who knows the property was unlawfully taken and engages in intentional conduct aimed at facilitating the purchase, sale, disposition or transfer of the stolen items which completely deprives the owner of possession in it. Actual possession of the stolen property is typically not required to satisfy the actus reus element of the offense so long as there is evidence that the perpetrator had control over it, that is, constructive possession and knew that it came from an illicit source. For instance, in accordance with the Model Penal Code that criminal act could be established by "acquiring possession, control or title, or lending on the security of the property" (Model Penal Code § 223.6(1).

The act of receiving stolen property, through one of those methods or another form specified under the applicable statute must be done with a purpose, knowing, reckless or negligent intent to move stolen goods in some way such as through a purchase, sale, acquiring, or transferring title to them that results in the owner involuntarily losing control over the property. The perpetrator must know that the items were stolen, and such knowledge could be actual such as when the person charged with receiving stolen property is the individual who organized the crime or constructive which means that such awareness is imputed in circumstances where a reasonable person would have known, and therefore it is assumed that the perpetrator did as well. Constructive knowledge can be demonstrated by evidence showing that the individual who is charged with receiving stolen property is a dealer of illicit goods or someone who is familiar with that individual's reputation for being involved in such activities. A dealer is generally defined by statute as a "person in the business of buying or selling goods including a pawnbroker" and that status must be substantiated by a pattern of receiving property that is stolen or exchanged for an amount that is far below the market value of the items (Model Penal Code § 223.6(2). The performance of some conduct that is intended to facilitate the receipt of stolen property establishes causation between those requisite elements and the resultant harm, the owner's property loss. Like the other nonviolent consolidated theft crimes, receiving stolen property is punished on a graded scale as a misdemeanor or felony crime depending on the value of goods taken.

## Crimes That Intrude on or Damage Property

This section explores crimes that intrude on or damage property, such as criminal trespass, burglary, arson, and criminal mischief. These offenses do not necessitate the use of violence but do involve the destruction of personal or real property, which can be devastating and cause serious injuries and even death to the owner and other individuals who are occupants or in possession of the affected property. Criminal trespass encompasses some preliminary steps toward the commission of burglary and may be charged in situations wherein some of the criminal intent or act elements of burglary are lacking; it is typically graded as a low-level misdemeanor offense to reflect that distinction in culpability. Burglary and arson are treated as felony crimes in states and federally, given the enhanced safety risks associated with them. In addition, modern laws largely depart from narrow common law conceptions of those offenses, which stifled the prosecution of acts of burglary and arson committed against nonresidential, unoccupied property or in the absence of certain attendant circumstances. Criminal mischief is a crime against property that can occur incidental to burglary or arson, since it is achieved through intentional mishandling of property or interference with necessities such as gas, electricity, or water by tampering, use of fire or explosives, or other intrusions that cause loss or damage to property owned by someone other than the individual who perpetrated those acts. The requisite intent driving such conduct can be general or specific, depending on the applicable statute. Criminal mischief is typically punished less harshly than burglary or arson as a low-grade felony or misdemeanor offense, based on how much the property was devalued. Distinctions among these crimes that intrude on or damage property will be discussed, along with the overlap between them, to provide a comprehensive overview of the associated harms and safety threats.

## Criminal Trespass and Burglary

Criminal trespass alone does not result in any damage to property, but it does contravene the owner's privacy interests as it involves the criminal act of entering or remaining on another person's real property without their consent. Culpability is established if the alleged trespasser knew or had reason to know they were accessing a building, structure, land, or other property that belonged to someone else without the owner's permission. Criminal trespass is complete once those basic elements are satisfied, and for that reason that offense is commonly punished as a misdemeanor crime to reflect the correspondingly low threats to property and personal

FIGURE 8.2 **Burglary**

safety. However, in some jurisdictions criminal trespass of an occupied residence can be charged as a felony offense, yet one that is less serious in nature compared to a burglary, a felony crime that begins with a criminal trespass but encompasses much more.

At common law, burglary was defined as the unlawful breaking and entering into the dwelling house of another at nighttime with the intent to commit a felony therein. That stringent standard is no longer a part of most contemporary statutes, which specify that burglary can occur during any time of the day and be perpetrated against various types of real property other than a home, including but not limited to an office building, structure, or vehicle, including a person's own property. The property no longer has to belong to someone else, and examples of when a person can be found guilty of burglarizing their own place can arise in situations in which entry into the premises is restricted by law under a lease agreement or restraining order. Some states impose an attendant circumstance, such as that the property must be locked or occupied. Burglary can be charged as a first- or second-degree offense based on aggravating factors, such as the property being in use as a residence and the use or possession of a deadly weapon during the commission of a burglary, and any death or injury caused by the weapon. Under modern laws, the breaking and entering component of burglary is broader compared to how it was construed under common law, since it can be established even if the property in question was not actually broken into or fully entered. To illustrate this point, consider the following example of Jeff, who devises a plan to steal jewelry from his neighbor Todd's home. He approaches the house with that intent, pushes the front door open, and steps through the doorway. But before he can get any further, Todd surprises him from inside and yells, "Get off of my property!" Startled, Jeff quickly runs away, assuming that he will not get in any trouble since he did not fully enter the house or steal anything. Unfortunately, Jeff is mistaken, because the incident occurred in a jurisdiction where breaking and entering constitutes the criminal act of burglary. This can be satisfied by the use of physical force, however slight, if it is accompanied by partial or complete entry in a structure, such as kicking a door open or lifting an unlocked window and inserting a body part, full body, or instrument into the property. Jeff accomplished that by pushing the front door open and stepping foot into the foyer of the home of another person uninvited. The fact that he did not fully enter the premises or steal anything does not diminish his culpability, but there is variance across state laws that require an unlawful breaking and entry, require only an entry, or criminalize the act of remaining in the property without permission after an unauthorized or legal entry (Fla. Stat. Ann. § 810.02, 2022; Model Penal Code § 221.1, 1962; N.Y. Penal Law § 140.20, 2014).

The criminal act of burglary can be accomplished by breaking and entering into another person's property and also lingering on those premises without the owner's permission, but such conduct must be performed with either a general or specific intent to commit a crime inside in order to be punishable under any applicable contemporary law. In New York a burglary must be committed with general intent as follows: "A person is guilty of burglary in the third degree when he knowingly enters or remains unlawfully in a building with intent to commit a crime therein" (N.Y. Penal Law § 140.20, 2014). Whereas the Model Penal Code requires such actions to be done with the "purpose to commit a crime therein" (Model Penal Code § 221.1). It is important to note that the intended offense need not be a felony, as was required at common law; however, unlawful access to or presence on a property that is done with that criminal intent could be considered an aggravating factor and basis for imposing a first-degree burglary charge. A burglary cannot occur unless there is concurrence between those criminal act and intent elements, but there could be sufficient basis to support a lesser offense such as larceny or criminal trespass. The following example is intended to demonstrate those points. Assume that Bob is a hiker who gets stranded in a desolate area during a severe snowstorm. He is in desperate need of basic necessities—food, shelter, and water—and believes that he will not survive unless he has access to those items soon. Bob sees a cabin in the near distance and makes his way to it. He turns the knob and walks through the door uninvited with the intent to warm up, change clothes, and find food. After being in the cabin for a few hours, Bob notices what he believes is valuable jewelry, puts it into his pocket, and walks out. Unbeknownst to Bob, the cabin is under surveillance, and the entire incident is captured on video.

Pause and reflect on actus reus and mens rea elements of burglary and what you have learned about how they must concur in time, and decide whether Bob could be charged with that offense. If not, are there any other theft or property-related crimes covered in this chapter that are more aligned with the evidence? Explain.

**PAUSE AND REFLECT**

The Model Penal Code and most states recognize the following affirmative defenses to burglary: the property was abandoned, it was open to the public, or the defendant had a license or other legal right to be present on the premises. These defenses are used to refute the unlawful access or entry component of burglary.

## Arson

Arson is a property crime that was strictly defined under common law as a malicious, intentional burning of another person's dwelling; that did not cover situations wherein only minimal fire damage was caused or the residence belonged to the person who started the fire. Contemporary criminal laws are more inclusive and provide standards for the actus reus requirement of arson to be satisfied by evidence of burning, as well as other less destructive outcomes of starting a fire, such as charring or explosions. In most jurisdictions the incendiary actions must be performed with general intent, knowing that they will lead to the resultant property damage, or with a specific intent or purpose to cause such harm. Unlike at common law, the damaged property does not have to belong to someone else, and it can be any type of building or structure, including but not limited to a residence, a vehicle, or other fixture as specified in the applicable statute. The intentional act of setting fire to the property must be both the actual and proximate cause of the destruction, which means the destruction is a foreseeable outcome of the fire. The New Mexico arsons statute aligns with other statutes, including the Model Penal Code, which embody modern conceptions of that offense; accordingly, a person is guilty of arson who

> maliciously or willfully starts a fire or causes an explosion with the purpose of destroying or damaging: a building, occupied structure or property of another person; a bridge, utility line, fence or sign; or any property, whether the person's own property or the property of another person, to collect insurance for the loss. (NM Stat. § 30-17-5, 2018)

Arson can be treated as a misdemeanor or felony offense, and those charging decisions and corresponding punishments are graded on a scale basis according to the value, extent, and type of property damage and whether any persons were injured or killed as a result.

## Conclusion

Crimes against property range in type and impact but can be organized into general categories based on the requisite elements of violence, intrusion, property loss, or damage. Nonviolent theft crimes include larceny, larceny by trick, false pretenses, embezzlement, and extortion and are criminalized under a single statute in most states and the Model Penal Code, given the commonalities between them. Nonetheless, they are distinguished by how the property is taken—through deceit, based on trust, or under the threat of harm—and in turn the corresponding extent of property loss suffered by the victim. The Bernie Madoff case was discussed to demonstrate the vulnerability inherent in fiduciary relationships and related acts of embezzlement. Another sensational case covered in this chapter centered on Abigail Catt and her conviction for aggravated robbery. As discussed, actual or threatened violence is inherent in robbery, and that element is enhanced through circumstances such as in Abby's case, in which a weapon was used to unlawfully obtain property within another person's possession. The final part of this chapter covers criminal trespass, burglary, arson, and criminal mischief, which are crimes that intrude on or damage property. Although these offenses are not commonly consolidated into a single statute as nonviolent theft crimes are, the reader is left to wonder whether perhaps they should be.

# THINK AND APPLY

Draw from what you have learned in this chapter about crimes that intrude on or damage property, including criminal trespass, burglary, arson, and criminal mischief. As discussed, these distinct offenses can occur as part of the same crime incident, given that criminal trespass readily culminates into burglary and can be charged in situations in which one or more elements of burglary are lacking. Similarly, an arson can be accomplished through acts of criminal mischief that involve the use of fire or explosives to tamper with property. Perhaps these parallels should be reflected in criminal laws that consolidate the elements of crimes that intrude on or damage property. Pursuant to federal law,

> a person is guilty of criminal mischief if he damages tangible property of another purposely, recklessly, or by negligence in the employment of fire, explosives, or other dangerous means; or purposely or recklessly tampers with tangible property of another so as to endanger person or property; or purposely or recklessly causes another to suffer pecuniary loss by deception or threat. (25 CFR § 11.410, 1999)

What language would you add to this statute so that it consolidates the elements burglary and arson?

*Credits*

Fig. 8.1: Copyright © 2014 Depositphotos/photographee.eu.
Fig. 8.2: Copyright © 2013 Depositphotos/rcreitmeyer.

# Chapter 9

# Justification Defenses

## Introduction to the Chapter

Every person charged with a crime is entitled to due process under the law as provided through the 5th and 14th Amendments to the U.S. Constitution, which afford opportunities for individuals to defend against such allegations by asserting their innocence or presenting other evidence that could otherwise mitigate culpability and punishment. An alibi defense is raised in situations wherein the defendant denies all responsibility for the crimes charged and substantiates those claims with details of their whereabouts during the crime commission that conflict with the time, place, and location of the crime incident. The focus of this chapter is on affirmative defenses, and more specifically justifications for crimes committed out of necessity, or with reasonable nondeadly or deadly force used in defense of self, others, or property and in law enforcement, with a particular emphasis on the accompanying elements and standards of proof as outlined in applicable criminal laws. Unlike alibi defenses, those crime justifications involve an affirmation of criminal wrongdoing and corresponding position that such conduct was nonetheless reasonable and should therefore be justified under the law as sufficient grounds for a reduced or no punishment. In criminal cases, the prosecutor has the burden of showing that the person charged with the crime(s) is guilty beyond a reasonable doubt and must present substantiating proof that they committed the criminal act with the requisite level of intention. Under the laws in most jurisdictions, that burden shifts to a defendant who raises an alibi or affirmative defense, since they are presumably in the best position to explain their experiences preceding and coinciding with the criminal incident and how those events justify their criminal conduct in accordance with the governing statute. Criminal laws contain various standards that are used to determine whether someone has successfully demonstrated a perfect defense: that their criminal actions and intent aligned with the qualifying specified conditions for the purported justification. A central component of justification defenses is reasonableness, which means the asserted criminal act is measured against an objective reasonable person standard and whether that figurative individual would have behaved in the same way; if so, it is considered justified and possible grounds for an acquittal. Therefore, a mistaken but unreasonable belief in the justifiability of criminal behavior may also be protected in some jurisdictions but to a lesser extent, because it is considered mitigating but not exculpatory evidence and can therefore only result in a conviction for a lesser offense like, for example, manslaughter instead of murder in homicide cases. This chapter also explores deep-rooted concerns about the extent to which fairness and justice are reflected in jury verdicts rendered in use-of-force cases and how those sentiments persist through time and contexts, as exemplified by the sensational outcomes of the racially charged shooting committed by Bernhard Goetz, spousal homicide inflicted by a battered wife and mother, Francine Hughes, and various incidents of police use of deadly force against persons of color.

## Necessity of Force: Self-Defense, Defense of Others, and Defense of Property

FIGURE 9.1. Use of force

The necessity of using force in self-defense and defense of others and property is one of the most revered and controversial justifications for crime. It has roots in traditional common law concepts and can be applied to prevent a homicide or other serious felony offenses, as outlined by statute. Criminal laws contain separate designations for when persons are justified in using nondeadly or deadly force to protect themselves, others, and property from threatened or actual harm, and in most jurisdictions those standards are measured by the totality of circumstances and objective reasonableness. Nondeadly force is generally considered reasonable when administered in response to a proportionate, immediate threat posed by the victim to the defendant, another person whom the defendant seeks to protect, or their property. Such harm may also be justified as part of a performed duty to protect that is implicit in family relationships, conferred through professional obligations, and in emergency situations. For example, nonlethal harm can legally be inflicted by a parent or legal guardian to exert control over a child or someone who is adjudicated incompetent, a physician during the provision of care or treatment for a patient in accordance with their informed consent, or in urgent situations in which such permission is unattainable.

Only nonfatal force used in defense of real or personal property is justifiable under the law, and it must emanate from a reasonable belief that such violence is necessary to protect the property from an impending trespass, theft, destruction, or some other intrusion by the victim.

In most states the exertion of violence in defense of property must be based on an objective belief that such a response is necessary, but the Model Penal Code also considers individualized, subjective threat perceptions a justifiable basis for the application of nondeadly force in that context. Real property is generally defined as buildings and other structures, such as homes that are permanently affixed to land, and includes the curtilage or areas surrounding it like backyards and enclosed spaces within fences, and personal property covers items that are movable in nature, such as jewelry, cars and clothes. The scope of justifiable force that can be used in defense of property is limited to nondeadly violence regardless of the type of property involved, but that restriction does not apply to actions taken to protect oneself or another person from an immediate threat of bodily injury or death. Although there is no concrete distinction between nondeadly and deadly force, typically harm is considered lethal even if it does not result in death but a reasonable person would perceive it as likely to cause serious bodily injury or fatality (10 CFR § 1047.7, 2016). Deadly force poses a heightened threat of harm to the victim and potentially others, and that is reflected in federal and state laws, which require more stringent standards to be used in evaluating whether it is reasonably applied in self-defense or the defense of others. Subject to statutory variations, deadly force is justified if executed during an unprovoked attack and in reaction to an imminent threat of serious physical harm or death, but only if that perceived fear is reasonable from an objective standpoint and proportionate to the amount and type of force used to thwart it. The distinct criteria needed to satisfy each of those components—that is, to prove the necessity of deadly force—will be discussed both in theory and context.

## Unprovoked Attack

A cardinal rule in deadly force cases is that the individual who perpetrates such actual or threatened harm must not have provoked the incident that precipitated the behavior. As such, any person who is the initial aggressor in a violent encounter will not be justified in using or attempting to use lethal harm against the victim, who is only using force for self-protection in a situation that the instigator incited, unless one of the commonly recognized exceptions to the unprovoked attack requirement applies. To illustrate that point, suppose that Ivan becomes angry with his friend Ted and pushes him to the ground. When Ted regains his balance, he displays a pocketknife that he had been wearing all along and has what is undoubtedly a menacing look in his eyes. Ivan, fearful of being stabbed, picks up a huge boulder and repeatedly strikes Ted with it. Luckily, Ted suffers non-life-threatening injuries from the attack, but Ivan is less fortunate, since they live in a jurisdiction where a large boulder is considered an instrument of deadly force. To make matters worse, Ivan cannot successfully claim that his actions were justified and done in self-defense since he initiated the confrontation, unless he could show that Ted subsequently used force against him that did not match the threat his preceding conduct posed, either in degree or timing, or they were engaged in a mutually agreed-upon fight. These exceptions to the unprovoked attack rule are included in most criminal laws, which specify that a defendant who is the initial aggressor of an encounter that escalates into a felony crime or homicide can still claim those actions were done for self-protection or the protection of others upon a showing that the victim reacted to that provocation with excessive force; the defendant withdrew from the conflict and communicated that withdrawal to the victim, who nonetheless persisted with inflicting an actual or threatened injury upon them; or the parties were participating in combat, which they agreed to even if not specifically authorized to do so under the law (e.g., C.R.S. § 18-1-704, 2020; N.Y. Penal Law § 35.15, 2014; Wis. Stat. § 939.48, 2014).

Recall the scenario between Ivan and Ted but with a slight change of facts to put these exceptions into context. Pretend now that Ivan's push prompts Ted to remove a lighter from his front pocket and use it in an attempt to set Ivan's clothing and body on fire. Ted's actions constitute an excessive use of force since it involved fire, which presents a risk of serious injury or death that is disproportionate to any minor or nonfatal harm that typically occurs from getting pushed. If Ivan were to respond to that fear of getting burned by choking Ted to death, he could defend the homicide as justified even though he started the altercation, because Ted escalated it with an excessive application of force. The withdrawal exception can be demonstrated using the same preliminary facts, but now assume that Ivan flees after pushing Ted and yells, "I'm done, I won't hurt you anymore!" If Ted continues pursuing Ivan and eventually finds him hiding outside, where he attempts to set him on fire, Ivan would be justified in applying an equal amount of deadly force to defend himself against that serious threat of physical injury or death. Finally, Ivan's initial act of aggression toward Ted may constitute a justifiable use of force if done as part of a physical encounter that they both agreed to participate in, such as martial arts, contact sports, or other similar activities even if proscribed by law.

## Imminent Threat

As discussed, a successful self-defense claim must begin with evidence showing that the use of deadly force was applied in an unprovoked attack, but it could still be asserted in limited situations in which the defendant was the initial aggressor if the victim used force in response to that provocation that exceeded the underlying threat or came after it had already expired.

The defendant must then demonstrate the unprovoked confrontation they had with the victim in context by showing that during it, the victim did something that posed an immediate threat of serious bodily injury or death to them or another person. A threat is imminent if it would inspire an urgent and particularized fear among reasonable persons faced by it, who would similarly feel that their own or someone else's safety was endangered. Past or anticipated intimidation does not suffice to satisfy that standard, and so violent conduct performed in response to such intangible threats would not be justified. However, in some jurisdictions, a present verbal communication of impending injury could constitute an imminent threat, but antagonizing statements unaccompanied by any threat of physical harm typically do not (Tex. Penal Code § 9.31, 1994). In theory, the imminent threat requirement is simply understood as an urgent threat of bodily injury, which may be expressed through menacing words or conduct that reflect such intent. But applying it in context can be more complicated, particularly in situations wherein deadly force is used to quell a threat that is continuous and serious in nature yet carries no risk of any current danger, at least from an objectively reasonable standpoint. For instance, intimate partner homicides are perpetrated by individuals who are abused by someone they share a close relationship with, and that connection is patterned by violent experiences that can inspire subjective beliefs about the necessity of using deadly force but that do not coincide with the objective imminent threat criteria for proving self-defense.

In 1977 Francine Hughes showcased key complexities surrounding this issue with her crime, which captivated the nation and sparked conversations about the imminent threat requirement, how it is supposed to be weighed against an objective reasonable standard, and the extent to which that evaluation should also account for threat perceptions that are peculiar to victims of intimate partner violence.

## Battered Wife Exception

On March 9, 1977, news of Francine Hughes sending her husband, James "Mickey" Hughes, to a fiery death blasted across the country, and decades later her crime was documented in *The Burning Bed*, which further sensationalized what she did, her reasons for doing it, and how that all contributed to a shift in how self-defense is conceptualized in contemporary American laws and evidentiary procedures. Francine turned herself in to authorities immediately after killing her husband and recalled her experiences of being persistently abused by her husband, in front of their children, for more than 13 years; because of that, she remained in constant fear of him attacking her even at times when he posed no immediate threat to her safety. At trial, her attorney framed the necessity of the deadly force she used against Mickey as objectively reasonable, in light of her traumatization as an abused wife and mother who was failed by the criminal justice system and more importantly her husband, on whom she was totally dependent for financial support. Francine was a teenager when she dropped out of high school to marry Mickey and became pregnant with the first of their four children. On several occasions leading up to the murder, Francine called police to report the domestic violence she suffered at the hands of her alcoholic husband, including incidents in which she was bloodied and bore other serious visible injuries of abuse. But Mickey was never arrested, which was a common police response to domestic abuse calls for service during the mid-1970s, since at that time abuse between intimate partners was considered a private, domestic matter outside the purview of formal law enforcement procedures (Boots, 2020; Langer, 2017).

Francine eventually sought advice from a social worker, who recommended that she divorce Mickey, which she did—but that did not stop the violent onslaughts. Mickey remained living in their former marital household, where he terrorized her daily, which all culminated in Francine believing that her only options were either to be killed by Mickey or kill him first. Indeed, she thought there was an urgent need to take his life, even though he was sleeping at the time that she did. Earlier that fateful night, Mickey had verbally and physically abused Francine in the presence of their children, forced her to burn her secretarial books, threw the dinner she prepared on the floor, pressed her face into it, and twisted her arm until she cleaned up the mess he caused. Mickey then raped Francine, his final act of abuse, before falling into a drunken stupor. It was in that moment that Francine decided to end the violence once and for all, believing that if she did not, the cycle of fear and victimization would continue once Mickey awoke. While Mickey slept, Francine placed their four children safely

Victim:
James "Mickey" Hughes

Defendant:
Francine Hughes

in her car outside and proceeded to set his bed on fire with him in it, and then she left him there to burn to death. She then drove directly to the police station, where she recounted those events, was placed under arrest, and later charged with first-degree murder for killing Mickey. She pleaded not guilty by reason of insanity, and her case went to trial. Her defense attorney explained that his decision to advise Francine not to claim self-defense was done out of concern that the jury would perceive the homicide as an unjustified act of lethal harm, since the facts clearly showed that Mickey did not provoke the attack that was inflicted on him and posed no imminent threat of danger to anyone in his sleep. Indeed, Francine Hughes exerted deadly force under circumstances that did not align with the traditional elements of self-defense (Grimes, 2017).

**PAUSE AND REFLECT**

Pause and reflect on the elements of a successful self-defense claim that have been discussed so far: an unprovoked attack and fear of harm emanating from the victim's words or actions, which reasonable persons would likely feel pose an imminent threat of bodily injury. Both were lacking in the Francine Hughes case. Regardless, pretend you were her attorney; would you still have tried to convince the jury that the objective reasonable person standard should be amenable to account for subjective factors such as sustained intimate partner violence and the psychological effects of it, which likely contribute to threat perceptions held by abused victims and their perceived need to inflict deadly harm on their abuser? Explain.

Ultimately, Francine Hughes was found not guilty by reason of temporary insanity, and her attorney presented evidence that she was a "battered woman" for over 13 years, subject to relentless verbal and physical abuse by her husband, to demonstrate that because of those experiences, she "lacked substantial capacity either to appreciate the nature and quality or the wrongfulness of her conduct, or to conform her conduct to the requirements of the law" (MCL § 780.972, 2006). By 1979 Lenore Walker, a renowned psychologist, published empirical data to show a need for reform in self-defense law to formally recognize what she called "battered woman's syndrome," under which victims of intimate partner violence experience cyclical phases of rising tension, systemic violence, and reconciliation. She further explained how that pattern of victimization and abeyance is perpetual, existing throughout the domestic or intimate partner relationship, and under those circumstances, victims often anticipate the ensuing violence, even during periods of rising tension and reconciliation, and thereby perceive it as impending even though other individuals would not

FIGURE 9.2 Intimate partner violence

objectively view it that way. With that, Walker (2016) established the battered woman's syndrome and corresponding framework for considering subjective threat perceptions in the evaluation of the reasonableness of deadly force. Her groundbreaking research has prompted some states to allow the admission of expert witness testimony in intimate partner homicide cases as relevant to proving the battered woman's syndrome defense; however, those decisions are made on a case-by-case basis, subject to state evidentiary rules and application to the specific facts and circumstances in which the deadly force was applied (e.g., *Hawthorne v. State of Florida*, 1985; *Ibn-Tamas v. United States*, 1979; *State v. Kelly*, 1984; *State v. Yusuf*, 2002). Walker's conception of the battered woman's syndrome and associated cycles of abuse and victimization has broadened the scope of understanding deadly force used in self-defense and in particular the intricacies of evaluating the imminence of threat perceptions from a reasonable person standard. But individuals who assert the battered woman's defense must demonstrate that any supporting evidence meets procedural standards for relevance, risk of prejudice, and qualifying expert witnesses before the substantive elements of their claim will be considered, and that could prove challenging and perhaps even fatal to the viability of an unconventional self-defense claim.

## Objectively Reasonable Fear and Proportionality

The justification of deadly force, whether used for self-protection or to prevent harm to others, is contextual and must be inspired by an unprovoked threat of bodily injury or death posed by the victim that is immediate in nature from an objective standpoint. The issue in some deadly force cases, such as those involving intimate partner homicide, is whether and to what extent being a victim of patterned abuse and violence could be perceived as an imminent threat by the abused defendant and others in similar situations. But that aside, it is more readily understood how intimate partner abuse, particularly when inflicted over a prolonged period of time, can

Victims: Barry Allen, Darrell Cabey, Troy Canty, and James Ramseur

Defendant: Bernhard Goetz

instill a reasonable fear of injury or death in the victim. In other incidents, such as the multiple shooting perpetrated by Bernhard Goetz, the reasonableness of the lethal harm used is framed by questions about how subjective biases and race might influence threat perceptions. On December 22, 1984, Goetz, a White man, committed one of the most remarkable racially charged crimes when he shot four unarmed Black youths—Barry Allen, Darrell Cabey, Troy Canty, and James Ramseur—on a crowded subway car and later defended his actions at trial as a reasonable, necessary use of deadly force. Even though all the youths sustained non-life-threatening injuries, Cabey experienced permanent brain damage and paralysis from the shooting. Goetz fled New York City but was arrested soon after and charged with attempted murder, assault, and possession of illegal firearms. He entered a not guilty plea, and the subsequent trial centered on whether, under the circumstances, it was reasonable for him to fear for his life and personal safety. It is important to note that the intimidation that motivates the use of deadly force can still be justified, even if based on perceived rather than actual danger posed by the assailant victim's behavior, so long as it is rooted in objective facts that would lead others to draw the same conclusions about the necessity of using force. At trial, there were certain uncontested details of the incident that were key to evaluating whether it was reasonable for Goetz to shoot four individuals in a public space. In the months leading up to the shooting, Goetz was mugged and assaulted by a group of Black teenagers. He reported the incident to police but grew disheartened by what he construed as their lack of serious devotion to the case. That first encounter prompted him to obtain a licensed handgun for self-protection, which he was known to always carry, especially when riding the subway including on the day of the infamous shooting (Latson, 2014).

After the shooting occurred, the media dubbed him the "Subway Vigilante," which reflected how he recounted his decision to fire five shots in rapid succession at four teenagers who approached him asking for money. At trial, the victims confirmed they were panhandling for money to play video games when Canty approached and said, "Give me $5" (Small, 2020). Eyewitnesses recalled how Goetz responded to that statement by immediately standing from his seat and opening fire on the four young men. Goetz admitted to that at trial and further explained that those actions were a justifiable response and based on his reasonable belief that the four victims were going to rob him and that their request for money was a prelude to that. Pursuant to the applicable New York Penal Code and U.S. criminal laws generally, the offense of robbery is defined as the forcible taking of property from within a person's possession or control (N.Y. Penal Law §§ 160.05, 160.10, 160.15, 2014). It is likely that Goetz had $5 or other items worth that amount, but the issue was whether Canty or any of his friends attempted to take that personal property by force. None of them were armed or carrying weapons, but that fact alone is not dispositive, since legitimate uses of force can be motivated by actual or perceived threats. So a central issue at trial was whether the four youths did or said something to indicate a present intent to rob Goetz. There was no evidence to indicate that he was faced with any form of verbal or physical intimidation, let alone an imminent one (Small, 2020).

**PAUSE AND REFLECT**

Pause and reflect on what the trial record did show in the Bernhard Goetz case, that he was confronted by Canty, who told him "Give me $5," a statement that he interpreted as a threat and justification for shooting Canty and the three friends who accompanied him (Small, 2020). This incident occurred in New York City, and under the applicable law, any use of deadly force in defense of self or others must be done in response to a proportionate threat of harm, specifically deadly force (N.Y. Penal Las § 35.15, 2014). Was it objectively reasonable for Goetz to shoot Canty in response to his demand for money? What about Allen, Cabey, and Ramseur—was Goetz justified in shooting them?

As indicated by that law, for the use of lethal harm to be legally justified, it must be proportionate to the threat posed by the victim so that reasonable persons would agree that it was necessary to prevent an impending physical injury or death. This proportionality requirement is measured from an objective standpoint and based on the nature of the actual or threatened violence initiated or exacerbated by the victim. Criminal laws do not distinguish between the specific methods of force that may constitute nondeadly or deadly harm, but the determining factor applied by courts is whether such underlying conduct creates a high risk of severe bodily harm or death, and if so, it will be considered fatal in nature. The way in which that imminent threat is classified, as nondeadly or deadly, is essential to establishing whether a justifiable amount of force was used to defend against it. Specifically, there must be a match between the seriousness of harm posed by the victim and presented by the defendant, and whether that proportionality exists is largely dependent on attendant circumstances, such as whether any of the disputants displayed or used an instrumentality during the violent encounter in question that is considered a dangerous weapon from an objective standpoint.

Decades after Bernhard Goetz shot four unarmed youths, there remain lingering questions about how and why a jury found him not guilty of attempted murder and assault and in turn justified his acts of force against those individuals who did not threaten his life in any way. Of particular importance was what the prosecutor revealed at trial, that during the incident Goetz told Cabey, who was seated and attempting to shield himself, "You don't look so bad, here's another" before firing his gun. Cabey was shot, and even though that bullet did not end his life, it drastically changed it forever, as it caused permanent paralysis and brain damage (Chambers, 1985). In 1996 Cabey won a civil lawsuit against Goetz and was awarded $43 million in damages for the personal injuries that he suffered from the shooting, which the jury in that case decided was an intentional tort, a harm driven by malicious intent. Despite that verdict, Cabey has not received any compensation from Goetz, who filed for bankruptcy shortly after he was found liable in that civil action. To date, the only punishment that Goetz has actually endured from the sensational shooting incident was an 8½-month jail sentence, which he served after being convicted of illegal possession of the firearm he used during the encounter. He was prosecuted and sentenced in New York, under Penal Law § 35.15(2)(b) (2014), which includes the standard approach taken by most other state statutes that define the use of deadly force as reasonable if inflicted in an unprovoked attacked and in response to an imminent fear of bodily injury or death, such as one posed during the commission or attempted commission of a "kidnapping, forcible rape, forcible criminal sexual act or robbery" or a forcible felony generally (see MCA § 45-3-102, 2009; Neb. Stat. Ann. § 28-1409, 2012). As discussed, Bernhard Goetz defended the shooting based on the claim that it was a justified reaction to Barry Allen, Darrell Cabey, Troy Canty, and James Ramseur, who were attempting to rob him of $5. The fact that a jury agreed with that position remains a point of fascination and concern in public discourse about the intricacies of self-defense laws, how those rules are applied to real life situations and weighed against objective standards of reasonableness (Gladwell, 1996; Tarmy, 2020).

## Attendant Circumstance: To Retreat or Not Retreat

A duty to retreat was imposed under common law as an attendant circumstance in justifying the use of deadly force, which meant defendants were required to demonstrate a failed attempt to safely avoid the infliction of lethal harm to prove that it was truly done out of necessity. Recall the true crime stories highlighted in this chapter surrounding Francine Hughes and Bernhard Goetz and how their asserted self-defense claims were framed by questions about deadly force justifications and whether in those and other similar situations the actual or threatened serious injury or death involved could have been avoided altogether. With that in mind, the laws in 15 states are reminiscent of common law and require a defendant to make some effort to retreat from the impending harm before executing lethal harm in response to it but contain exceptions for encounters that occur in the home, vehicle, or workplace. The castle doctrine refers to that exception to the duty to retreat requirement, which applies to deadly force incidents that occur within a home or private dwelling and is specified in applicable laws (National Conference of State Legislators, 2020). For example, pursuant to the Maine Revised Statutes, there is a duty to retreat, "except if the person is in a dwelling place and not the initial aggressor" (M.R.S. § 108, 2007). An important qualification on the duty to retreat, no matter the context of the encounter, is that the actor must be able to disengage from the encounter in a peaceful, nonviolent manner, and if not, then it does not apply. Interestingly, New York is among the states where there is a duty to retreat and where Bernhard Goetz was acquitted of first-degree murder for what a jury decided was a justifiable shooting that he perpetrated without first seeking to avoid what he perceived as an impending robbery. That is despite the letter of the applicable law, which states, "the actor may not use deadly physical force if he or she knows that with complete personal safety, to oneself and others he or she may avoid the necessity of so doing by retreating" (N.Y. Penal Law § 35.15, 2014). Whereas in the state of Michigan, where Francine Hughes was prosecuted for first-degree murder, there is a stand-your-ground law, which vitiates that duty for defendants who while engaged in lawful conduct are presented with a reasonable fear of bodily harm or death and use lethal harm to prevent it. As per that statute,

> an individual who has not or is not engaged in the commission of a crime at the time she uses deadly force may use deadly force against another individual anywhere she has the legal right to be with no duty to retreat if the individual honestly and reasonably believes that the use of deadly force is necessary to prevent the imminent death, great bodily harm or sexual assault to herself or to another individual. (MCL § 780.972, 2006)

Although Francine Hughes had ample reason to stand her ground in the face of what she perceived as a recurring, imminent physical and sexual danger to herself, she was found not guilty on the basis of her asserted temporary insanity defense, on which the jury was not required to reach a decision regarding self-defense. The goal in presenting those case outcomes in the context of the duty to retreat or not retreat is to further illustrate deep complexities surrounding the application of self-defense laws to actual cases and more importantly jury deliberations.

PAUSE AND
REFLECT

Pause and reflect on distinctions between state laws that impose a duty to retreat and those that do not and instead allow defendants to stand their ground in the face of an imminent threat to themselves or another person. Which approach seems to be the most reasonable in deadly force cases, a duty to retreat with or without a castle doctrine exception, or rather a stand-your-ground rule with no duty to retreat at all? Explain.

## Police Use of Deadly Force

Daunte Wright, Andre Hill, Manuel Ellis, Rayshard Brooks, Daniel Prude, George Floyd, Atatiana Jefferson, Breonna Taylor, Aura Rosser, Stephon Clark, Botham Jean, Philando Castile, Alton Sterling, Freddie Gray, Janisha Fonville, Eric Garner, Michelle Cusseaux, Akai Gurley, Gabriella Nevarez, Tamir Rice, Michael Brown, and Tanisha Anderson. Chances are that you recognize some or all of these names of Black individuals who were killed by police use of deadly force in separate incidents, which captured public attention and spurred ongoing conversations over when those decisions are justified or instead motivated by a subjective, extralegal factor such as racial bias (Ater, 2020; McPhillips, 2020). Your opinion, no matter what it is, should be informed by the U.S. Constitution and U.S. Supreme Court decisions, which provide well-established standards for when it is reasonable for federal, state, and local police officers to use force against citizens. The Fourth Amendment to the U.S. Constitution is central to inquiries about whether police used excessive force in a particular instance, since it provides citizens protection from unreasonable searches and seizures, which are essentially unjustified intrusions on one's body or property. Police must have either a warrant or probable cause to justify an interference with a citizen's reasonable expectation of privacy in their person or belongings. Probable cause is needed to secure an arrest or search warrant and is defined as a reasonable belief that a crime has occurred, is in progress, or is about to occur and the items or person to be searched and seized is directly connected to that suspected law violation. The U.S. Supreme Court, in two landmark rulings—*Tennessee v. Garner* (1985) and *Graham v. Connor* (1989)—interpreted the scope of the Fourth Amendment protection against unreasonable searches and seizures in the context of police use-of-force decisions to apprehend persons, search and seize their bodies to make an arrest, or kill them to avoid an imminent danger. The court in both cases was presented with the issue of when police are justified under the Fourth Amendment in using deadly or nondeadly force and which standards should be applied in making those determinations on a case-by-case basis.

In *Tennessee v. Garner* (1985), it was decided that police use of deadly force under the common law fleeing felon rule constituted an unreasonable seizure under the Fourth Amendment and is therefore unjustified. Prior to that ruling, some states, including Tennessee, had laws that reflected this traditional standard and allowed for law enforcement officers to apply lethal harm against any citizen who was attempting to avoid police apprehension and who they had reason to believe had committed a felony or was about to. The applicable statute gave officers the authority to "use all the necessary means to effect the arrest" of any person who flees or forcibly resists after the officer informs them of an intent to make an arrest. The U.S. Supreme Court ruled that an effort to capture a fleeing felon in itself does not suffice to justify the use of deadly force in the process, and there must also be probable cause or reason to believe that such lethal harm is necessary to avoid an imminent danger to life posed by the victim. With that, *Tennessee v. Garner* heightened the standard law enforcement officers must satisfy to show that a deadly force decision is justified, and it is measured from an objective standpoint. But as exemplified by the sensationalism and controversy surrounding police use of deadly force incidents, applying that standard in context is complex, to say the least, particularly because reasonable persons share different perspectives on what a citizen must do or say to objectively warrant a fatal officer response.

**PAUSE AND REFLECT**    Pause and reflect on the *Tennessee v. Garner* standard for determining the justifiability of police use of deadly force. Also recall one of the sensational cases highlighted in this section or another that involved a citizen who was killed during an encounter with a law enforcement officer. Applying the *Garner* rule to those case facts, explain whether it was a justified or excessive use of force.

In *Graham v. Connor* (1989), the U.S. Supreme Court reinforced objective reasonableness as essential to establishing whether law enforcement decisions to use force to effectuate a search or seizure is justified in a particular instance and outlined the scope of that standard by the totality of circumstances. The justices ruled in favor of the police officers who used physical force to restrain a citizen who they observed exhibiting behaviors that they believed were indicative of being under the influence of alcohol or drugs. The court ruled that even though that conclusion was wrong, it was a reasonable one since they saw the citizen who was diabetic and experiencing low blood sugar exhibiting erratic and sudden movements that included running around his car and going in and out of a store suddenly due to a failed effort to buy orange juice. Despite the citizen explaining to the officers his urgent need of medical care, given the totality of circumstances, the officers' decision to use nondeadly force to subdue and arrest him was considered reasonable. The citizen sustained bruising, broken limbs, and other non-life-threatening injuries during his encounter with the officers, which he claimed constituted an unreasonable seizure and violation of his Fourth Amendment rights. Since the court disagreed, *Graham v. Connor* exemplifies police nondeadly force in context and that such decisions are justified if done on the basis of objective circumstances that law enforcement officers observe or otherwise learn through their interactions with the citizen, and an honest but mistaken belief about the necessity of using such force can still be considered reasonable from that perspective.

## Conclusion

This chapter discussed the necessity of using force for self-protection or in defense of others or property, which was first recognized at common law as a justifiable defense to crime. Under contemporary law, the defendant has the burden of asserting the elements of a defense claim, which generally require a showing of proportionality between the threatened or actual harm presented by the victim and their violent response, that such impending danger was imminent and presented in an unprovoked attack, and under those circumstances an objective reasonable person would have also believed it was necessary to employ the same force to protect themselves from bodily harm or death. Either nondeadly or deadly force can be employed to defend oneself or another person; however, lethal harm is only justified in response to a form of intimidation that carries a risk of severe bodily injury or death. Imminent threats that do present that level of danger can be quelled with nondeadly force instead. But context matters under the law, and accordingly, reasonable force used in protection of real or personal property is limited to harm that is nondeadly in nature. In some states and under common law, the defendant has a duty to retreat from the harm if possible to safely do so, unless the encounter occurs in a home, vehicle, or workplace. Other jurisdictions allow persons to stand their ground in the face of an unprovoked, imminent danger regardless of place, as long as they have a legal right to be present in that space. Finally, those concepts were examined using examples from sensational cases surrounding Bernhard Goetz, Francine Hughes, and incidents of police use of force to further enhance understanding of the elements and complexities of justification defenses in context.

## THINK AND APPLY

As discussed, only nondeadly force could be applied in defense of property, in situations wherein the initiating threat does not involve any risk of harm to persons. But some statutes also recognize a justification defense based on necessity absent any use of force. For example, if someone is in dire need of shelter from freezing temperatures and unlawfully enters another person's house to avoid death, they might be able to defend their illegal actions. But the homeowner can also defend against that trespass with nondeadly force. From an objective reasonable perspective, which action is more justifiable, the trespass or the nondeadly force?

*Credits*

Fig. 9.1: Copyright © 2013 Depositphotos/leremy.
Fig. 9.2: Copyright © 2014 Depositphotos/lifeinapixel.

# Chapter 10

# Excuse Defenses

## Introduction to the Chapter

There are legal justifications and excuses for crime that can be raised in defense of criminal charges as grounds for reduced or no punishment; these are contingent on a sufficient demonstration of certain personal characteristics and/or offense circumstances that can substantiate the elements of that claim. As discussed in Chapter 9, justification defenses are measured by an objective reasonableness standard, which requires any accompanying act of necessity; use of force in self-defense, defense of others, or defense of property; or law enforcement to be proved by evidence showing that other people in that situation would have responded similarly, therefore justifying the otherwise criminal conduct. The focus of this chapter is on excuse defenses related to legal insanity, infancy, intoxication, duress, entrapment, and mistake of law and fact, which are recognized under state and federal laws that require the defendant to affirm criminal wrongdoing and explicate some reason why their mental state during the crime commission was absent the requisite criminal culpability. In evaluating the validity of excuse defenses, courts must consider any subjective characteristics of the person who committed the crime, along with situational factors that are presented and relevant to their asserted reason for doing it in accordance with the governing statute. What constitutes a legal excuse to crime is outlined by law and subject to statutory variations, but all such defenses are commonly linked to mens rea. More specifically, successful criminal excuses require proof that the underlying act was performed without criminal intent due to some dysfunction in the mind or body or the influence of some factor outside the actor's control. From that standpoint, criminal conduct may be legally excused in situations wherein the individual actor was unable to comprehend the gravity of their illicit behavior or otherwise prevent it, irrespective of whether such outcome is seen as justified among reasonable persons in general.

FIGURE 10.1. Excuses to crime

## Legal Insanity

The insanity defense is recognized federally and in most states except for Idaho, Kansas, Montana, and Utah under criminal laws that specify one of these four standards used for determining legal insanity: McNaughten test, irresistible impulse, substantial capacity, and the Durham test. Each imposes distinct requirements for measuring whether the defendant committed the criminal act with a diminished or no culpability while suffering from some mental disease or defect at the time. It is irrelevant whether such impairment persisted thereafter, like during the criminal prosecution, since legal competence to stand trial is established if the defendant "has sufficient present ability to consult with his lawyer with a reasonable degree of rational understanding ... and has a rational as well as factual understanding of the proceedings against him" (*Dusky v. United States*, 1960), and that encompasses a relatively lower threshold of proof. All tests for legal insanity are centered on the extent to which the criminal actor lacked or possessed a compromised ability to understand the law and/or conform their conduct in accordance with it when they committed the crime. The underlying rationale behind this defense and the corresponding methods for evaluating it is that if someone is accordingly deemed to have been legally insane at the time of their crime commission, such conduct should be excused from traditional punishments like incarceration, which presumably would not serve to reduce their unfettered propensity for crime. The consequences of a not guilty by reason of insanity verdict reflect this and include confinement to a mental health institution, for persons like Andrea Yates, Lorena Bobbitt, and John Hinckley Jr., who as discussed in this chapter were adjudicated legally insane and acquitted of criminal acts that they performed while in that psychological state. In other cases in which the defendant does not successfully demonstrate their insanity, a jury may return a verdict of guilty or guilty but mentally ill; both decisions lead to incarceration, but the latter one entitles opportunities to psychological treatment services during imprisonment. The burden of proof for legal insanity is established by varying criminal laws, which impose it on the prosecution to refute insanity or the defense to demonstrate it in accordance with the applicable standard. Whatever the outcome, when a defendant enters a plea of not guilty by reason of insanity, their freedom and fate are largely dependent on which of the four tests is applied to evaluate that defense, and accordingly whether evidence of complete or partial cognitive or impulse control impairment will suffice to satisfy it.

## McNaughten Test

In American jurisprudence, the insanity defense was born from the McNaughten rule, a common law standard that originated in Britain after Daniel McNaughten was acquitted in the shooting death of Robert Peele back in 1843. That verdict sent shock waves across the British Parliament and citizenry alike because Peele was a high-ranking official, but even more appalling was the fact that since there was no established rule for determining insanity at the time, the jury in *R. v. McNaughten* (1843) reached that conclusion based only on scarce testimonial evidence that he committed that crime with a delusional state of mind. The

McNaughten test, is aptly named after that infamous case, and was developed in response to that outcome. It imposes a heightened, rigid standard for proving legal insanity—that the defendant was suffering from a mental disease or defect and because of that did not know their conduct was wrong or the general difference between right and wrong from a moral or legal standpoint. The successful application of that standard in context can be challenging since it only accounts for cognition, specifically whether a person was aware of their actions or the law, and there is no allowance for anything else such as behavioral influences. However, a textbook example of a successful insanity claim under the McNaughten test is the Andrea Yates case and others wherein a criminal act is excused based on facts that the defendant committed it to serve what they believed was the will of God or a higher being and therefore did not understand the gravity of their actions or that such actions were even wrong. Pursuant to the narrow language and application of the McNaughten test, crimes that are committed with mental awareness of the resultant harm but with low or no impulse control are inexcusable. The irresistible impulse test addresses that gap since it allows for insanity to be demonstrated based on evidence that the defendant had a psychological illness and because of it could not resist a compulsion to break the law, even if they knew the difference between right and wrong or that their actions were illegal.

## Irresistible Impulse Test

When most people hear the name Lorena Bobbitt, they think of the woman who infamously severed the penis of her husband, John Bobbitt, while he slept, tossed the mutilated body part out her car window, and kept on driving. A far-less-popular point of discussion related to those outrageous events is that the irresistible impulse test for insanity served a central role in the criminal prosecution against Lorena on charges of malicious wounding. Lorena faced a maximum of 20 years in prison and deportation for the crime, which she admitted to doing, but her attorneys argued that she was legally insane when she performed those actions and that therefore they should be excused under the law. She was charged in Virginia, and in that state legal insanity is measured by a standard that encompasses elements of both the McNaughten and irresistible impulse tests. Under it, persons can be excused from criminal culpability for legal insanity if, due to having a mental disease or defect, they lacked mental awareness about either the criminal nature of their actions or the difference between criminal and legal conduct generally, or were otherwise unable to control their behavior at the time of the crime commission (Margolick, 1994).

Victim:
John Bobbitt

Defendant:
Lorena Bobbitt

Lorena's defense centered on the irresistible impulse portion of that standard, under which evidence of a complete breakdown in self-control at the time of the crime can suffice as grounds for a successful legal insanity defense. She pleaded not guilty by reason of insanity, and at trial her attorneys presented evidence that John had physical and sexually abused her for the duration of their 4-year marriage. He had been arrested for assault and battery on prior occasions, but the couple always reunited, and the alleged domestic violence continued. It was under those circumstances that Lorena claimed that she was unable to resist the impulse to cut off John's penis to protect herself from any further victimizations, which allegedly included marital rapes, with the last one occurring just before the castration. The jury returned a not guilty verdict by reaching the conclusion that Lorena was temporarily insane and acting on an irresistible impulse when she disfigured her husband. She was subsequently acquitted of malicious wounding and avoided deportation but was court ordered to spend 45 days in a mental institution. John underwent a successful genital reattachment surgery and was acquitted on charges of marital sexual assault. But the American public has not fully recovered from the scandalous Lorena Bobbitt story, as the details of her crime and acquittal remain embedded in popular culture decades after they happened. Those events also illustrate the application of the irresistible impulse test for legal insanity in context, and perhaps to some, good reason why it is not employed in most state and federal cases, since it offers no guidance for understanding what it takes for someone who knows right from wrong to become totally unhinged in their ability to control their actions (Gearan, 1994; Sorrentino, et. al., 2019).

**PAUSE AND REFLECT**

Pause and reflect on the components of the irresistible impulse test for determining legal insanity that was applied in the Lorena Bobbitt case pursuant to Virginia law. It allows for proof of insanity based on either cognitive or volitional deficits that result from a mental disease or defect that existed at the time of the crime commission. Under it, persons who claim insanity must demonstrate that they either did not understand their conduct was wrong, did not understand the difference between right and wrong behavior, or were otherwise unable to suppress an impulse to commit the crime. Lorena's insanity defense was based on the latter component, which can be satisfied by evidence that the criminal actor lacked the capacity to control their actions. So her attorneys called psychiatrists to testify that Lorena had no control over her actions when she severed her husband's genital, due to the prolonged effects of domestic abuse. In most jurisdictions, irresistible impulse is not recognized as a legitimate basis for proving legal insanity, since it is challenging to verify a lack of volitional will, and more importantly what evidence suffices to substantiate that.

What do you think about the irresistible impulse test?

## Substantial Capacity Test

Victim:
Former president
Ronald Reagan

Defendant:
John Hinckley Jr.

The substantial capacity test is part of the Model Penal Code, which was drafted by the American Legal Institute (ALI) in 1962; because of that, it is also commonly referred to as the ALI or Model Penal Code test for insanity (Model Penal Code § 4.01, 1962). By 1980 most states and the federal government used it to measure insanity, but that drastically changed 2 years later when John Hinckley Jr. was found insane under it and acquitted of attempting to assassinate former president Ronald Reagan. But during 1980 to 1982, the substantial capacity test was largely considered the preferred approach to proving insanity over the McNaughten and irresistible impulse tests, which taken together require a showing that the defendant committed a crime while suffering from a psychological condition that completely debilitated their mental or physical capacity to make controlled, rational choices or bodily movements within the confines of the law. It can also be challenging for attorneys and triers of fact to quantify the symptoms of a psychological disease or defect as causing a complete dysfunction in awareness or action, especially if the defendant suffers from a mental illness that is exhibited through intermittent periods of manic and stable behavior. So the substantial capacity test provides a buffer to those stringent requirements imposed under the McNaughten and irresistible impulse tests. Under it, criminal actions are excused if committed by persons who lacked a substantial capacity to understand their conduct was wrong or to act in a lawful manner, and so a complete breakdown in cognition or bodily control need not be shown.

By 1982 the substantial capacity test was in the public spotlight, along with Hinckley during his widely publicized trial for shooting and wounding former president Reagan and two of his aides. Hinckley entered a plea of not guilty by reason of insanity, which was substantiated by evidence that he attempted to assassinate Reagan to attract the attention of the actor Jodie Foster, with whom he proclaimed to be obsessed. Prior to the incident, he had written countless poems, letters, and other correspondence to Foster, all of which went unanswered; so, as he documented in his last letter sent, he intended the shooting to be the final effort to gain her affection, all of which his attorney explained indicated that he lacked a substantial capacity to control himself. The jury agreed and acquitted Hinckley on all charges, and he was sentenced to a federal psychiatric facility, where he received mental health treatment until his release in 2016. People were shocked by that case outcome and attributed it to the substantial capacity test and the perceived ease with which it could be satisfied (Finley, 2021; Glass, 2018). In response, on October 12, 1984, then-president Reagan signed the Insanity Defense Reform Act into law, which heightened the standard for proving insanity in federal cases to require a showing that "at the time of the commission of the acts constituting the offense, the defendant, as a result of a severe mental disease or defect, was unable to appreciate the nature and quality or the wrongfulness of his acts." It also eliminates a diminished capacity defense as it stated, "mental disease or defect does not otherwise constitute a defense" (18 U.S. Code § 17, 1984). Similarly, most states shifted away from the irresistible impulse test by adopting standards for determining legal insanity that were reminiscent of the McNaughten rule and the associated challenges to proving insanity under it.

## Durham Test

The Durham test, also known as the "product test," is by far the least popular standard for measuring insanity, since it is rejected by the federal government and all states except for New Hampshire. Under it, legal insanity can be proved based on evidence that the "unlawful conduct was a product of a mental disease or defect" (*Durham v. United States*, 1954). There is no accompanying explication of what constitutes a product of a mental disease or defect or even what factors could be considered in making that determination. It only requires proximate causation between the psychological condition and the crime, which is established if there is a foreseeable connection between that cause and effect. This makes the Durham test a very broad standard, which in theory could be applied to excuse a wide array of crimes that have a causal link to and are a product of a mental disease or defect.

**PAUSE AND REFLECT**

Pause and reflect on the Durham, or product, test for measuring legal insanity, which requires that the "unlawful conduct was a product of a mental disease or defect" (*Durham v. United States*, 1954). A major criticism of it is that crimes committed by individuals who are suffering from a drug or compulsion addiction such as gambling can be excused as a product of a mental defect and in turn insanity.

What do you think about the Durham test?

## Infancy

Just like legal insanity, the infancy defense has common law roots and is used to negate criminal intent on the basis that the defendant had no or a diminished criminal culpability; however, due to age, and not some mental disease or defect. Individuals who are below a certain age designated by statute at the time of their crime commission can avoid punishment for such conduct entirely or in part since it is well established that children possess underdeveloped mental and emotional faculties, which can hinder rational and productive decision making. The purpose of the infancy defense is to excuse juveniles from criminal punishment, since that outcome would not serve to reduce crime among them, who by virtue of their age are presumed to have violated the law because of immaturity and not a criminal intention to do so. The infancy defense provides only limited protection, specifically from criminal convictions and sentences imposed through the adult criminal justice system—but even that is subject to varying statutory waiver policies that stipulate when children can be charged as adults in accordance with listed age, offense, and offender characteristics. For instance, the Model Penal Code stipulates that the juvenile court has exclusive jurisdiction over persons who were younger than 16 at the time of their crime commission (§ 4.10(1)(a), 1962). State laws impose distinct minimum age requirements and additional qualifying criteria for determining when juvenile and adult courts have exclusive or concurrent powers to process cases involving a child who is arrested for a crime. For instance, in Georgia any offenses committed by individuals who are younger than 13 years old must be adjudicated in juvenile court. But accordingly, 13- or 14-year-olds can be charged as an adult for a capital crime or one that causes the victim to endure a serious physical injury, and other juvenile felony crime commissions are only subject to adult court jurisdiction if performed by individuals who are at least 15 years of age (GA Code § 15-11-561, 2014). In other jurisdictions, no criminal culpability is presumed if certain age, offense severity, and criminal history criteria are met, and that can be rebutted with sufficient proof that the child broke the law with criminal intention and as a consequence should be tried as an adult. At common law, mens rea was also linked to age at the time of the crime commission in accordance with these standards: persons younger than

7 years old did not have the capacity to form criminal intent and were exempt from criminal punishment; a rebuttable presumption of no culpability among persons 7 to 14-years old; and anyone older than 14 years old has the ability to act with a criminal mind and face prosecution in adult court for doing so. There are distinct statutory and common law rules for determining the scope of criminal liability among juvenile offenders, which taken together create a framework for the infancy defense, particularly when it could excuse someone from the jurisdiction of adult court.

## Intoxication

Intoxication is generally defined as a disruption to mental or physical capacities caused by the ingestion of drugs, legal or not, or alcohol, and evidence of those effects can excuse criminal conduct in whole or part, depending on whether it happened voluntarily (Model Penal Code § 2.08(5)(a), 1962). Involuntary intoxication is a valid defense to crime under most state laws and to some extent in federal court, and successful proof of it can negate the requisite criminal intent and excuse any accompanying behavior as a complete or partial defense (*United States v. Nix*, 1974). The involuntary nature of the resultant intoxication is an essential element of the validity of the defense, but state laws offer varying guidance on what constitutes involuntariness. For example, in the Tennessee Code, "involuntary intoxication means intoxication that is not voluntary," T.C.A. § 39-11-503, 2019 but other statutes expound that definition by specifying that the intoxicating substance must have been ingested unknowingly, due to trickery, fraud, duress or other coercion (MCA § 45-2-203, 2009;). Evidence of involuntary intoxication must be substantiated by facts showing that the influence of it rendered the defendant incapable of forming the requisite criminal intent at the time that they violated the law. In some states and the Model Penal Code, that requirement is satisfied if "the person lacked substantial capacity either to appreciate the wrongfulness of the person's conduct or to conform that conduct to the requirements of the law allegedly violated," and that is the same standard used to measure legal insanity in jurisdictions that still apply the substantial capacity test in such cases (11 Del. C. § 423, 1953; T.C.A. § 39-11-503, 2019). That is a reflection of how legal insanity and involuntary intoxication defenses offer distinct grounds for excusing crime, yet both are satisfied by evidence that the crime commission was done with diminished or no criminal intent. In contrast, intoxication that is voluntary occurs from the knowing and intentional consumption of a substance that is known or likely to have that effect, and for that reason it is not a complete defense to crime and can solely be introduced to reduce criminal punishment when permitted under the applicable statute and subject to any corresponding limitations. In *Montana v. Egelhoff* (1996), the U.S. Supreme Court confirmed common law and contemporary legal practices in ruling that there is no inherent right under the 14th Amendment to the U.S. Constitution to the admission of evidence of voluntary intoxication as an excuse to crime, so states have the discretion to decide when that information can be presented at trial and the extent to which it can influence punishments. Accordingly, in states like Delaware, evidence of voluntary intoxication is inadmissible even as a mitigating circumstance of guilt for the crime charged (11 Del. C. § 421, 1953). Other jurisdictions take a different approach and allow the trier of fact to consider intoxication caused by the voluntary ingestion of drugs or alcohol in very limited circumstances, such as to negate the mens rea element of crimes that require a level of culpability that is defined by purposeful, knowing, or deliberate intent or when it is relevant to an effort to downgrade a murder charge to a lower degree or manslaughter (Cal. Penal Code §§ 29.4, 2001; 18 Pa. C.S. § 308, 2014; T.C.A. § 39-11-503, 2019).

| | |
|---|---|
| **PAUSE AND REFLECT** | Pause and reflect on how voluntary intoxication is generally defined as the intentional consumption of drugs or alcohol that are known or likely to have an intoxicating effect. Consider a situation in which someone chooses to take prescription drugs to treat a newly developed health condition instead of undergoing occupational therapy. It turns out that this person is allergic to some of the products contained in the medicine, which they were not previously aware of. After taking the prescribed dose of medication, they begin driving and suddenly become intoxicated, but before they can pull over, they run into the back of another car, killing the passengers inside. There were no warning labels on the medication that advised against driving. The driver is subsequently charged with involuntary manslaughter. |
| | Can that crime be excused as a result of involuntary intoxication? |

## Ignorance and Mistake

Criminal conduct may be excused from punishment if it was committed with a mistaken belief about a fact essential to the law violation or an applicable law, if that misperception negates the requisite purposeful, knowing, reckless, or negligent intent or is otherwise considered a state of mind that constitutes a defense to the crime under the law (11 Del. C. § 441, 1953; Model Penal Code § 2.04(1), 1962; NH Rev. Stat. § 626:3, 2015). Generally, ignorance or mistake is no defense to strict liability offenses, since punishment for such crimes are solely imposed on the basis of the crime commission, regardless of whether it was performed with any specific or general intent; however, as discussed previously, state laws contain exceptions to this. There are also specifications under the law according to how the mistake is classified as one related to a pertinent fact surrounding the offense or a governing law. If the defendant committed an act that they believed was legal but was actually not, due to a recent or unpublished change in a statute or judicial opinion or incorrect advice from a judicial or administrative official who is acting in a professional capacity, their conduct may be excused if that misunderstanding sufficiently reflects an absence of the required criminal intent. Reliance on a misrepresentation of law made by a private attorney is inexcusable. Furthermore, any misperception of law must be reasonable in nature, and courts may consider a variety of factors in making that determination, such as the amount of time between the change in law and criminal conduct and the specific details of the incorrect legal guidance. The scope of the mistake of law defense is limited to these circumstances, since plain ignorance of the law is not a valid excuse for criminal conduct pursuant to the doctrine of statutory clarity, which is a core component of the American legal system. Accordingly, it is presumed that adults of sound mind are aware of the law and any corresponding prohibitions under it so long as such rules are clearly written and already established.

For that reason, a mistake about a fact that constitutes an element of the offense might provide more accessible grounds for an excuse defense, depending on the offense charged and the reasonableness of the defendant's factual misperception related to it. Statutory rape provides a good example of how the mistake of fact defense is applied in context. It is a strict liability offense, which means the underlying act is punishable regardless of the level of culpability with which it was performed; this makes ignorance or mistake irrelevant and not a valid defense. However, some statutes contain exceptions to this default rule that make certain crimes, including strict liability offenses, excusable based on a sufficient showing of a critical factual mistake. For instance, in some states like Pennsylvania,

> when criminality of conduct depends on the child being below a critical age older than 14 years, it is a defense for the defendant to prove by a preponderance of the evidence that he or she reasonably believed the child to be above the critical age (18 Pa. C.S. §§ 3102, 2014).

As such, a reasonable mistake about the victim's age can excuse what would otherwise constitute a statutory sexual assault, which in that state is defined as sexual intercourse between the defendant and a complainant to whom they are not married and who is younger than 16 years old but older than 13. Age is a crucial element of that offense, since there must also be at least a 4-year age difference between the defendant and minor victim in order for the sexual encounter to constitute a statutory sexual assault (18 Pa. C.S. §§ 3102, 3122.1, 2016. In Pennsylvania, mistake of age can only be raised in those specific circumstances because if

> criminality of conduct depends on a child being below the age of 14 years, it is no defense that the defendant did not know the age of the child or reasonably believed the child to be the age of 14 years or older (18 Pa. C.S. §§ 3102, 2016).

This means that mistake of age is no defense to child rape, which is defined as "sexual intercourse with a complainant who is less than 13 years old" (18 Pa C.S. §§ 3102, 3121(c), 2016.

**PAUSE AND REFLECT**

Pause and reflect on the fact that in Pennsylvania and other states, mistake of age can be raised in defense to statutory sexual assault, or sexual intercourse with a minor who is ages 13 to 16 years old. The defendant has the burden to demonstrate that mistaken belief by a preponderance of evidence or showing that it is more likely than not (51%) that they committed the crime with such a false impression of the other participant's age, but that it was reasonable under the circumstances.

What are some examples of evidence that you would consider sufficient to satisfy that burden and excuse a statutory sexual assault based on mistake of age?

## Entrapment

A successful entrapment defense is a complete excuse to crime and any corresponding punishments because "government agents may not originate a criminal design, implant in an innocent person's mind the disposition to commit a criminal act, and then induce commission of the crime so that the Government may prosecute" (*Jacobson v. United States*, 1992). When someone charged with a crime asserts entrapment as an excuse for it, the trier of fact must determine whether the intent to commit it originated from their mind or the government official who was involved in the incident and whether that agent also coerced them into executing that desire, whomever it came from. The focus of that inquiry is on either the defendant's criminal predisposition or the law enforcement officer's behaviors, particularly whether it would likely sway a reasonable person's mind toward a crime commission, and the application of each standard is governed by statute.

## Subjective Test

Most state and federal laws measure entrapment according to the subjective test, which balances relevant evidence of the defendant's character traits and conduct before and during the crime, along with any other inclinations toward violating the law, against their claim that a police officer or other government actor forced them to commit a crime. In some jurisdictions, the prosecution may admit evidence of the defendant's criminal history to infer their predisposition for crime and intent to carry out the current offense; however, the existence and nature of a criminal record is not dispositive to that inquiry. Alternatively, the defense has the burden to show that (a) the government induced the defendant to engage in criminal behavior, and (b) the defendant possessed no criminal plan independent of that persuasion so but for it, would not have performed the criminal act. The subjective test for entrapment is centered on the defendant, specifically whether that person had a predisposition for crime; however, government inducement must still be proved from the outset of trial (*Matthews v. United States*, 1988). Government inducement is broadly defined as persuasion or coercion that is facilitated through words or actions, which can be mild in nature but must be substantial enough to overcome a person's will to obey the law (*State v. Nations*, 1985). Federal case law provides useful examples of it and distinguishes conduct that falls within the constitutional scope of law enforcement. For instance, police officers may use deceit, decoys, false pretenses, solicitation, and other forms of trickery to obtain crime information or a confession, apprehend a suspect, and otherwise conduct a criminal investigation, and for that reason such behaviors are not considered inducement or the first step to an entrapment (*Sherman v. United States*, 1958; *Sorrells v. United States*, 1932; *United States v. Johnson*, 1989).

## Objective Test

The Model Penal Code and a few states—including California, Michigan, and Texas—take a different approach and use an objective test to determine whether criminal conduct resulted from entrapment and should therefore be excused. Pursuant to those laws, the sole basis of an entrapment defense is government inducement; any evidence tending to show a defendant's criminal inclination, such as criminal history, is considered irrelevant and inadmissible at trial for that purpose. For example, the Texas Penal Code provides that "it is a defense to prosecution that the actor engaged in the conduct charged because he was induced to do so by a law enforcement agent using persuasion or other means likely to cause persons to commit the offense" (Tex. Penal Code § 8.06, 1994). The latter portion of that standard, indicating that the inducement must be likely to convince "persons" to violate the law, is key to the objective test, which weighs the governmental conduct at issue against a reasonable person standard. Accordingly, government inducement is conduct that would convince a reasonable person to perform a criminal act, irrespective of their subjective criminality. The trier of fact may account for attendant circumstances of the crime, such as interactions between the agent and defendant preceding and coinciding with it, but not the defendant's character or inclination toward crime (CALCRIM No. 3408, 2020).

## Duress

Duress is a defense that can be asserted as an excuse for crime that is shown to be a necessary and reasonable response to an actual or imminent threat of serious bodily injury or death that could not be safely avoided. That prefatory physical force can still amount to duress even when it is inflicted on someone other than the criminal actor, so long as there is a close connection between it and the defendant's crime commission. More specifically, such undue influence must be a proximate cause of the criminal act and can be communicated through words, gestures, or actions that express or imply a level of coercion that would have also compelled any person of ordinary, sound mind to violate the law.

FIGURE 10.2. Duress

Those conditions must be present in the moment when the defendant commits the crime, so any duress that precedes or happens after it is inexcusable under the law. A classic example that satisfies those elements is when someone performs a criminal act while a gun or knife is being held to their head or otherwise directed toward them in a menacing way. But that along with similar forms of duress are framed by state and federal rules, which impose general exceptions to when crime resulting from such undue influence can be legally excused. In federal cases duress is only a defense to crime committed under extraordinary compulsion, but to the exclusion of criminal acts performed by a prison escapee who encountered such a threat while on the run, if they left prison on their own volition. In context, that is a very stringent standard to meet (*United States v. Bailey*, 1980; *United States v. Bryan*, 1979; *United*

*States v. Michelson*, 1977). In most jurisdictions, homicide cannot be excused even if done under duress; however, some courts allow evidence of the undue influence to be admitted as a mitigating factor in sentencing.

## Conclusion

This chapter covered excuses to crime that are linked to insanity, infancy, intoxication, ignorance/mistake, entrapment, and duress; conditions that can interfere with a person's ability to develop and execute criminal intent. The sensational crimes committed by Andrea Yates, Lorena Bobbitt, and John Hinckley Jr. were discussed to highlight some intricacies surrounding the insanity defense in the context of various tests for evaluating such claims that emanate from and vary by statute. The infancy defense is also framed by criminal laws that determine the exclusive and/or concurrent jurisdiction of juvenile and adult courts over juvenile defendants based on age, offense, and criminal history criteria. Criminal acts performed while under the influence of drugs or alcohol may also be excused if that intoxication was involuntary and deprived the defendant of a substantial capacity to make independent, rational decisions. However, voluntary intoxication is generally no excuse for criminal conduct, but it may be introduced as a mitigating factor at sentencing in some jurisdictions. Even though voluntary drunkenness is no defense for crime, some criminal laws do account for the reality that people make mistakes and because of that might unintentionally violate the law. Mistakes of law and fact are both grounds for excusing crime as determined by statute, but it can be more challenging in context to prove a mistake of law, since adults are expected to have notice of any prohibitions contained in statutes that are clearly written and established. Entrapment and duress are distinct in that both excuses arise from situations in which the defendant is placed under the influence of a threatened or actual physical force exerted by a government official or private person, respectively, which can only be resisted by committing the crime. Subjectivity is a key component of all excuse defenses; however, criminal laws impose objective rules for measuring whether the defendant nonetheless had the ability to formulate and act on a criminal intention.

### THINK AND APPLY

Draw from what you have learned in this chapter about excuse defenses. Which one do you think is the most difficult to demonstrate at trial? Explain your position and also provide recommendations for how that defense can be modified to alleviate some of those challenges.

*Credits*

# Chapter 11

# Crimes Against the Public

## Introduction to the Chapter

This chapter covers prostitution, drug crimes, and disorderly conduct, which fall into a distinct category of offenses against the public generally, and in that respect involve harms that can seem less tangible than those resulting from crimes that are inflicted on specific persons or property. Therefore, some people perceive those acts as victimless crimes, particularly if engaged in voluntarily by adults, and in turn believe they should not be criminalized at all, or at least less harshly than other types of crimes. State laws that legalize marijuana for medicinal and/or recreational purposes exemplify that perspective but also conflict with federal statutes, which prohibit that and other controlled substances under all circumstances. The dichotomy between state and federal regulation of marijuana is discussed to illustrate how competing interests in crime control, health, and state police powers can contribute to the development of unparalleled laws on drugs across local, state, and federal governments. Marijuana aside, the production, use, and distribution of controlled substances, along with prostitution and disorderly conduct, are consistently criminalized federally and under state and local laws, which reflect a general yet fractured consensus that such crimes are offensive and threatening to the moral fabric of society.

For instance, prostitution is legal in Nevada when conducted within the scope of time, place, and manner restrictions designated by statute, but outside of particular jurisdictions in that state, engaging in that activity or any related conduct such as pimping and pandering are consistently punished, with no exceptions. As explained in this chapter, that is precisely what happened to Heidi Fleiss, otherwise known as the "Hollywood Madam," who pandered countless women to celebrity clients during the early 1990s in California, where doing so is a punishable as a felony-level offense. The attendant circumstances of crimes against the public are crucial factors in how they are classified as a misdemeanor or felony, and the corresponding requisite level of intent. That is evident in drug laws, which outline punishments for use, possession, distribution, cultivation, and manufacturing of controlled substances by type, quantity, intent, and other conditions that are deemed to aggravate or mitigate the severity of it. In this chapter, what Lori Arnold did to earn the title of "Queen of Meth" is explained to put that in context for readers, as is Shia LaBeouf's drunken behavior one fateful day in 2017, which offended onlookers and violated disorderly conduct and public intoxication laws.

## Prostitution

Prostitution is generally defined as the procurement or participation in sex-related acts in exchange for something of value, such as money, property, or services, and it is criminalized in all states except certain rural counties in Nevada. Although prostitution is legal in the state of Nevada, it is subject to statutory restrictions on the time, manner, and place in which those encounters can lawfully be conducted. According to Nevada law, it is only legal to solicit a prostitute and engage in prostitution within a licensed house of prostitution, which means such behavior is unlawful if performed elsewhere (NRS 201.354, 2021). But it is a felony to abet or conduct prostitution even in those places if any of the participants tested positive for HIV (human immunodeficiency virus) through a state-approved test and received notice of those results prior to engaging in such conduct (NRS 201.358, 2021). Most statutes include that circumstance among penalty enhancement criteria for prostitution that also specify other offense and offender characteristics, such as habitual offending, encouraging, or participating in prostitution near school buildings or other places where minors are likely to be present. Subject to statutory variation, the criminal act of prostitution is broadly defined by an array of conduct that includes the solicitation of a prostitute for hire, offering or agreeing to pay someone for a sexual favor, and engaging in a sex-related activity performed in exchange for money. Any individual who facilitates prostitution, as either a sex worker or client, can face punishment for engaging in those and similar behaviors if performed with the requisite *mens rea*, if there is one, as indicated in the governing statute. Many jurisdictions treat prostitution as a knowing or general intent crime that "consists of knowingly engaging in or offering to engage in a sexual act for hire" (NM Stat § 30-9-2, 2020). The Model Penal Code distinguishes conduct that precedes or is incidental to prostitution, such as loitering, which is only punishable if done with a specific purpose to engage in or promote the sexual act in exchange for money (Model Penal Code § 251.1, 1962). However, in a few states like New York and Washington, prostitution is a strict liability offense, so punishment is based solely on that criminal act, and there is no required showing of corresponding intent. Accordingly, under New York Penal Law § 230.00 (2014), "a person is guilty of prostitution when such person engages or agrees or offers to engage in sexual conduct with another person in return for a fee," and so those acts alone are punishable regardless of the level of intention behind them (RCW 9A.88.030, 2011).

FIGURE 11.1 **Nevada Brothel**

A Nevada brothel is pictured here.

Pause and reflect on the distinct legalization of prostitution under Nevada law compared to the laws in other states and federally, which prohibit it under all circumstances. The 9th Amendment to the U.S. Constitution confers the individual right to autonomy in intimate, private affairs, including those that are sexual in nature, and is an integral part of the 14th Amendment due process protections (*Griswold v. Connecticut*, 1965). Do you believe consensual sexual acts between consenting healthy adults that are performed in exchange for money reflect that fundamental constitutional right and therefore should be legalized nationally? Or instead, do you agree with the dominant perspective that even under those circumstances, prostitution denigrates public health and welfare and therefore should be prohibited under the law? Explain your position.

## Pimping and Pandering

Criminal laws qualify a wide range of conduct as prostitution, which include actions taken by individuals who are involved with hiring a prostitute or working as one. That was the downfall of the "Hollywood Madam," who is otherwise known as Heidi Fleiss. On June 9, 1993, she was charged with five counts of pandering for her role in orchestrating the prostitution of hundreds of women to celebrity clients, like Charlie Sheen, who testified against her at trial. The media had an insatiable appetite for the details surrounding

Victims:
The Public

Defendant:
Heidi Fleiss

her ascent to power as one of the most successful madams known in American history, and the public consumed every part of the story, including the rich and famous clientele, how the sex workers were groomed to appear as stereotypical Beverly Hills natives, and the exorbitant profits that Fleiss made on a weekly basis. Fleiss was charged with pandering pursuant to California law, which makes it a felony crime when someone "receives any money for procuring another person for the purpose of prostitution" (Cal. Penal Code § 266i(a)(6), 2001). As reflected in that statute, pandering is typically classified as a specific intent crime, which means it must be done with a purpose—in this case, to facilitate a paid sexual encounter. At trial, the prosecutor showed how Fleiss did just that and in essence became the infamous Hollywood Madam by hiring an exorbitant number women to work as prostitutes and service high-profile clientele for a price up to $1,500 for one-night encounters. She organized the provision of payments and sexual acts between them with a clear goal: to make money. And that is in fact what she did, keeping over 40% of all proceeds that her sex workers made. At the height of Fleiss's success, she was earning an estimated $300,000 on a weekly basis. To that point, Sheen testified that he spent about $53,000 on sex-related services that the Hollywood

Madam provided through her escort business. His story was sensational but more importantly impactful, likely contributing to the jury conviction against her on three counts of pandering. Fleiss was subsequently sentenced to 3 years in prison but was released in 1996 when the verdict was overturned due to the revelation of jury misconduct that took place during the deliberation process (Abramovitch, 2018; Meyer, 1996). She moved to Nevada after getting released from prison, where ironically prostitution is legal.

PAUSE AND<br>REFLECT

Pause and reflect on the rise and fall of Heidi Fleiss, the Hollywood Madam, and particularly that she was convicted of pandering, which is typically classified as a specific intent felony offense. As discussed, pandering occurs through the procurement of prostitutes for the purpose of receiving money. There is no doubt that Fleiss did just that, but a point of reflection is the subtle distinction between her conduct and pimping, which is also treated as felony crime in most jurisdictions. Pimping happens when someone receives money or other valuable items from a prostitute, knowing or with the general understanding that it was obtained from an act of prostitution. The accompanying levels of intent for pimping and pandering are distinct, but both crimes encompass similar acts that are aimed at facilitating prostitution. Sentences for pandering and pimping can be enhanced by statute on the basis of aggravating circumstances such as threatened or actual use of force to compel an act of prostitution, or if the person engaged in the sexual interaction is a minor (Or. Rev. Stat. § 167.017, 2019).

Should pandering and pimping be consumed into a single offense under all criminal laws? Discuss related pros and cons.

## Drug Crimes

The Controlled Substances Act (CSA) is a federal statute that incorporates a five-tier system to be used federally and among the states in determining which narcotics can be used at all or only in certain instances, depending on the quantity, source, and reason for the consumption (21 U.S.C. § 812, 2012). It provides a framework for the development of criminal laws that regulate the manufacturing, cultivation, distribution, possession, and use of drugs, which state governments are required to adopt in accordance with the supremacy clause contained in Article VI of the U.S. Constitution. That constitutional standard embodies federalism, which is an integral component of the American legal system that requires state governments to comply with federal rules for governance, including the CSA. The Controlled Substances Act of 1970 comprises Schedules I, II, III, IV, and V, and each includes a group of specified drugs organized by tier in descending order based on potential for abuse and corresponding eligibility for prescription distribution and usage. For instance, marijuana is a Schedule I drug listed among heroin, ecstasy, and other substances that are deemed to carry a strong potential for dependency and not authorized for any legal use, including medical treatment. Federalism mandates that state laws reflect that categorization and prohibit the distribution, possession, and use of marijuana under all circumstances. Yet most state criminal codes exempt those marijuana-involved activities from criminal prosecution if it is obtained and consumed for recreation or medicine within the scope of any time, place, and manner regulations imposed under the applicable law. For example, in Pennsylvania and more than 30 other states, it is illegal to have marijuana unless it is possessed along with a valid medical identification card that authorizes it to be administered by a state-approved physician and dispensary (35 P.S. § 10231.303, 2016). In nearly half of all states, marijuana is permitted for casual consumption among persons at least 21 years old in small quantities within nonpublic settings. State laws authorize recreational or medicinal marijuana usage, or both, and there is even legislation underway to decriminalize it in

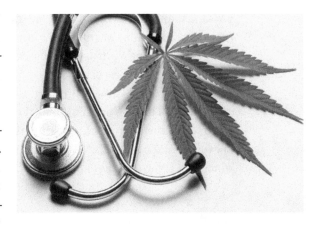

FIGURE 11.2. **State legalization of marijuana**

Idaho and Nebraska, the last remaining states to fully impose the Schedule I classification of marijuana set forth in the CSA (Dunker, 2021; Jaeger, 2021; NRS 453.336, 2021). Although controversy remains over the dichotomy in federal and state laws on marijuana, the various state criminal codes are consistent in regulating other controlled substances in accordance with the CSA.

## Cultivation, Possession, and Use

There are a host of state and federal laws that define criminal liability for the cultivation, manufacturing, possession, distribution, or use of drugs that emanate from the CSA. Those drug-related offenses are graded as felonies or misdemeanors depending on the accompanying level of intent, the type of scheduled drug, and amount of drug retrieved during an arrest or incidental search and seizure. For example, cultivating and possessing marijuana in small quantities are generally treated as low-level infractions since in most states it is legal to grow and keep cannabis, subject to applicable statutory limitations, even though it remains a Schedule I drug federally. New Jersey is among those states, where

> it is unlawful for any person, knowingly or purposely, to obtain, or to possess, actually or constructively, a controlled dangerous substance or controlled substance analog, unless the substance was obtained directly, or pursuant to a valid prescription or order form from a practitioner. (N.J. Rev. Stat. § 2C:35-10, 2013)

Otherwise, drug cultivation is punishable if done with a general intent or awareness that the produced substance is illicit. Drug possession can occur through actual contact, such as carrying the illicit substance on the body, clothing, or constructively, like storing it in a place that is within a person's control or immediate reach. Simple possession is just that, simply possessing a scheduled drug with a general or knowing intent to carry the controlled substance, and it is typically graded as a misdemeanor offense. If that same act is done with a specific intent or purpose to distribute the drugs, it is elevated under the law to a felony crime. Whether drugs are possessed for personal use or public distribution, whoever consumes it can also be criminalized for doing so if they engage in conduct related to that consumption that is also prohibited under the law, such as disorderly conduct or public intoxication. The U.S. Supreme Court ruled in *Robinson v. California* (1962) that someone cannot be punished for being a drug user, because addiction alone is a status that involves no overt criminal action. As a result, criminal laws prohibiting drug use must specify any coinciding behaviors that are punishable.

## Manufacturing and Trafficking

Victim:
The Public

Defendant:
Lori Arnold

Lori Arnold, the sister of famous comedian Tom Arnold, built one of the largest known crystal methamphetamine empires, which was featured in the 2021 documentary titled *Queen of Meth*. She earned that nickname, since her Iowa-based operation produced more than 30 pounds of methamphetamine and hundreds of thousands in profits per week at its peak during the late 1980s. Arnold was a meth user and also distributed it for sale to other users across the United States, which eventually caught the attention of federal law enforcement agents. Drug manufacturing and trafficking is illegal in Iowa, the central location of Arnold's methamphetamine operation, as well as in other states and under federal law. In 1990 federal agents arrested the Queen of Meth on drug trafficking charges, and more specifically for violating federal law, which makes it "unlawful for any person knowingly or intentionally to manufacture, distribute, or dispense or possess with intent to manufacture, distribute or dispense a controlled substance" (21 U.S.C. § 841, 2018). Crystal methamphetamine is also a Schedule II listed drug under the CSA, among other controlled substances like cocaine and PCP that are categorized as carrying a high potential for abuse and cannot be manufactured, distributed, possessed, or used for any lawful purpose. Arnold was convicted of multiple federal drug crimes and sentenced to 15 years in federal prison, a punishment that was imposed because of her law violations and more generally the ravaging effect that methamphetamine distribution and use have on communities, rural ones in particular (Baker et al., 2021). That is, in essence, the rationale behind quality-of-life crimes, to penalize actions that are offensive to people and society in general and involve victimizations that are actual but not always easy to precisely quantify.

## Disorderly Conduct

Statutes that prohibit disorderly conduct must be narrowly tailored to directly serve an important governmental interest, such as one related to the preservation of peace in public spaces and aimed at fostering environments where citizens can safely and effectively conduct regular activities. Such laws that regulate how individuals can lawfully conduct themselves in nonprivate settings must clearly reflect and delineate the underlying safety or public welfare rationale; otherwise, they can be voided for vagueness or overbreadth. The void for vagueness and overbreadth doctrines requires any statutory restriction on the time, place, and manner in which someone can conduct themselves in an area open to the general public to be limited and specific enough to still allow individuals to exercise freedoms of speech, expression, and assembly conferred under the First and Fourteenth Amendments to the U.S. Constitution. The U.S. Supreme Court has ruled that protected speech may include pure (or actual) speech, symbolic speech such as flag burning, along with physical gestures and other nonverbal displays so long as those expressions do not contain obscenity, fighting words, true threats, or otherwise contravene the safety of another person or the public generally. For example, in *Texas v. Johnson* (1989), the court invalidated a Texas ordinance for its overbreadth since the law made it illegal for anyone to "desecrate a venerated object," with no exceptions. Gregory Lee Johnson was arrested for violating it when he burned his own American flag while standing outside of a municipal building, to express his discontent with the U.S. involvement in a war that was ongoing at that time. He was convicted, sentenced to 1 year in jail, and required to pay a $2,000 fine. On appeal, the U.S. Supreme Court ruled that he had the freedom to express symbolic speech in that manner, which as the justices acknowledged was likely offensive to many but did not threaten public welfare in any way, and therefore the governmental infringement on it constituted a violation of his constitutional rights. Drawing from other landmark legal precedent, the case outcome would have likely been different had Johnson burned the flag and also engaged in conduct that incited the crowd to violence, with words or gestures that went beyond mere results (*Brandenburg v. Ohio*, 1969; *Hess v. Indiana*, 1973; *NAACP v. Claiborne Hardware Co.*, 1982).

Disorderly conduct must be defined by laws that carefully balance governmental concerns in maintaining a peaceful and healthy quality of life for citizenry against individual rights to engage in protected forms of speech and expression afforded under the U.S. Constitution. As specified by statute, disorderly conduct can occur through actions such as loud noises that are antagonizing or reach an excessive volume; displays of obscenity like indecent exposure; and words or gestures that would incite a reasonable person to violence, make them feel threatened, or create a hazardous condition. Any behaviors that are classified as disorderly conduct must be performed with the specific purpose to disturb the public or recklessness; that is, a conscious disregard for how it might diminish the quality of life enjoyed by other people who encounter such behaviors. Under most laws, place matters and is included as an attendant circumstance of disorderly conduct, which must be done with the requisite level of intent in a public area that is open and accessible to anyone or privately owned property. The following excerpts from state laws illustrate how those key elements of disorderly conduct are distinctly specified by statute. For example, in Alabama, "a person commits the crime of disorderly conduct who with intent to cause public inconvenience, annoyance or alarm, or recklessly creating a risk thereof … in a public place uses abusive or obscene language or makes an obscene gesture" (AL Code § 13A-11-7, 2013). But in Alaska, disorderly conduct that occurs in nonpublic contexts is also punishable, if for instance "a person refuses to comply with an order of a peace officer to leave premises" (AS § 11.61.110, 2007) that they have no legal right to occupy. Michigan law reflects a different approach, since under it, "being a disorderly person" is criminalized and defined by a broad array of conduct that includes various forms of expression that are similarly prohibited in other states, as well as activities like being "able-bodied but failing to support your family, a prostitute or loitering in or near places of prostitution" (MCL § 750.167, 2006). Across all states, it is illegal to engage in disruptive behaviors with a specific or general intent to disturb the peace or interfere with regular activities, and although there is variation in the specific acts that are prohibited, public intoxication is certainly listed among them (Brockington, 2017).

## Public Intoxication

Victims:
The Public

Defendant:
Shia LaBeouf

Public intoxication, no matter how it is specifically defined by statute, must involve some display of disorderly conduct, since as mentioned no person can be criminalized for a status alone, such as having an alcohol or drug addiction or being under the influence of a controlled substance (*Robinson v. California*, 1962). Recall from Chapter 4 that there must be some overt voluntary action that accompanies one of those underlying states, such as driving while under the influence of alcohol, use of profanity, or other behavior that creates a nuisance or threat to another person and/or the general public welfare. One of the main rationales behind such quality-of-life offenses is to deter more serious and potentially violent crime commissions, such as assault, battery, and incitement. Disorderly conduct and public intoxication are precipitatory and overlapping crimes and from that perspective may be considered victimless by nature. For example, in Georgia any person who is inebriated while in a public place, private residence, or immediate area surrounding it that they do not own or have an invitation from the lawful owner or occupant to be in can be found guilty of public intoxication if such inebriation is accompanied by boisterousness, indecent condition or act, or vulgar, profane, loud, or unbecoming language (O.C.G.A. § 16-11-41, 2010). However, those offenses truly come to life when put in context—particularly of real, sensationalized cases involving celebrities like Shia LaBeouf, who is known for his role in the *Transformers* franchise movies, among others. In 2017 the public spotlight shifted to his arrest in Georgia for public drunkenness, obstruction, and disorderly conduct. Everything started with a cigarette that LaBeouf requested from a stranger but never received. It appeared to others that he was under the influence of alcohol, as he became visibly upset by that rebuffed quest for nicotine. LaBeouf reportedly began cursing and using vulgar language in front bystanders, including a police officer, before fleeing into a hotel lobby, where he continued to display an onslaught of disruptive behaviors. His story, as retold through the media, exemplifies the risks of physical harm to individuals and disruption to public health and welfare associated with public intoxication and disorderly conduct and also that those crimes, which are typically classified as misdemeanors, can be charged as felonies if committed in an aggravated manner such as in the presence of a law enforcement officer.

## Conclusion

In this chapter, readers learned about the elements of quality-of-life crimes that involve prostitution, drugs, disorderly conduct, and public intoxication in the context of sensational cases, which were used to illustrate how those offenses disrupt the public welfare and also carry potential for more serious crime commissions. Discrepancies in federal, state, and local laws that regulate prostitution and drugs were also discussed to provide a comprehensive overview of how those activities are criminalized—but also made legal under specific circumstances designated by statute. Nevada is an exception to other state and federal laws, which prohibit prostitution regardless of the time, place, and manner in which that activity is carried out. There is a more glaring distinction in the state and federal regulation of marijuana, which is classified as a Schedule I controlled substance under the federal CSA and therefore prohibited for any purpose, yet it is allowed for medicinal and/or recreational use under limited conditions in most states. Those differences were explained and also presented alongside important ties that bind criminal laws enacted at the federal, state, and local levels and impose punishments for the possession, cultivation, use, or distribution of controlled substances, aside from marijuana; pimping; pandering; disorderly conduct; and public intoxication. Since the rationale for punishing those crimes against the public is to protect quality of life, in a general sense, the consequences for committing them are framed by circumstances such as quantity, time, place, and manner of execution that are attendant to those offenses and present a serious risk of impairment to public safety, health, and welfare. So, while crimes that involve prostitution, drugs, disorderly conduct, public intoxication, and other harms to the public are typically classified as misdemeanor offenses, they can be charged as felonies depending on how, when, and where the underlying law violations occurred; that is, how offensive they are to others, from either a literal or figurative standpoint. After finishing this chapter, readers possess the knowledge to comprehend the fundamental components of crimes against the public and also how those offenses impact quality-of-life conditions. Remember to draw from the contextual examples presented, which cover the rise and fall of Heidi Fleiss, the Hollywood Madam; Lori Arnold, the Queen of Meth; and Shia LaBeouf's viral display of public disorder and intoxication to enhance understanding of that material in context.

## THINK AND APPLY

Draw from what you have learned in this chapter about crimes against the public that are perpetrated through acts of prostitution, drug use and distribution, disorderly conduct, and public intoxication. As discussed, some believe those crimes present actual and threatened harms to quality of life, while others might perceive them as victimless and therefore unnecessarily criminalized. Perhaps the inclusion of a contemporary, uniform definition of "quality of life" in relevant criminal laws could help reconcile those differences by facilitating understanding what quality of life means and more importantly what it means to offend it.

Could you think of one?

*Credits*

# Chapter 12

# Hate Crimes

## Introduction to the Chapter

The focus of this chapter is on the elements and commission of hate crimes inflicted on individuals because of their race, color, sex, ethnicity, national origin, religion, disability, sexual orientation, or gender identity, and on and the host of laws that create civil and constitutional protections against such harms and impose criminal sanctions for violations. It begins with an overview of landmark federal legislation, including the Civil Rights Act of 1964, Voting Rights Act of 1965, and Civil Rights Act of 1968. Together, these acts mandate that states desegregate public schools and afford access to voting, public housing, and other governmental services to all citizens without discrimination on the basis of any of those protected statuses, but the acts contain no explicit mention of sexual orientation or gender identity. Other statutes embody corresponding constraints on private individuals by prohibiting any intentional interference with those conferred rights to voting, housing, and access to public services and also limit freedoms to exercise religion, speech, or expression in ways that would hinder those protections (18 U.S.C. § 245, 1970; 42 U.S.C. § 3631, 2012). The First Amendment to the U.S. Constitution provides all individuals the freedom to engage in public discourse and communication—whether done to express themselves, a particular viewpoint, or religion—and the government cannot infringe on this freedom unless there is a legitimate, neutral need to do so for the preservation of public safety, health, or welfare. But certain categories of speech and expression—such as fighting words, true threats, and obscenity—fall outside the scope of that protection and are per se prohibited, and the government does not have to demonstrate any reason for censoring such speech.

Hate crimes are manifested through unprotected speech, since those offenses are in essence bias directed toward an individual or group of persons and expressed through some verbal and/or physical intimation akin to true threats or fighting words that actually come to fruition. This chapter frames the U.S. Constitution and federal civil rights legislation as foundational components in the emergence of the Matthew Shepard and James Byrd Jr. Hate Crimes Prevention Act, as well as contemporary state-based hate crime laws also inspired by tragic and sensational crimes motivated by hate (18 U.S.C. § 249, 2009). Readers will learn details about the murders of James Byrd Jr., Matthew Shepard, Scott Amedure, Nikki Kuhnhausen, and other known devastating acts of hate, which remain subject to nationwide attention and influential factors in the

FIGURE 12.1 **Hate crime**

development of more comprehensive and stringent civil rights protections and criminal laws that reinforce them. Although hate crimes are underreported, official crime data reflect a link between those crime incidences and bias perceptions constructed within American society and perpetuated through major news outlets. That phenomenon is highlighted in a discussion of the disproportionate increase in violent crimes committed against actual or perceived immigrants and transgendered persons, triggered by hatred toward their national origin and gender identity respectively.

**PAUSE AND REFLECT**

What are some factors that courts should consider in determining whether an offense should be categorized as a hate crime and subject to enhanced punishment? In your response, explain whether those criteria should focus on the perpetrator's conduct and intention behind their acts, harm suffered by the victim, or a combination of both.

## Civil Protections Against Hate

Hate can be expressed through crime inflicted on one or more persons, fueled by prejudice or dislike for them and an entire group which they belong to and share in common some personal characteristic(s) such as sex, race, ethnicity, color, national origin, religion, sexual orientation, gender identity, or disability; such conduct is likely to have a discriminatory impact or marginalizing effect on those targeted individuals. From that standpoint, there is an intersection between discrimination, which constitutes a civil rights violation, and incidents of hate violence; this intersection could feasibly begin with those unwarranted exclusions from employment, voting, housing, and other opportunities to which people are entitled to have equal access. Federal antidiscrimination laws protect all persons from being treated unequally, without due process, in employment, voting, housing, and other public sectors and are rooted in the due process and equal protection clauses contained in the 5th and 14th Amendments to the U.S. Constitution. Due process rights are conferred through both the 5th and 14th Amendments to the U.S. Constitution and together restrict federal and state governments from denying any person life, liberty, and property unless warranted and done through the legitimate, fair, and neutral decision-making procedures set forth under the law. The U.S. Supreme Court has interpreted those protections, through the selective incorporation doctrine, as requiring state and federal governments to afford all persons the rights and freedoms created through the Bill of Rights, which are the first 10 amendments to the U.S. Constitution.

Therefore, the equal protection clause provides that no law constrain those and other conferred privileges and immunities or otherwise deny equal protections under the law. It is important to note that those constitutional rules only apply to governmental actions and individuals who are acting in an official capacity to administer, interpret, create, or enforce the law and government sponsored programs. But there are federal and state-enacted statutes along with local ordinances that also frame the conduct of private citizens, interactions between them, and what constitutes discriminatory and hate violence in those contexts and will be discussed later in this chapter.

FIGURE 12.2 Discrimination

The mid-1960s was a pivotal era in the development of civil rights and protections created to reinforce and reflect the U.S. Constitution in both theory and application, and Congress divested with the power to pass the underlying federal legislation had front and center stage.

The bedrock of those civil liberties consists of the Civil Rights Act of 1964, Voting Rights Act of 1965, and Civil Rights Act of 1968, which prohibit discrimination in public sectors; those protections also guard against other prejudicial actions, including those that are criminal in nature (18 U.S.C. § 245, 1970; 42 U.S.C. § 2000, 1964; 52 U.S.C § 10101, 2015). For example, those laws also make it a crime for any individual to engage in conduct that is intended to intimidate someone or interfere with their civil rights, because of their appearance, who they are, or religious beliefs (42 U.S.C. § 3631, 2012).

## Contemporary Hate Crime Laws

### Penalty Enhancement Statutes

Nearly every state has a law that imposes enhanced penalties for crime commissions that are bias driven, and in that way such laws supplement federal antidiscrimination laws and corresponding punishments faced by individuals who victimize others because of who they are (Morava & Hamedy, 2021). Most states have adapted existing hate crime penalty enhancement statutes in response to certain fatal incidents of hate that captured the attention of the nation, including the U.S. Supreme Court, and sent rippling effects around the world. For instance, state legislators have modified vaguely written hate crime laws so that race, national origin, religion, sex, disability, sexual orientation, and gender identity are all explicitly listed as protected categories and have heightened punishments for criminal victimizations fueled by prejudice against persons who possess one or more of those innate characteristics. Yet some individuals on the receiving end of such sanctions who have been charged with committing a hate crime have challenged those laws as an unconstitutional infringement on their First

Amendment rights to express their feelings, albeit hate filled ones, and the U.S. Supreme Court answered those claims in a series of landmark rulings. Those decisions, along with the sensational cases that sparked them, are the framework for the structure and application of state penalty enhancement laws in hate crime prosecutions.

## National Origin and Religion

**PAUSE AND REFLECT**

Xenophobia is prejudice toward individuals who are from a different country, on the sole basis of their immigrant status. There are well-documented examples throughout American history that illustrate how such feelings infiltrate public opinion, are sustained through the media, and trigger hate crime incidents against persons who are connected to the targeted group through religion, ethnicity, race, color, and/or national origin. Following are two prominent ones.

On September 11, 2001, more than a dozen Islamist extremists from the Middle East conducted a terrorist attack on the United States that decimated the Twin Towers, the Pentagon, and so many lives. In the weeks following that horrific event, there were an unprecedented number of hate crime incidents committed against Muslims, increasing 1617% from 2000 to 2001 and manifested through actual and threatened violence against persons and property connected to Islam. Decades later, Islamophobia remains a prevalent fear among Muslim Americans (Alfonseca, 2021; Mekouar, 2021).

The coronavirus (COVID-19) pandemic struck the United States in 2020 a historic event that coincided with a new wave of hate expressed toward Asians and Pacific Islanders. They were blamed by virtue of their national origin for the ensuing health, political, and socioeconomic crises in an onslaught of tweets made by then-president Donald Trump. Coincidentally, anti-Asian hate crimes sharply increased across the entire nation by 73% in 2020 through the perpetration of verbal and physical acts of violence against Asian Americans (Do, 2021; Venkatraman, 2021).

Pause and reflect on those hate crime phenomena. What is the root cause: preexisting prejudice, socially constructed prejudice, or both?

## Race

The period from 1990 to 2000 is certainly a decade to remember, at least in the context of criminal law and hate crimes in particular. By that time there was a well-established delineation, in theory, between free speech and unlawful expressions of fighting words and true threats that fall outside the purview of constitutional protection (*Chaplinsky v. New Hampshire*, 1942). In *Chaplinsky*, the U.S. Supreme Court explained that fighting words are determined from a reasonable person standpoint and include any communication so inherently inflammatory that an even-tempered person of sound mind would be incited to violence or a breach of peace upon hearing it. By 1992 lingering questions about how that rule should apply in real-life interactions were brought to life in *R.A.V. v. St. Paul*. In that case, the U.S. Supreme Court considered the constitutionality of an ordinance that made it illegal for any person to burn a cross or swastika anywhere with the intent to "arouse anger or alarm on the basis of race, color, creed or religion" (Minn. Legis. Code § 292.02, 1990).

Robert A. Viktora was among a group of others charged with violating that law after they burned a makeshift cross on a Black family's yard. His attorneys claimed the statute imposed a content-specific limitation on freedom of expression, which was an unconstitutional encroachment on First Amendment protections. The court agreed with that position, since the ordinance only restricted expression that targeted people who were of a particular race, ethnicity, or religion, which was not only specific but an unnecessary means to achieve the legitimate governmental interest in maintaining the peace and order. Therefore, cross or swastika burning done for any purpose other than what was explicitly prohibited under the law, say to arouse political discourse or express discontent with a governmental action, was permitted. For that reason, the U.S. Supreme Court struck down the Minnesota ordinance (Minn. Legis. Code § 292.02, 1990) in a landmark decision that strengthened individual rights to freely engage in expressions and speech, including communications that convey bias or prejudice. But even that and other forms of protected speech are subject to reasonable and neutral government censorship, and of course there remain whole categories of expression unprotected by the Constitution.

Just 1 year later, in *Wisconsin v. Mitchell* (1993), the U.S. Supreme Court had to decide when crimes perpetrated through hate-fueled words or actions cross that legally constructed threshold between protected and unprotected speech. That case centered on a statement made by a Black youth, who along with other Black individuals attacked a White teenager, rendering him unconscious and in coma. The victim later recovered, but his attackers were found guilty of assault and sentenced to 4 years' imprisonment, an enhanced punishment from the 2 years typically imposed for that crime in the state of Wisconsin. That sanction was determined in accordance with the hate crime law applicable to that and other incidents wherein the defendant selected the victim because of their "race, religion, color, disability, sexual orientation, national origin or ancestry" (Wis. Stat. § 939.645, 2021). Todd Williams appealed the conviction and relied on the court's ruling in *R.A.V. v. St. Paul* to support his position that the Wisconsin law was unconstitutional on its face and a violation of his First Amendment rights. He further argued that his statement—"Do you all feel hyped up to move on some white people? There goes a white boy, go get him"—which he made to friends before committing the assault should not have been admitted as evidence to show that the victim was selected because of his race. But the U.S. Supreme Court disagreed and affirmed the validity of the statute as a legitimate censorship of unprotected expression. In *Wisconsin v. Mitchell*, the court distinguished the governing statute from the one at issue in the *R.A.V.* case, since that law restricted conduct and speech expressed to target persons because of an innate personal characteristic and to effectuate an accompanying crime against them. Similar to fighting words and true threats, those types of hate-filled expressions can precipitate a violent crime occurrence, which the court reasoned could be criminalized under the law, in accordance with the U.S. Constitution. The race-centered law violations surrounding *R.A.V. v. St. Paul* (1992) and *Wisconsin v. Mitchell* (1993) appealed to U.S. Supreme Court justices in more

Victim:
James Byrd Jr.

Defendants:
Shawn Berry,
Lawrence Russell
Brewer, and John
King

ways than one. But the murders of James Byrd Jr. and Matthew Wayne Shepard had even more of a far-reaching effect worldwide, sparking an unprecedented awareness about hate crime victimization and leading to the enactment of a federal law in honor of those victims.

In the summer of 1998, James Byrd Jr. became a household name because of his tragic death inflicted by White supremacists: Shawn Berry, Lawrence Russell Brewer, and John King. Decades later, even if that name has faded, what happened to Byrd is likely to resonate with most people. He was the Black man who was assaulted, chained by the ankles, and then dragged to his death from the back of a pickup truck driven by Berry. For their part, Brewer and King were riding together with Berry when he offered Byrd a ride. All three men together contributed to the murder, by luring first Byrd into the vehicle and then to a remote area, where they rendered him helpless with alcohol and beatings. After dragging him from the back of the truck for 3 miles, Berry, Brewer, and King stopped to collect his remaining body parts and toss them into the front yard of a Black Baptist church, where they were found the next morning. That along with their association with a White supremacy group led many, including the local sheriff at the time, to speculate that "they killed him [James Byrd Jr.] because he was black" (Goodwyn, 2019). Still other residents of the already racially divided Texas community believed the crime was a result of a drug deal gone wrong. Regardless, all three men were convicted of capital murder; Brewer and King were sentenced to death and Berry to life imprisonment, and the incident has been ruled a hate crime in the court of public opinion and as reflected in criminal laws subsequently enacted in response to it (Burch, 2018; Goodwyn, 2019). In 2001 former Texas governor Rick Perry passed the James Byrd Jr. Hate Crimes Act, which grants trial court judge's discretion to weigh bias in a crime commission as an aggravating factor in punishment and impose enhanced sentences in cases wherein the victim(s) was targeted because of their "race, religion, color, sex, disability, sexual preference, age, or national origin" (The Associated Press, 2001). That explicit list of protected statuses diversifies protections from hate crime victimizations compared to prior legislation in that state, but it excludes gender identity and sexual orientation. Recent data show increased vulnerability to biased violence among individuals who identify as part of the LGBTQ+ community, which only confirms what the 1998 murder of Matthew Shepard had already revealed—that hatred expressed toward individuals because of their sexual orientation could have fatal consequences unless tempered by the law.

## Sexual Orientation and Gender Identity

Victim:
Matthew Wayne
Shepard

Defendants:
Russell Henderson
and Aaron McKinney

As the world still grappled with the shock of James Byrd Jr.'s racially motivated and horrific murder, Matthew Wayne Shepard's 21-year-old lifeless body was found tied to a log fence in a remote Wyoming area just a few months later. Russell Henderson and Aaron McKinney killed Shepard and left no doubt that it was because he was an openly gay man. They targeted him on the basis of his sexual orientation and even admitted to pretending to also be gay in order to gain his trust. Once they did, Shepard willingly entered their vehicle, where he was robbed for $20. Henderson and McKinney then drove him to a desolate location, where they pistol whipped his head more than a dozen times, rendering him unconscious. Their beatings left Shepard in a coma with severe blunt force head trauma and skull fractures, which one of the investigators compared to injuries typically inflicted during high-speed car crashes. His near lifeless body was discovered 18 hours after Henderson and McKinney left him in the cold, shoeless and tied to the fence, to die. Matthew Wayne Shepard was an activist for gay rights in life and in legacy, which endures decades after his death (Bindel, 2014; Sheerin, 2018). In 2009 former president Barack Obama passed the Matthew Shepard and James Byrd Jr. Hate Crimes Prevention Act, a federal statute that provides funding to state, local, and tribunal governments to investigate and prosecute violent crimes committed "because of the actual or perceived race, color, religion, national origin gender, sexual orientation, gender identity, or disability of any person" (18 U.S.C. § 249, 2009). As the statutory language indicates, it is a comprehensive supplement to state hate crime legislation and inclusive of gender identity and sexual orientation, which are absent from state laws such as in Texas. Equally important is that the Matthew Shepard and James Byrd Jr. Hate Crimes Prevention Act is a namesake for both individuals whose lives were ended prematurely by acts of hate. Unfortunately, since their untimely deaths in 1998, there have been countless other violent hate crime incidents that disproportionately impact transgendered individuals.

Hate crimes perpetrated against individuals because they are transgender deserve special attention, in general to enhance public awareness about the distinct vulnerabilities faced by members of that population and, more importantly, to ensure efficient and adequate legal protections for those potential crime victims. Transgendered persons are more likely to be impacted by hate violence, including homicide, compared to members of other at-risk populations who are singled out on account of race, color, national origin, religion, sex, or another status. More specifically, such individuals whose personal identity and appearance do not correspond to their biological sex face a slightly higher than 8% risk of being murdered in a serious crime incident that is motivated by transphobia, or hatred toward that trait, and trans females of color are especially vulnerable to that fate. In contrast, there is less than a .01% chance that nontransgendered persons will become a hate crime victim (Carlisle, 2021; Srikanth, 2020). The Matthew Shepard and James Byrd Jr. Hate Crimes Prevention Act is among other legislation that explicitly criminalizes hate violence motivated by gender identity and sexual orientation. But those protections are buffered against provisions in other laws, which defendants can draw from to mitigate potential punishments they face for perpetrating such acts.

Pursuant to the "gay/trans panic" defense, individuals who are charged with committing a bias-motivated crime against a homosexual or transgendered person can defend that conduct by shifting blame to the victim and their personal trait that inspired the violence. More than a quarter of states have banned that defense and acknowledged it as a form of victim shaming, but it is still permitted in some jurisdictions in accordance with the applicable standard of law, which varies but generally requires a sufficient showing of insanity, provocation, or self-defense. Those standards are distinct, but all necessitate that the defendant carry the burden in proving that the victim's sexual orientation or gender identity contributed to their criminal act in such a substantial way that it excuses their behavior and warrants a charge reduction or lesser punishment.

That is precisely what Russell Henderson and Aaron McKinney attempted to do in response to the murder charges they faced for killing Matthew Shepard because he was a gay man. Recall how they murdered Shepard in 1998 after engaging him in a conversation at a bar. Henderson and McKinney asserted that it was Shepard's homosexuality that made them feel an irresistible impulse to murder him, and therefore the homicide should be excused as a product of their temporary insanity. That crime and trial occurred in Wyoming, a state where the insanity defense is measured by the substantial capacity test, under which

> a person is not responsible for criminal conduct if at the time of the criminal conduct, as a result of mental illness or deficiency, he lacked substantial capacity either to appreciate the wrongfulness of his conduct or to conform his conduct to the requirements of law. (WY Stat. § 7-11-304, 1997)

The trial court judge excluded evidence that Henderson and McKenney presented to show that Shepard's sexual orientation created such an emotional disturbance within them that it caused them to lose control and kill him as a result. The judge reasoned that such information did not adequately demonstrate a substantial lack of mental capacity, which is a higher standard and requirement under Wyoming law for insanity claims. Although the gay/trans panic defense was not successful in that case, it might be in others, since Wyoming remains among the majority of states where individuals charged with a hate crime can assert fear or bias toward their victim on account of that person's sexual orientation or gender identity as a defense.

*Gay/Trans Panic Defense*

FIGURE 12.3 **Transphobia**

In Michigan there is no law prohibiting the admission of evidence to show that a hate crime was motivated by the victim's sexual orientation or gender identity, and in that context, Jonathan Schmitz explained why he murdered Scott Amedure in 1995. Just a few days before the incident, the pair appeared on *The Jenny Jones Show* in an episode featuring guests who were invited to reveal their secret homosexual crushes. Amedure, who was openly gay and a friend of Schmitz, was aware of the topic for conversation and shared on air, before a live audience and in explicit detail, how he desired for that platonic relationship to be a romantic one. Schmitz, who is heterosexual, was asked to come on the show to meet an ex-girlfriend who wanted to rekindle their love. He appeared visibly surprised to see Amedure there instead and very embarrassed by his intimate public admission, stating, "You lied to me" and clarifying that he was "completely heterosexual" (Smith, 2020). The episode never aired, but that interaction was released in a clip shared by major news outlets after Amedure's death.

**Victim:**
Scott Amedure

**Defendant:**
Jonathan Schmitz

Schmitz confessed to the fatal shooting after finding a sexual note from Amedure in his driveway, and he was subsequently charged with first-degree murder, the most serious form of homicide, which requires premeditation. Certainly, there was evidence to support that charge, since Schmitz purchased a gun after finding the note for the purpose of killing Amedure and deliberately executed that plan. But at trial he defended the murder on the grounds that it was provoked by Amedure's sexual orientation and affection toward him, which he expressed in such a public way. Schmitz further argued that the shame he felt from that experience was exacerbated by the note, and those combined incidents, which centered on the victim's homosexuality, provided an adequate provocation and excuse for a heterosexual man to commit murder. That in essence is the gay/trans panic defense. After hearing it the jury found Schmitz guilty of the lesser offense of second-degree murder, and he was sentenced to 20–50 years in prison. Schmitz was released on parole in 2017, a time when transphobia-driven violence and reform in state hate crime laws were coincidentally rising (Dart, 2018; Smith, 2020).

More than a dozen states have passed laws that prohibit defendants from using sexual orientation or gender identity bias to defend their criminal conduct. Washington State is among those jurisdictions where the gay/trans panic defense and supporting evidence is considered an affront to the LGBTQ+ community and per se excluded from trial for that purpose.

Washington was the 10th state to pass such legislation, yet that law drew nationwide attention because of the 2019 sensational murder of Nikki Kuhnhausen, a transgender female, that inspired it. On June 6, 2019, she was killed at age 17 years by David Bogdanov, whom she met for the first time in person after they had talked on Snapchat. Bogdanov later claimed that he killed Kuhnhausen in self-defense after she reached for his gun when he grew enraged from discovering that she was born a biological male. He even testified at his murder trial, revealing his hatred for all LGBTQ+ persons and fear that his family would be humiliated to learn that he was intimate with someone from that community. But the jury was not swayed by that self-defense ideation of gay/trans panic and found him guilty of second-degree murder and malicious harassment, which is considered a hate crime in Washington. Bogdanov is currently serving a 19½-year prison sentence, and his victim's family has ensured that others who commit similar crimes in that state will receive the same fate, through their relentless efforts that contributed to the successful passage of Washington's ban on the use of the gay/trans panic defense in criminal prosecutions for hate crimes (Prokop, 2021; Truesdall, 2021).

## Conclusion

In this chapter, readers learned about hate crimes along with various laws that are in place to protect individuals from being victimized because of some personal, innate characteristic or trait that is also subject to systemic discrimination or marginalization. Race, color, national origin, religion, disability, and sex are the enumerated categories that traditionally have been afforded protection from discrimination through bedrock civil rights legislation, which includes but is not limited to the Civil Rights Act of 1964, Voting Rights Act of 1965, and Civil Rights Act of 1968. There are also federal and state hate crime statutes that are used to escalate sentences for persons who are convicted of bias-motivated crimes and explicitly indicate sexual orientation and gender identity among the other statuses already specified in civil rights legislation. The U.S. Supreme Court has played a pivotal role in interpreting those laws in the context of the First Amendment to the U.S. Constitution, particularly whether the accompanying censorships apply to protected or unprotected speech and the constitutionality of such limitations. Another key element in the development of hate crime legislation is the sensational and tragic prejudice-driven incidents that literally transformed America. As discussed, the names Matthew Shepard and James Byrd Jr. are synonymous with hate violence among people who experienced the worldwide attention those victims received and as evidenced by the Matthew Shepard and James Byrd Jr. Hate Crimes Prevention Act of 2009, the first federal hate crime penalty enhancement statute. Remember them along with countless others like Scott Amedure and Nikki Kuhnhausen, who lost their lives in bias-motivated acts of violence. Finally, it is important to consider hate crimes in context, and especially factors known to influence such violence like xenophobia, racism, transphobia, and widespread biases against entire groups that emerge from those feelings, along with incessant media coverage of major news events. The highlighted experiences faced by Muslims following the September 11, 2001, attacks and then by Asians and Pacific Islanders during the COVID-19 pandemic reflect that.

## THINK AND APPLY

Refer to what you have learned in this chapter about various sources of federal legislation that prohibit discrimination in public sectors on the basis of race, color, national origin, disability, religion, and sex. Also reflect on the disproportionate risk of hate victimizations that transgender individuals face. The Equality Bill is a law proposed in response to those threats that in effect would amend the Civil Rights Act of 1964 to explicitly include sexual orientation and gender identity among the other categories of protection.

Would you support the enactment of a similar law that would impose a nationwide ban on the gay/trans panic defense? Explain your position.

### Credits

# Chapter 13

# Serial Killers and Crime Intersectionality

## Introduction to the Chapter

American popular culture is inundated with serial killer stories told and retold in documentaries, books, shows, and other forms of media consumption, and perhaps that mirrors a deep fascination many people have with individuals who are classified as serial killers and the crimes they committed. Serial killing is by definition distinct from other crimes against persons since it is the intentional commission of two or more murders in separate incidents. Those elements distinguish it from mass murder events, which also involve multiple homicides, but the fatalities occur during a single crime occurrence. In contrast, serial killing, or a series of murders, is done more than one time and through a pattern of conduct that is unique to the perpetrator and becomes known as their modus operandi, or mode of operation (MO). In fact, details of how a serial killer selects victims, preys on them, executes murders, handles victims after their death, makes any communications with law enforcement, and any common demographic victim characteristics are often sensationalized in the media. That type of persistent, widespread news coverage and accompanying public consumption of it largely influence the social construction and assignment of nicknames to multiple murderers that coincidentally correspond to some publicized element of their modus operandi.

Do the names "Son of Sam," and the "Killer Clown" sound familiar? They are colloquial names used for David Berkowitz and John Wayne Gacy, respectively, in public discourse, academia, psychology, and various other contexts. In this chapter, readers will learn how the two earned those monikers, along with details of other serial killer stories featuring Jeffrey Dahmer, Ted Bundy, Aileen Wuornos, and Charles Manson. A central component of serial killing and the patterned conduct it follows is crime intersectionality in that multiple murderers tend to commit another crime against either persons or property that is simultaneous or incidental to each homicide, and in that regard such offenses are part of their MO. This chapter features the already mentioned serial killers, details surrounding their infamous murders and key intersections between those homicides, and their commission of other offenses such as sexual assault, robbery, prostitution, aggravated assault, and conspiracy that are distinctly linked to them and their fatal crimes. It also explores capital punishment statutes that are used to determine life imprisonment or death penalty sentences in cases wherein the defendant is

FIGURE 13.1 **Serial killers and crime intersectionality**

found guilty of committing a series of first-degree murders and coinciding felony offenses that are weighed as aggravating evidence against mitigating factors such as mental impairment. Finally, this chapter provides insight into how the legal insanity defense has been applied to serial killing, which can help readers reconcile why none of the serial killers discussed in this chapter were found not guilty by reason of insanity; some did not even take that plea, and yet they all had some diagnosed mental defect and/or intellectual disability at the time of their crime commissions.

## Sexual Assault

Sexual assault, as discussed in Chapter 6 on nonfatal crimes against persons, is prohibited under state and federal laws and is broadly defined as nongendered, unwanted, offensive bodily contact or penetration that is intimate in nature and achieved by actual or threatened force. This section expounds those concepts in the context of the serial murders committed by notorious killers Jeffrey Dahmer, John Wayne Gacy, and Ted Bundy. Together those three serial killers literally terrified America by senselessly murdering boys, girls, young men, and young women and sexually assaulting them during and after each homicidal event. Although Dahmer, Gacy and Bundy each had a signature method of serial killing, their modes of operation included forced sexual contact characterized by one or more elements of necrophilia, pedophilia, and rape.

### Necrophilia

**Victims:**
17 young men of color

**Defendant:**
Jeffrey Dahmer

Necrophilia, cannibalism, lobotomies, body dismemberments, and skull and genitalia souvenirs are all the things that Jeffrey Dahmer's serial killings were made of, and coincidentally his namesake and what distinguishes him from other multiple murderers. He committed a series of homicides and sexual assaults during 1978 to 1991, but the shock and horror of what he did continues to live on, decades later. Dahmer, a slim, meek-looking White man, drugged and strangled 17 young men and boys of color to death, and then sexually assaulted their lifeless bodies, which he documented with polaroid photographs, and made keepsakes from the victims' skulls and genitals that police uncovered at the time of his arrest. Autopsies showed those skulls ridden with holes that he had drilled and then filled with acid during botched brain surgeries (lobotomies), which were a ritual part of his killings. Investigators who searched Dahmer's apartment also made a gruesome discovery in his kitchen—frozen and half cooked body parts—and with that they came to the realization that Dahmer sought more than sexual gratification from torturing and killing his victims. Indeed, Dahmer confirmed what police suspected, that he preserved, cooked, and consumed the remains of 17 people. As more of their bodies were found, it also became evident that Dahmer directed his murderous desires for necrophilia and cannibalism toward a very specific group: homosexual men of color who were unemployed, homeless, or otherwise had weak connections to society. Dahmer preyed on those individuals at gay bars and lured them back to his home, where he incapacitated them with drinks laced with drugs. That mode of operation went smoothly until Tracy Edwards escaped from Dahmer's apartment and reign of terror. While drugged with sleeping pills, and with one wrist in handcuffs, he managed to run into the street and alert neighbors to call police, who immediately learned there were other victims upon discovering a decomposing body in Dahmer's bedroom (Holewa, 1991; Walsh, 1992).

Dahmer pleaded not guilty by reason of insanity to multiple counts of first-degree murder. Since there is no death penalty in the state of Wisconsin, he faced either life imprisonment if found guilty or confinement to a mental institution if the jury agreed that he was mentally insane at the time of each crime commission. Dahmer admitted to knowing his actions were wrong, but under Wisconsin law, legal insanity can be shown by evidence that while suffering from a mental defect, a person lacked a substantial capacity to either appreciate the wrongfulness of their conduct or otherwise act within the boundaries of the law (Wis. Stat. §§ 971.15, 2021). At trial, the defense argued that Dahmer was insane in accordance with the latter part of that standard because he suffered from a progressive mental illness, and with that defect came an overwhelming impulse to sexually assault young males after their death. However, the jury did not agree that Dahmer lacked a substantial capacity to control himself when he performed each of the 17 overlapping incidents of murder and sexual assault and found him guilty on all counts. He received consecutive life sentences in 1992 but was stabbed to death by another prisoner just 2 years later (Jentzen, 2017).

Pause and reflect on learning that Jeffrey Dahmer was convicted of 17 first-degree murders and received consecutive life sentences because the jury rejected his insanity plea. Recall that pursuant to Wisconsin law, insanity must be proved by evidence showing that the defendant lacked a substantial capacity to conform conduct or mentality within the confines of the law. As discussed in this book, a major criticism of the substantial capacity test is that it is difficult for jurors to precisely measure how much mental impairment equates to a lack of substantial capacity and in turn legal insanity.

Consider the details of Dahmer's crimes discussed. Identify and explain some possible challenges jurors might have encountered in applying the substantial capacity test in the context of his case. Explain.

**PAUSE AND REFLECT**

## Pedophilia

**Victims:**
33 male adolescents

**Defendant:**
John Wayne Gacy

More than 40 years have passed since John Wayne Gacy, the "Killer Clown," sexually assaulted and murdered 33 male adolescents in a quiet suburban town in Chicago, where he lived and worked as a well-respected businessperson. Gacy was particularly known in the community for hosting kid-themed parties at his house and wearing a clown costume for the festivities. He wore that now infamous clown costume to mask his appearance in the literal sense, but more importantly his pedophilia, which in the 1970s was unseen, especially behind the facade of that party disguise. That was the first step in his modus operandi, to gain the trust of partygoers and community residents, especially among young males who fell victim to his serial killing, torture, and sexual assault. Gacy was known as a trusted, kid-friendly, local businessperson, and so when he approached children and teenagers while driving around town, they readily accepted his offer for a ride. Once his victims entered his vehicle, he either sedated them with chloroform or administered alcohol and drugs to them at his home to subdue them. Nearly all the victims' remains were uncovered from a crawlspace in Gacy's home, and their bodies showed evidence of strangulation and sexual assault. Gacy would later reveal how he methodically wrapped a rope or cord around each victim's neck and used a pipe to tighten it and block circulation to their airways. Gacy confessed these details to police when he was finally arrested on December 21, 1978 (Associated Press, 2021b; Rumore, 2021).

As a result, at his trial 2 years later, the issue was not whether he was a pedophilia-driven serial killer but rather whether he was legally insane when he performed each of those acts. Gacy pleaded not guilty by reason of insanity, and under the applicable Illinois statute, that defense is measured by a narrow version of the substantial capacity test, which excludes diminished impulse control as sufficient grounds for legal insanity. Instead, "a person is not criminally responsible for conduct if at the time of such conduct, as a result of mental disease or mental defect, he lacks substantial capacity to appreciate the criminality of his conduct" (§ 720 ILCS 5/6-2, 2012). The defense called psychiatric witnesses to testify that Gacy did not possess the ability to fully understand the wrongfulness of his actions due to having a multiple personality disorder and exhibiting schizophrenic behaviors. His attorney inferred how that disability persisted through each crime incident, using the testimony of Jeff Rignall, a surviving victim. On the stand, Rignall recalled how Gacy victimized him, by first forcing him to inhale chloroform and then raping and tormenting him for hours. But the jury did not make the same inference as the defense from that evidence. Gacy was found guilty of all counts of kidnapping, assault, and first-degree murder and sent to death by lethal injection on May 19, 1994 (Sneed, 2021).

## Rape

Ted Bundy is sometimes called "Lady Killer" or "Campus Killer," but neither of those cheeky monikers reflect why he is also known as one of the most prolific serial killers in American history. His murders spanned approximately 5 years from 1975 to 1980 across the nation, and while he confessed to killing and raping at least 28 young women and girls in various states, federal investigators believe there are countless other victims whose identities and bodies have never been uncovered. Bundy, a former law student, had the likeness of a stereotypical all-American White male, just like John Wayne Gacy, and used that appeal as part of his modus operandi. Bundy and Gacy also selected victims in similar ways, using their cars as a vehicle for kidnapping and torture; however, there are also stark differences in their crime patterns. Bundy targeted women and attracted their attention and sympathy by stopping to ask for their assistance with a feigned injury, and then utilized a variety of instruments to strangle or bludgeon them. He sexually assaulted or raped each murder victim, but only after that person had lost consciousness or died from their inflicted injuries. Bundy admittedly took great pleasure in dressing them up and doing their makeup postmortem before committing those sex crimes, which were ongoing until decomposition made it impossible to continue. Both Ted Bundy and Jeffrey Dahmer were necrophiliacs and shared a habit of keeping mementos of their victim's remains, such as polaroid pictures, skulls, and other body parts, which they also consumed (Lavender, 2020; Yang et al., 2019).

Bundy stands out as a methodical serial killer and rapist who planned out each murder and intersecting sexual assault or rape by scouting a location to dispose of the bodies and securing weapons and tools needed to complete those crimes. That level of careful deliberation persisted throughout his crime spree, and so did his charming good looks, and those combined factors largely contributed to his ability to avoid police detection for years—until he was finally arrested and convicted of aggravating kidnapping and assault in two separate cases in 1974 and again in 1977. Bundy managed to escape from prison both times, and after the second escape, he escalated his serial crimes to a level that earned him the nickname "Campus Killer," along with multiple death sentences. On January 15, 1978, he unlawfully entered a Chi Omega sorority home located on Florida State University campus and proceeded to attack, rape, and sexually assault four women, strangling and beating two of them to death, all within a 15-minute span. Less than 1 month later, he abducted and murdered a 12-year-old girl. Bundy was arrested a week later for driving a stolen car, and while in police custody he confessed to murdering the two college students, Margaret Bowman and Lisa Levy, and the little girl, Kimberly Leach. He pled not guilty but refused to assert an insanity defense, against the advice of his attorneys. The jury was uncharmed by Bundy and found him guilty on all charges and sent him to death by electrocution on January 24, 1989 (Flores, 1987; Pruitt, 2019).

> **Victims:**
> 28 or more young women
>
> **Defendant:**
> Ted Bundy

## Prostitution and Robbery

Victims:
Seven middle-aged
White men

Defendant:
Aileen Wuornos

Was Aileen Wuornos a monster? That is certainly how she was portrayed in the 2003 film *Monster*, which is based on her life and contains all the appeal of a sensational yet different kind of true crime drama: salacious crimes, serial killings, and a female with a starring role. Recent data show that only 5%–7% of known multiple murder incidents are committed by women, and that disproportionality is also reflected in most media depictions of serial killers, which feature White men, who are predominantly responsible for such crimes (Cottier, 2020; Sterbenz, 2015). Naturally, the movie *Monster* aroused public interest in Aileen Wuornos, a White woman who looked monstrous in the film, courtesy of Charlize Theron with heavy makeup and whose homicidal acts matched those of Wuornos without any exaggeration. Wuornos killed seven White middle-aged men in separate events spanning from 1989 to 1990; some of their bodies were discovered nude or partially disrobed, which is indicative of how she used the promise of sex and sexual acts to lure her victims into a vulnerable position and then rob them. She admittedly worked as a prostitute, and it was in that capacity that she met the seven men, who had agreed to pay her in exchange for sexual gratification, which is criminalized in all states except for certain counties in Nevada as a quality-of-life violation and affront to public health, safety, and welfare. Prostitution was essential to how Wuornos conducted her serial murder operation in central Florida, where it is unlawful to give or receive money in exchange for sexual activity. It is unclear whether Wuornos actually engaged in any sexual behaviors with her victims, but at the very least she used the promise to do so as a facade to mask her other criminal intentions. Even inchoate acts such as those, involving the solicitation of prostitution or offer to commit it, are prohibited (Fla. Stat. § 796.07, 2021). But the prosecutor assigned to Wuornos's case did not charge her with prostitution, an offense typically punished as a misdemeanor crime unless it is accompanied by one or more of the attendant circumstances specified in the statute that warrant an enhanced felony classification and penalty. Instead, he sought punishment for the more serious, violent crimes that she inflicted on her victims (Stockton, 2021; Wright, 2021).

The 1990 arrest of Wuornos came with the revelation that she was a serial killer who was responsible for taking the lives of seven men. She was charged with six counts of first-degree murder and confessed to killing another man, whose body was never found; for that reason she escaped punishment for his death. Wuornos pleaded guilty or no contest to deliberately killing all of them except for one, Richard Mallory, who also happened to be her very first victim. Mallory was last seen alive riding along a busy interstate Florida highway, as his friends revealed, in pursuit of a prostitute. Investigators found him dead, with multiple bullet wounds in his chest. Wuornos was charged with first-degree murder, armed robbery with a firearm or other deadly weapon, and possession of a firearm by a convicted felon in connection with Mallory's death. She pleaded not guilty, and her subsequent trial as highlighted in the movie *Monster* was a prime-time event. At trial, the state introduced key evidence to demonstrate that Wuornos robbed Mallory and how that crime was instrumental in his death. It was revealed at trial that investigators found Mallory's belongings and items from his car in local pawn shops and traced them back to Wuornos. The prosecutor presented that information in tandem with the shooting death of Mallory to prove that he was also a victim of armed robbery, for which Wuornos was responsible (Jacob, 2020; Wade, 2021).

Pursuant to Florida law and consistent with federal and state jurisdictions, robbery is defined as the forceful taking of property from another person or their custody with the intent to permanently deprive them of it. The use of a firearm or other dangerous weapon during the commission of such a crime is considered armed robbery and sufficient grounds to escalate it to a first-degree felony (Fla. Stat. § 812.13, 2021). Wuornos testified on her own behalf, and because of that she was subjected to a line of cross-examination that challenged the veracity of her claim that the murder was done in self-defense, in response to being violently raped by Mallory. However, the jury had no reasonable doubt about her guilt and convicted her of first-degree murder, armed robbery, and illegal possession of a firearm, which taken together made her eligible for a death sentence. In Florida an unlawful killing, which is a homicide that not justified or excused, is considered capital murder if it is premeditated or achieved through the commission or attempted commission of a robbery or other serious felony (Fla. Stat. § 782.04, 2021). In accordance with the corresponding law, the jury found those aggravating factors outweighed the one fact that by statute mitigates guilt—mental impairment, and more specifically that Wuornos was diagnosed with borderline personality disorder. That decision sent her to death in the electric chair, a fate that was executed on January 31, 1992, and remains a source of concerns and controversies over capital punishment, intellectual disability, and legal insanity (Cottier, 2020).

**PAUSE AND REFLECT**

Pause and reflect on what you learned about Aileen Wuornos, who while working as a prostitute met seven men whom she shot to death in separate incidents and committed an armed robbery against at least one of those victims. An equally important but less sensationalized part of her story is the psychological, social, and environmental risk factors that she experienced from a young age, which are known to contribute to criminal pathways and offending (Wikström, 2020). Wuornos endured a childhood fraught with parental abandonment, alcoholism, alleged abuse, molestation, and prostitution. She was also diagnosed with an antisocial/personality disorder and had an 80 IQ, just slightly more than 71, which is the threshold measure of intellectual disability used to protect otherwise eligible persons from capital punishment (*Atkins v. Virginia*, 2002). In accordance with Florida's capital murder statute, the jury could only consider the personality disorder as a mitigating factor in punishment. The presiding judge acknowledged those other nonstatutory risk factors mentioned but nonetheless approved the jury's recommended death sentence.

Should Aileen Wuornos have been sentenced to life imprisonment? Explain.

## Inchoate Offenses

In Chapter 4 readers learned about actus reus and how that criminal act element of crime can occur through voluntary conduct or culpable omissions that are prohibited under the law. Accordingly, criminal conduct is punishable regardless of whether the intended result is completed. Incomplete or inchoate offenses encompass acts of solicitation, attempts, and conspiracy, and each type of crime is established by distinct elements of proof set forth under the law. This section puts that content in the context of serial killings that were perpetrated by David Berkowitz and Charles Manson and explores how those multiple homicides intersect with attempted murder and conspiracy.

### Attempted Murder

**Victims:**
**13 New York City Residents**

**Defendant:**
**David Berkowitz**

During the late 1970s, David Berkowitz, a 23-year-old postal worker, terrorized New Yorkers with his serial shooting rampages that resulted in numerous murders and attempted murders. His crimes shook America to the core and even caused wig sales to skyrocket as women with brown hair who lived in or near New York City scrambled to conceal their heads for self-preservation. Berkowitz used a .44 caliber gun to shoot both men and women, but most were females with brunette hair, and those details are considered key attributes of his modus operandi. There were 13 victims in total, and 7 were fortunate to survive both the shooting and fires that Berkowitz set to divert law enforcement efforts. People were terrified by that violence but even more horrified by how it was executed. Berkowitz shot his victims in random public places throughout the New York City greater area, and most of them were in their cars, en route home or otherwise engaged in mundane activities. Those circumstances were part of each crime commission and in that regard created a palpable sense of vulnerability and panic among residents, who were afraid to be out past dark since the shootings were done mainly during the evening or nighttime (Hockenberry, 2004).

Although Berkowitz's shootings were patterned by that mode of operation, there seemed to be no clear motive behind those victimizations, as none of the people injured or killed knew him personally, professionally, or in any other capacity. That all changed when Berkowitz began mailing letters to various newspapers and media outlets that contained cryptic, taunting messages related to the shooting incidents. The first one had the most sensational panic effect and influence in shaping Berkowitz's serial killer legacy. In it, Berkowitz wrote that the "Son of Sam" was responsible for the shooting deaths, explaining that Sam was his neighbor, who had a "son," a demon-possessed dog named "Harvey," that commanded him to commit the killings. From that letter and the ensuing media frenzy, Berkowitz became known as the Son of Sam, .44 caliber killer. Berkowitz, the Son of Sam, pleaded guilty to all six murders, which shocked many who speculated that the Son of Sam story was a product of his mental illness and a foreshadowing to an insanity plea. Not surprisingly, he was convicted on all six counts of second-degree murder and several counts of attempted murder for shooting with an intent to kill the victims who were fortunate to survive those bullets (Bonn, 2021; Quindlen, 1978). Accordingly, in New York an attempted crime is defined as any intentional conduct "which tends to effect the commission" (N.Y Penal Law § 110.0, 2014) of a crime. After years in prison, Berkowitz recanted the Son of Sam story, but that nickname is still alive and well courtesy of countless documentaries, books, movies, and more. One example of the indelible mark his crimes left on society are Son of Sam laws, which exist in most states and severely restrict opportunities for individuals with felony convictions to earn profits from books, movies, and other creations based on their crime commission(s). Instead, victims and civil litigants who bring a successful lawsuit against the defendant have prioritized rights to those proceeds.

**PAUSE AND REFLECT**

Pause and reflect on what you learned about the Son of Sam, otherwise known as David Berkowitz. Ironically, New York is among several states where Son of Sam laws have been invalidated as unconstitutional, in violation of First Amendment freedom of expression protections.

Explain whether you support or oppose Son of Sam laws.

## Conspiracy

Picture pregnant Hollywood actress Sharon Tate dead along with four of her friends, blood splattered throughout her residence, and the word "PIG" written in blood on the front door to her residence. That might sound like the plot for a horror movie, but it was the unfortunate reality that Los Angeles Police Department officers discovered in 1969 upon their arrival at Tate's home. The details of what would become known as the Sharon Tate murder were covered by major news outlets, much to the horror and chagrin of Los Angeles residents. The ensuing public fear of crime was fueled the

> Victims:
> Seven Los Angeles Residents
>
> Defendant:
> Charles Manson

very next day when a local couple, Leno and Rosemary LaBianca, were also found murdered in their home. The homicides, which the media called the LaBianca–Tate murders, went unsolved—that is, until self-proclaimed members of a cult confessed to their involvement in the homicides and identified Charles Manson as the ringleader. As the story goes, or least one version of it, Manson acquired a cultlike group of followers called "the Manson Family," composed mostly of women who worshipped him and Satan.

It is unknown what exactly motivated members of the Manson Family to kill multiple people in separate incidents, but there is plenty of speculation that the culprit was drugs, satanism, or an ill-conceived attempt to incite a race war. That aside, one important fact is clear, that four individuals who claimed to be members of a cult run by Manson claimed that they participated in the LaBianca–Tate murders because he told them to. They even explained that Manson instructed them to write something ominous in blood at the Tate home and even accompanied them to the second murder to ensure that the operation went smoothly. That is what a conspiracy is made of, at least under the applicable California law, which makes it illegal for two or more persons to conspire to commit a crime by forming an agreement to do so and engaging in some overt act to achieve it. In that state and most others, conspiracy does not merge with the completed crime that was conspired (Cal. Penal Code § 182, 2001). But the prosecutor only charged Manson and four of his cult followers with multiple counts of murder, for which they received the ultimate punishment, death, pursuant to the California capital murder statute in existence at the time. Accordingly, serial deliberate homicide was considered a qualifying aggravating factor for the death penalty, but capital punishment was abolished statewide in 2016, and as a result their sentences were commuted to life imprisonment. Manson's life ended at age 83 from heart failure, but his mark on true crime popular culture is still beating. The beat goes on in an array of media artifacts, most notably *Helter Skelter: The True Story of the Manson Murders*, a best seller book coauthored by Vincent Bugliosi, who was the prosecutor in the Manson trial (Grow, 2019; Iati, 2019; Lenoir, 2019).

## Conclusion

This chapter features six of the most infamous serial killers in history—Jeffrey Dahmer, John Wayne Gacy, Ted Bundy, Aileen Wuornos, David Berkowitz, and Charles Manson—and the footprints their crimes left on American culture and jurisprudence. They were sentenced to life or death for committing separate series of murders, which were all horrifying yet distinguishable by modus operandi (MO). As discussed, each of those individuals had a unique modus operandi, or method for killing, which lives on decades after their homicides in the public psyche, fueled by sensational media coverage in documentaries, books, movies, academia, and more. Particular attention is devoted to the patterned characteristics of how those serial killers operated with respect to their weapon choice, victim selection and demographics, postmortem tortuous acts and crime intersectionality. This chapter outlined those and other distinctive details of the serial homicides covered by drawing connections between them and offenses that were perpetually committed in tandem with the murders. That approach gives readers a deeper understanding of the featured serial killers in the context of the one or more crimes of sexual assault, prostitution, arson, robbery, attempted murder, and conspiracy they habitually committed to facilitate those fatal outcomes and/or as a personal reward for taking lives. Now you are prepared to watch *The Sons of Sam: A Descent into Darkness, Monster, Conversations with a Killer: The Ted Bundy Tapes, John Wayne Gacy: Devil in Disguise,* and other serial killer inspired shows through a comprehensive lens, to see those murders along with any intersecting crimes that are a collective part of modus operandi.

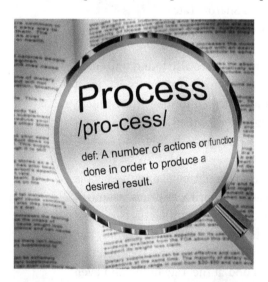

FIGURE 13.2 **Modus operandi**

## THINK AND APPLY

Refer to what you learned in this chapter about notorious serial killers Jeffrey Dahmer, John Wayne Gacy, Ted Bundy, Aileen Wuornos, David Berkowitz, and Charles Manson and how their murders intersected with other crimes against persons and property. Can you name at least two other individuals who committed multiple murders and identify a pattern of other offenses they perpetrated while inflicting those homicides? Explain the elements of those incidental crimes and ways that committing them were used as a tool in the serial murders.

### Credits

# References

Abrahamson, A. (1995, August 2). *Menendezes can use abuse defense, judge says: Courts: Prosecutors had sought to preclude evidence that dominated the brothers' first murder trial. The jurist says he will sharply limit testimony on minutiae of the defendants' lives, however.* Los Angeles Times. https://www.latimes.com/archives/la-xpm-1995-08-02-me-30580-story.html

Abramovitch, S. (2018, June 7). *Heidi Fleiss reflects on 25th anniversary of her arrest, ex Tom Sizemore and what Charlie Sheen really spent on girls.* The Hollywood Reporter. https://www.hollywoodreporter.com/lifestyle/lifestyle-news/heidi-fleiss-her-arrest-macaw-cause-drug-addict-tom-sizemore-1117449/

Aho, C. (2021, June 15). *The story behind the Menendez brothers.* Inquirer. https://usa.inquirer.net/74455/the-story-behind-the-menendez-brothers

AL Code § 13A-11-7 (2021). https://law.justia.com/codes/alabama/2021/title-13a/chapter-11/article-1/section-13a-11-7/

Alfonseca, K. (2021, September 11). *20 years after 9/11, Islamophobia continues to haunt Muslims.* ABC News. https://abcnews.go.com/US/20-years-911-islamophobia-continues-haunt-muslims/story?id=79732049

American Law Institute. (1985). Model Penal Code: Official draft and explanatory notes: Complete text of Model Penal Code as adopted at the 1962 annual meeting of the American Law Institute at Washington, D.C., May 24, 1962.

Andone, D., McLaughlin, E. C., Spells, A., & Sayers, D. M. (2022, January 8). *Ahmaud Arbery's killers sentenced to life in prison for 25-year-old Black man's murder.* CNN. https://www.cnn.com/2022/01/07/us/ahmaud-arbery-sentencing-killers-mcmichael-bryan/index.html

AS§ 11.61.110 (2020). https://law.justia.com/codes/alaska/2020/title-11/chapter-61/article-1/section-11-61-110/

Asokan, T.V. (2007). Daniel McNaughton (1813-1865). Indian J Psychiatry. 49(3): 223–224. doi: 10.4103/0019-5545.37328

A.R.S § 13-1103 (2021). https://law.justia.com/codes/arizona/2021/title-13/section-13-1103/

Assefa, H. (2013, December 13). *Former 'Sopranos' actor Lillo Brancato Jr. released from prison.* CNN. https://www.cnn.com/2013/12/31/showbiz/former-sopranos-actor-release/index.html

Associated Press. (2021, April 6). *Police testimony: Derek Chauvin was trained to avoid neck pressure.* Politico. https://www.politico.com/news/2021/04/06/police-derek-chauvin-george-floyd-479404

Associated Press. (2021, October 25). *Victim killed by John Wayne Gacy in 1970s finally identified.* Fox 59. https://fox59.com/news/john-wayne-gacy-victim-identified-after-45-years/

Ater, R. (2020, May 29). In memoriam: I can't breathe. *Renée Ater.* https://www.reneeater.com/on-monumentsblog/tag/list+of+unarmed+black+people+killed+by+police

*Atkins v. Virginia,* 536 U.S. 304 (2002).

Baker, R., Leichtling, G., Hildebran, C., Pinela, C., Waddell, E. N., Sidlow, C., ... Korthuis, P. T. (2021). "Like yin and yang": Perceptions of methamphetamine benefits and consequences among people who use opioids in rural communities. *Journal of Addiction Medicine, 15*(1), 34–39.

Biden, J. (2021, April 20). *Remarks by President Biden on the verdict in the Derek Chauvin trial for the death of George Floyd.* The White House. https://www.whitehouse.gov/briefing-room/speeches-remarks/2021/04/20/remarks-by-president-biden-on-the-verdict-in-the-derek-chauvin-trial-for-the-death-of-george-floyd/

Bindel, J. (2014, October 26). *The truth behind America's most famous gay-hate murder.* The Guardian. https://www.theguardian.com/world/2014/oct/26/the-truth-behind-americas-most-famous-gay-hate-murder-matthew-shepard

Bonn, S. (2021, May 19). *What are "Son of Sam" laws?* Wicked Deeds. https://www.psychologytoday.com/us/blog/wicked-deeds/202105/what-are-son-sam-laws

Boots, A. (2020, July 9). *"The burning bed" recalls the case that changed how law enforcement treats domestic violence.* The New Yorker. https://www.newyorker.com/culture/video-dept/the-burning-bed-recalls-the-case-that-changed-how-law-enforcement-treats-domestic-violence

Borden, T. (2020, May 4). *One murder-for-hire plot, 5 husbands, and 176 tigers: Meet Joe Exotic, the man Nicolas Cage will play in an upcoming TV series.* Insider. https://www.businessinsider.com/who-is-joe-exotic-maldonado-passage-tiger-king-netflix

*Brandenburg v. Ohio*, 395 U.S. 444 (1969).

Brockington, A. (2017, July 8). *Actor Shia LaBeouf arrested on public drunkenness, disorderly conduct charges.* NBC News. https://www.nbcnews.com/pop-culture/celebrity/actor-shia-labeouf-arrested-public-drunkenness-disorderly-conduct-charges-n780936

Bruney, G. (2021, June 24). *Ghislaine Maxwell knows more about Jeffrey Epstein than anyone. Now, she's facing federal charges.* Esquire. https://www.esquire.com/entertainment/tv/a32714413/ghislaine-maxwell-now-jeffrey-epstein-madam/

Burch, A. (2018, July 9). *In Texas, a decades-old hate crime, forgiven but never forgotten.* The New York Times. https://www.nytimes.com/2018/07/09/us/james-byrd-jasper-texas-killing.html

Burke, N. (2020, July 16). *Case dismissed against social workers charged in death of 8-year-old California boy.* NBC News. https://www.nbcnews.com/news/us-news/case-dismissed-against-social-workers-charged-death-8-year-old-n1234089

CALCRIM No. 3408 (2020). https://www.justia.com/criminal/docs/calcrim/3400/3408/

Cal. Penal Code §§ 29.4 (2013), 31 (2008), 182 (2011), 187 (1996), 188 (2019), 189 (2020), 189.5 (1989), 190 (1998), 192 (2015), 211 (1872), 266i(a)(6) (2020), 273(d) (2011), 11164 (2001) https://leginfo.legislature.ca.gov/faces/codes_displaySection.xhtml?lawCode=PEN&sectionNum=29.4; https://leginfo.legislature.ca.gov/faces/codes_displaySection.xhtml?lawCode=PEN&sectionNum=31;https://leginfo.legislature.ca.gov/faces/codes_displaySection.xhtml?sectionNum=182&lawCode=PEN https://leginfo.legislature.ca.gov/faces/codes_displaySection.xhtml?sectionNum=187.&lawCode=PEN#:~:text=(a)%20Murder%20is%20the%20unlawful,a%20fetus%2C%20with%20malice%20aforethought; https://leginfo.legislature.ca.gov/faces/codes_displaySection.xhtml?sectionNum=188.&nodeTreePath=4.7.1&lawCode=PEN; https://leginfo.legislature.ca.gov/faces/codes_displaySection.xhtml?sectionNum=189.5.&nodeTreePath=4.7.1&lawCode=PEN; https://leginfo.legislature.ca.gov/faces/codes_displaySection.xhtml?sectionNum=190.&nodeTreePath=4.7.1&lawCode=PEN; https://leginfo.legislature.ca.gov/faces/codes_displaySection.xhtml?lawCode=PEN&sectionNum=192; https://leginfo.legislature.ca.gov/faces/codes_displaySection.xhtml?lawCode=PEN&sectionNum=211; https://leginfo.legislature.ca.gov/faces/codes_displaySection.xhtml?lawCode=PEN&sectionNum=266I; https://leginfo.legislature.ca.gov/faces/codes_displaySection.xhtml?lawCode=PEN&sectionNum=273d https://leginfo.legislature.ca.gov/faces/codes_displayText.xhtml?chapter=2.&part=4.&lawCode=PEN&title=1.&article=2.5

Carlisle, M. (2021, December 30). *Anti-trans violence and rhetoric reached record highs across America in 2021.* Time. https://time.com/6131444/2021-anti-trans-violence/ 32 CFR § 750.21 (1998). https://www.law.cornell.edu/cfr/text/32/750.21

Chambers, M. (1985, February 28). *Goetz spoke to one youth and then shot again, police say.* New York Times. https://www.nytimes.com/1985/02/28/nyregion/goetz-spoke-to-one-youth-then-shot-again-police-say.html

Chang, R. (2020, November 17). *JonBenét Ramsey's murder: Timeline of the child pageant star's death and investigation.* Biography. https://www.biography.com/news/jonbenet-ramsey-murder-investigation-timeline

*Chaplinsky v. New Hampshire*, 315 U.S. 568 (1942).

Chiacchia, K. B. (2000). Insanity defense. In *Gale Encyclopedia of Psychology*. Gale Group.

CNN. (2020, July 2). *Andrea Yates fast facts.* https://www.cnn.com/2013/03/25/us/andrea-yates-fast-facts/index.html

Collman, A. (2020, October 11). *From a happy pregnancy announcement to a shallow grave: The full timeline of the Chris Watts murder case.* Insider. https://www.insider.com/chris-watts-murder-timeline-2018-12

Cottier, C. (2020, December 3). *Female serial killers exist, but their motives are different.* Discover. https://www.discovermagazine.com/mind/female-serial-killers-exist-but-their-motives-are-different

CO Rev. Stat. §§ 18-3-102, 18-3-104, 18-4-203, 18-3-302, 18-8-407, 18-1-704 (2020).; https://codes.findlaw.com/co/title-18-criminal-code/co-rev-st-sect-18-3-102.html; https://codes.findlaw.com/co/title-18-criminal-code/co-rev-st-sect-18-3-104.html; https://codes.findlaw.com/co/title-18-criminal-code/co-rev-st-sect-18-4-203.html; https://codes.findlaw.com/co/title-18-criminal-code/co-rev-st-sect-18-3-302.html https://codes.findlaw.com/co/title-18-criminal-code/co-rev-st-sect-18-8-407.html; https://codes.findlaw.com/co/title-18-criminal-code/co-rev-st-sect-18-1-704.html

Dart, T. (2018, May 12). *After decades of "gay panic defense" in court, US states slowly begin to ban tactic.* The Guardian. https://www.theguardian.com/us-news/2018/may/12/gay-panic-defence-tactic-ban-court

Dearen, J. (2011, August 2). *Video shows Nancy Garrido luring girl into van.* NBC News. https://www.nbcnews.com/id/wbna43993012

De Fabrique, N. (2011). M'Naghten rule. In J. S. Kreutzer, J. DeLuca, & B. Caplan (Eds.), Encyclopedia of clinical neuropsychology. Springer. https://doi.org/10.1007/978-0-387-79948-3_839

Deutsch , L. (2014, June 10). *OJ Simpson Murder Trial: "If It Doesn't Fit, You Must Acquit."* NBC News.https://www.nbclosangeles.com/news/local/oj-simpson-20-years-later-glove-fit-darden-dunne-murder-trial-of-the-century/1976992/

11 Del. C. §§ 421, 423, 441 (2018). https://delcode.delaware.gov/title11/c004/index.html

Dibdin, E. (2019, April 3). *A complete timeline of Dee Dee Blanchard's murder and Gypsy Blanchard's trial.* Harper's Bazaar. https://www.harpersbazaar.com/culture/film-tv/a26887708/the-act-dee-dee-gypsy-blanchard-murder-trial-timeline/

Do, A. (2021, June 30). *Hate crimes against Asians jumped 107% in California in "an epidemic of hate."* Los Angeles Times. https://www.latimes.com/california/story/2021-06-30/california-attorney-general-hate-crimes

Drucker, E. (2002). Population impact of mass incarceration under New York's Rockefeller drug laws: An analysis of years of life lost. *Journal of Urban Health Bulletin of the New York Academy of Medicine*, 79(3), 434–435.

Dunker, C. (2021, September 9). *Nebraskans for Medical Marijuana files language for two new petition drives.* Lincoln Journal Star. https://journalstar.com/news/state-and-regional/govt-and-politics/nebraskans-for-medical-marijuana-files-language-for-two-new-petition-drives/article_23362439-c49b-5568-88a6-f541611d2da9.html

*Durham v. United States*, 214 F.2d 862 (1954).

*Dusky v. United States*, 362 U.S. 402 (1960).

Esterbrook, J. (2002, February 28). *Yates' husband takes stand.* CBS News. https://www.cbsnews.com/news/yates-husband-takes-stand/

ESV Economy Bible. (2017). Exodus 20:2–17.

Finley, B. (2021, September 27). *John Hinckley, who shot Reagan, to be freed from oversight.* AP News. https://apnews.com/article/courts-ronald-reagan-jodie-foster-john-hinckley-c97c9e5f09d8f10e1b42290164965a0d

Fischer, C. (2019, June 28). Witnesses recall 2012 bank heist involving family at center of 20/20 documentary. Eyewitness News. https://abc13.com/bank-robber-abigail-catt-parole-prison/5370439/

FL Stat. §§ 782.04, 796.07, 810.02, 812.13, 812.014 (2021) http://www.leg.state.fl.us/statutes/index.cfm?App_mode=Display_Statute&Search_String=&URL=0700-0799/0782/Sections/0782.04.html http://www.leg.state.fl.us/statutes/index.cfm?App_mode=Display_Statute&URL=0700-0799/0796/Sections/0796.07.html; https://law.justia.com/codes/florida/2021/title-xlvi/chapter-812/section-812-012/; http://www.leg.state.fl.us/statutes/index.cfm?App_mode=Display_Statute&URL=0800-0899/0812/Sections/0812.13.html; http://www.leg.state.fl.us/statutes/index.cfm?App_mode=Display_Statute&Search_String=&URL=0800-0899/0812/Sections/0812.014.html

Fleeman, M. (1995, March 13). *Fuhrman tells how bloody glove was found in walkway—defense is expected to push claims that he planted evidence.* The Seattle Times. https://archive.seattletimes.com/archive/?date=19950313&slug=2109961

Flores, I. (1987, October 23). *Lawyers testify Bundy sabotaged defense efforts.* AP News. https://apnews.com/article/789cd3cb7ffa6bb761dbb8299e6e81de

GA Code § 15-11-561 (2020). https://law.justia.com/codes/georgia/2020/title-15/chapter-11/article-6/part-9/section-15-11-561/

Gajanan, M. (2019, July 17). *Here's what to know about the sex trafficking case against Jeffrey Epstein.* Time. https://time.com/5621911/jeffrey-epstein-sex-trafficking-what-to-know/

Gearan, A. (1994, January 23). *Lorena Bobbitt found innocent; jury cites temporary insanity: Law: Judge places her in custody to undergo psychiatric evaluation after she severed mate's penis.* Los Angeles Times. https://www.latimes.com/archives/la-xpm-1994-01-23-mn-14584-story.html

Gladwell, M. (1996, April 24). *Goetz told to pay $43 million, but plaintiff to get little of that.* The *New York Times.* https://www.sun-sentinel.com/news/fl-xpm-1996-04-24-9604240006-story.html

Glass, A. (2018, June 21). *Jury finds Hinckley insane in Reagan shooting, June 21, 1982.* Politico. https://www.politico.com/story/2018/06/21/jury-finds-hinckley-insane-in-reagan-shooting-june-21-1982-653299

Goodwyn, W. (2019, April 24). *Texas executes man convicted in 1998 murder of James Byrd Jr.* NPR. https://www.npr.org/2019/04/24/716647585/texas-to-execute-man-convicted-in-dragging-death-of-james-byrd-jr.

*Graham v. Connor*, 490 U.S. 386 (1989).

Grimes, W. (2017, March 31). *Francine Hughes Wilson, 69, domestic violence victim who took action, dies.* The *New York Times.* https://www.nytimes.com/2017/03/31/us/francine-hughes-wilson-dead-burning-bed-defendant.html

*Griswold v. Connecticut*, 381 U.S. 479 (1965).

Goldman, R. (2009, September 2). *Nancy Garrido: Was Jaycee Dugard's female abductor a victim too or an accomplice?* ABC News. https://abcnews.go.com/US/story?id=8476500

Grow, K. (2019, August 9). *Charles Manson: How cult leader's twisted Beatles obsession inspired family members.* Rolling Stone. https://www.rollingstone.com/feature/charles-manson-how-cult-leaders-twisted-beatles-obsession-inspired-family-murders-107176/

Harris, A. (2019, May 30). *The Central Park Five: We were just baby boys.* The *New York Times.* https://www.nytimes.com/2019/05/30/arts/television/when-they-see-us.html

*Hawthorne v. State of Florida*, 470 So.2d 770 (1985).

Henry, K. (2020, June 19). *H.E.R. questions indifference to black agony on "I Can't Breathe."* NPR. https://www.npr.org/sections/we-insist-a-timeline-of-protest-music-in-2020/2020/09/02/903233585/h-e-r-questions-indifference-to-black-agony-on-i-can-t-breathe

Henry, L. (2020, March 31). *5 things* Tiger King *doesn't explain about captive tigers*. World Wildlife Fund. https://www.worldwildlife.org/stories/5-things-tiger-king-doesn-t-explain-about-captive-tigers

*Hess v. Indiana*, 414 U.S. 105 (1973).

History.com Editors. (2019, May 14). *The Central Park Five*. A&E Television Networks. https://www.history.com/topics/1980s/central-park-five

History.com Editors (2009, November 13). *The Menendez brothers murder their parents* A&E Television Networks. https://www.history.com/this-day-in-history/the-menendez-brothers-murder-their-parents

Hockenberry, J. (2004, July 2). *Did "Son of Sam" really act alone?* NBC News. https://www.nbcnews.com/id/wbna5351509

Holcombe, M., & Vera, A. (2021, April 29). *Federal indictment for Ahmaud Arbery's accused killers is one step closer to justice, mother says*. CNN. https://www.cnn.com/2021/04/29/us/ahmaud-arbery-shooting-indicted-thursday/index.html/

Holewa, L. (1991, September 10). *Jeffrey Dahmer pleads not guilty to murder by reason of insanity*. The Seattle Times. https://archive.seattletimes.com/archive/?date=19910910&slug=1304624

Holtzman, M. (1969). Criminal insanity—another M'naghten? *University of Miami Law Review, 23*(1969), 644–652.

*Ibn-Tamas v. United States*, 407 A.2d 626 (D.C. 1979). §720 ILCS 5/6-2 (2021). https://law.justia.com/codes/illinois/2021/chapter-720/act-720-ilcs-5/title-ii/

Insurance Information Institute. (2021). *Facts + statistics: Aggressive driving*. https://www.iii.org/fact-statistic/facts-statistics-aggressive-driving

Jacob, A. (2020, June 29). *Damsel of death: The Aileen Wuornos story*. The Sun Daily. https://www.thesundaily.my/spotlight/damsel-of-death-the-aileen-wuornos-story-MB2636169

Jacobo, J., & Smith, J. (2020, January 23). *Michelle Carter, convicted in texting-suicide case, released early for good behavior*. ABC News. https://abcnews.go.com/US/michelle-carter-convicted-texting-suicide-case-released-good/story?id=68450833

*Jacobson v. United States*, 503 U.S. 540, 548 (1992).

Jaeger, K. (2021, August 24). *Idaho Supreme Court gives 2022 marijuana legalization initiative a boost with ruling on signature requirements*. Marijuana Moment. https://www.marijuanamoment.net/idaho-supreme-court-gives-2022-marijuana-legalization-initiative-a-boost-with-ruling-on-signature-requirements/

Jentzen, J. M. (2017). Micro disasters: The case of serial killer Jeffrey Dahmer. *Academic Forensic Pathology, 7*(3), 444–452. https://doi.org/10.23907/2017.037

Kettler, S. (2021, June 3). The story of Gypsy Rose Blanchard and her mother. *Biography*. https://www.biography.com/news/gypsy-rose-blanchard-mother-dee-dee-murder

Killelea, E. (2017, May 19). Flashback: Amy Fisher becomes "Long Island Lolita." *Rolling Stone*. https://www.rollingstone.com/culture/culture-news/flashback-amy-fisher-becomes-long-island-lolita-193012/

Langer, E. (2017, April 1). *Francine Hughes Wilson, whose "Burning Bed" became a TV film, dies at 69*. The Washington Post. https://www.washingtonpost.com/national/francine-hughes-wilson-whose-burning-bed-became-a-tv-film-dies-at-69/2017/03/31/a1799db8-161c-11e7-ada0-1489b735b3a3_story.html

Latson, J. (2014, December 22). Two shootings, 30 years apart, linked by fear. Time. https://time.com/3640967/bernhard-goetz-history/

Lavender, J. (2020, November 24). *Ted Bundy had sex with decapitated corpses and kept victims' heads as trophies. The Mirror*. https://www.mirror.co.uk/news/us-news/ted-bundy-sex-decapitated-corpses-23050616

Lenoir, A. (2019, July 17). *What did Charles Manson do? The little-known story of the thin case against him*. All That's Interesting. https://allthatsinteresting.com/who-did-charles-manson-kill

Letman, S. T. (1982). Future of the defense of legal insanity. Anderson Publishing CO. In G. Stephens (Ed.), *Future of criminal justice* (pp. 178–186).

Levenson, E. (2021, April 20). *The charges against Derek Chauvin in the death of George Floyd, explained.* CNN. https://www.cnn.com/2021/04/19/us/derek-chauvin-charges-explain/index.html

Lezon, D., & O'Hare, P. (2006, June 26). *Jurors hear Yates' chilling call to 911.* Chron. https://www.chron.com/news/article/Jurors-hear-Yates-chilling-call-to-911-1866104.php

Malone, N., & Demme, A. (2015, July 26). *"I'm no longer afraid": 35 women tell their stories about being assaulted by Bill Cosby, and the culture that wouldn't listen.* The Cut. https://www.thecut.com/2015/07/bill-cosbys-accusers-speak-out.html

*Mapp v. Ohio*, 367 U.S. 643 (1961).

Margolick, D. (1994, January 22). *Lorena Bobbitt acquitted in mutilation of husband.* The New York Times. https://www.nytimes.com/1994/01/22/us/lorena-bobbitt-acquitted-in-mutilation-of-husband.html

Margolick, D. (1995, January 25). *As Simpson trial opens, state tells jury of long blood trail.* The New York Times. https://www.nytimes.com/1995/01/25/us/as-simpson-trial-opens-state-tells-jury-of-long-blood-trail.html

Marriot, M. (1989, February 20). *After three years, crack plague in New York only gets worse.* The New York Times. https://www.nytimes.com/1989/02/20/nyregion/after-3-years-crack-plague-in-new-york-only-gets-worse.html

MA Gen L ch 265 § 13 (2020) https://law.justia.com/codes/massachusetts/2020/part-iv/title-i/chapter-265/section-13/

*Matthews v. United States*, 485 U.S. 58, 63 (1988)

McCann, M. (2015, March 3). *Circumstantial evidence proves powerful on day 15 of Hernandez trial.* Sports Illustrated. https://www.si.com/nfl/2015/02/26/aaron-hernandez-trial-day-15-circumstantial-evidence

McKinley C. (2016, October 28). *Ex-DA opens up about why she cleared the Ramsey family of JonBenet's murder.* ABC News. https://abcnews.go.com/US/da-opens-cleared-ramsey-family-jonbenets-murder/story?id=43106426

MCL §§ 750.167, 780.972 (2006). http://www.legislature.mi.gov/(S(kblv3qthovqqnodc1z05emhi))/mileg.aspx?page=getObject&objectName=mcl-750-167; http://www.legislature.mi.gov/(S(sv2qavos3lii2zcxjrrufjv1))/mileg.aspx?page=getobject&objectname=mcl-780-972

McLellan, F. (2006). Mental health and justice: The case of Andrea Yates. *The Lancet, 368*(9551), 1951–1954.

McPhillips, D. (2020, June 3). *Deaths from police harm disproportionately affect people of color.* U.S. News & World Report. https://www.usnews.com/news/articles/2020-06-03/data-show-deaths-from-police-violence-disproportionately-affect-people-of-color

Mekouar, D. (2021, September 10). *How 9/11 changed Arab and Muslim Americans.* Voice of America. https://www.voanews.com/a/6222700.html

Menza, K. (2017, September 26). *The Menendez murders.* Town & Country. https://www.townandcountrymag.com/society/money-and-power/a12231370/menendez-brothers-murders-trial-why-they-did-it-story/

Meyer, J. (1996, May 30). *Court of appeal reverses Heidi Fleiss' pandering conviction.* AP News. https://apnews.com/article/c82b91fb8194a337e2cadc1b703262d5

Minn., Legis. Code § 292.02 (1990).

MINN STAT §§ 609.19, 609.195, 609.205, 609.223 (2021). https://www.revisor.mn.gov/statutes/cite/609.19; https://www.revisor.mn.gov/statutes/cite/609.195; https://www.revisor.mn.gov/statutes/cite/609.205 https://www.revisor.mn.gov/statutes/cite/609.205; https://www.revisor.mn.gov/statutes/cite/609.223

Model Penal Code §§ 2.04(1), 2.06(3), 2.07, 2.08(5)(a), 4.01, 5.01(2), 5.03, 210.3, 211.1(1), 221.1, 222.1(1), 223.1, 223.4, 223.6(1), 251.1 (1962). https://archive.org/stream/ModelPenalCode_ALI/MPC%20full%20%28504%20pages%29_djvu.txt

*Montana v. Egelhoff*, 518 U.S. 37 (1996).

Morava, M., & Hamedy, S. (2021, March 17). *49 states and territories have hate crime laws—but they vary*. CNN. https://www.cnn.com/2021/03/17/us/what-states-have-hate-crime-laws-2021-trnd/index.html

Moyer, L. (2008, December 17). *Why The SEC missed Madoff*. Forbes. https://www.forbes.com/2008/12/17/madoff-sec-cox-business-wallst-cx_em_bw_1217ponzi.html?sh=7a62e782631317 M.R.S. § 108 (2017). https://legislature.maine.gov/statutes/17-A/title17-Asec108.html

MT Code §§ 45-3-102, 45-2-203 (2017) https://law.justia.com/codes/montana/2017/title-45/chapter-3/part-1/section-45-3-102/; https://law.justia.com/codes/montana/2017/title-45/chapter-2/part-2/section-45-2-203/

*NAACP v. Claiborne Hardware Co.*, 458 U.S. 886 (1982).

National Conference of State Legislators. (2020). *Self-defense and "stand your ground."* https://www.ncsl.org/research/civil-and-criminal-justice/self-defense-and-stand-your-ground.aspx

NE Code § 28-1409 (2021) https://law.justia.com/codes/nebraska/2021/chapter-28/statute-28-1409/

Nesterak, E. (2014, October 21). Coerced to confess: *The psychology of false confessions*. Behavioral Scientist. https://behavioralscientist.org/coerced-to-confess-the-psychology-of-false-confessions/

Neuman, S. (2020, June 4). *Medical examiner's autopsy reveals George Floyd had positive test for coronavirus*. NPR. https://www.npr.org/sections/live-updates-protests-for-racial-justice/2020/06/04/869278494/medical-examiners-autopsy-reveals-george-floyd-had-positive-test-for-coronavirus

NH Rev. Stat. § 626:3 (2020). https://law.justia.com/codes/new-hampshire/2020/title-lxii/title-626/section-626-3/

N.J. Rev. Stat. §§ 2C:11-3, 2C:11-4, 2C:15-1, 2C:35-10 (2021). https://law.justia.com/codes/new-jersey/2021/title-2c/section-2c-11-3/; https://law.justia.com/codes/new-jersey/2021/title-2c/section-2c-11-4/; https://law.justia.com/codes/new-jersey/2021/title-2c/section-2c-15-1/; https://law.justia.com/codes/new-jersey/2021/title-2c/section-2c-35-10/

NM Stat. §§ 30-9-2; 30-17-5 (2020). https://law.justia.com/codes/new-mexico/2020/chapter-30/article-9/section-30-9-2/; https://law.justia.com/codes/new-mexico/2020/chapter-30/article-17/section-30-17-5/

Nolasco, S. (2018, March 22). "Sopranos" actor Lillo Brancato talks getting sober after life in jail, returning to acting. *Fox News*. https://www.foxnews.com/entertainment/sopranos-actor-lillo-brancato-talks-getting-sober-after-life-in-jail-returning-to-acting

NRS 201.354, 201.358, 453.336 (2021) https://law.justia.com/codes/nevada/2021/chapter-201/statute-201-354/; https://law.justia.com/codes/nevada/2021/chapter-201/statute-201-358/; https://law.justia.com/codes/nevada/2021/chapter-453/statute-453-336/

N.Y. Penal Law §§ 20.10, 35.15, 110.0, 140.20, 160.05, 160.10, 160.15, 230.00 240.10 (2021). https://law.justia.com/codes/new-york/2021/pen/part-1/title-b/article-20/20-10/; https://law.justia.com/codes/new-york/2021/pen/part-1/title-c/article-35/35-05/; https://law.justia.com/codes/new-york/2021/pen/part-3/title-g/article-110/110-00/; https://law.justia.com/codes/new-york/2021/pen/part-3/title-i/article-140/140-20/; https://law.justia.com/codes/new-york/2021/pen/part-3/title-j/article-160/160-05/; https://law.justia.com/codes/new-york/2021/pen/part-3/title-j/article-160/160-10/; https://law.justia.com/codes/new-york/2021/pen/part-3/title-j/article-160/160-15/; https://law.justia.com/codes/new-york/2021/pen/part-3/title-m/article-230/230-00/; https://law.justia.com/codes/new-york/2021/pen/part-3/title-n/article-240/240-10/

O.C.G.A. §§ 16-5-21, 16-5-40, 16-5-41, 16-11-41 (2020). https://law.justia.com/codes/georgia/2020/title-16/chapter-5/article-2/section-16-5-21/; https://law.justia.com/codes/georgia/2020/title-16/chapter-5/article-3/section-16-5-40/; https://law.justia.com/codes/georgia/2020/title-16/chapter-5/article-3/section-16-5-41/; https://law.justia.com/codes/georgia/2020/title-16/chapter-11/article-2/section-16-11-41/

O'Leary, F. (2020, October 6). *Final moments: Killer dad Chris Watts reveals grisly details of pregnant wife's murder.* The U.S. Sun. https://www.the-sun.com/news/1590564/chris-watts-grisly-details-shannan-watts-murder-colorado/

OR. Rev. Stat. § 167.017 (2019). https://oregon.public.law/statutes/ors_167.017

18 Pa. Con. Stat. §§ 306(c), 306(g), 308, 901, 1102; 2502, 2503, 2701, 2702, 3102, 3121, 3122.1, 3125, 3701, 3903, 3927 (2020) https://law.justia.com/codes/pennsylvania/2020/title-18/chapter-3/section-306/; https://law.justia.com/codes/pennsylvania/2020/title-18/chapter-3/section-308/; https://law.justia.com/codes/pennsylvania/2020/title-18/chapter-9/section-901/; https://law.justia.com/codes/pennsylvania/2020/title-18/chapter-11/section-1102/; https://law.justia.com/codes/pennsylvania/2020/title-18/chapter-25/section-2502/; https://law.justia.com/codes/pennsylvania/2020/title-18/chapter-25/section-2503/; https://law.justia.com/codes/pennsylvania/2020/title-18/chapter-27/section-2701/; https://law.justia.com/codes/pennsylvania/2020/title-18/chapter-27/section-2702/; https://law.justia.com/codes/pennsylvania/2020/title-18/chapter-31/section-3102/; https://law.justia.com/codes/pennsylvania/2020/title-18/chapter-31/section-3121/; https://law.justia.com/codes/pennsylvania/2020/title-18/chapter-31/section-3122-1/; https://law.justia.com/codes/pennsylvania/2020/title-18/chapter-31/section-3125/; https://law.justia.com/codes/pennsylvania/2020/title-18/chapter-37/section-3701/; https://law.justia.com/codes/pennsylvania/2020/title-18/chapter-55/section-5505/ https://law.justia.com/codes/pennsylvania/2020/title-18/chapter-39/section-3903/ https://law.justia.com/codes/pennsylvania/2020/title-18/chapter-39/section-3927/

35 P.A. § 10231.303 (2016) https://casetext.com/statute/pennsylvania-statutes/statutes-unconsolidated/title-35-ps-health-and-safety/chapter-64-medical-marijuana-act/subchapter-3-program/section-10231303-lawful-use-of-medical-marijuana

42. Pa. C.S. § 5552 (2020). https://law.justia.com/codes/pennsylvania/2020/title-42/chapter-55/section-5552/

Pearson, M., & Valiente, A. (2017, January 5). *Lyle and Erik Menendez's cousin who testified about their sexual abuse speaks out for 1st time.* ABC News. https://abcnews.go.com/US/lyle-erik-menendezs-cousin-testified-sexual-abuse-speaks/story?id=44420173

*People v. Swanson-Birabent,* 114 Cal. App. 4th 733 (2003).

Peter, J. (2020, June 15). *Cashing in on George Floyd: T-shirts, pillows, running shoes and even underwear are being sold, some of it through Amazon.* USA Today. https://www.usatoday.com/story/money/2020/06/15/george-floyd-death-protests-lead-merchandise-sales-amazon/5337489002/

*Pinkerton v. United States,* 328 U.S. 640 (1946).

Pocklington, R. (2020, March 9). *Gabriel Fernandez pleaded for help 8 times and told teacher he was shot & punched.* The Sun. https://www.the-sun.com/news/510383/8-times-gabriel-fernandez-pleaded-for-help-from-telling-teacher-he-was-shot-punched-to-showing-guard-horror-injuries/

Prokop, J. (2021, August 27). *Bogdanov found guilty of murder in death of Nikki Kuhnhausen. The* Columbian. https://www.columbian.com/news/2021/aug/27/bogdanov-found-guilty-of-murder-in-death-of-nikki-kuhnhausen/

Pruitt, S. (2019, January 25). *Was Ted Bundy diagnosed with a mental illness?* Oxygen. https://www.oxygen.com/martinis-murder/was-ted-bundy-diagnosed-with-a-mental-illness-ted-bundy-manic-depressive

Quindlen, A. (1978, May 9). *Berkowitz pleads guilty to six "Son of Sam" killings.* The New York Times. https://www.nytimes.com/1978/05/09/archives/berkowitz-pleads-guilty-to-six-son-of-sam-killings-reference-to.html/

*R v. McNaughten* (1843) 8 E.R. 718.

*R.A.V. v. St. Paul*, 505 U.S. 377 (1992).

RCW §§ 9A.08.020, RCW 9A.88.030 (2005). https://law.justia.com/codes/washington/2005/title9a/9a.08.020.html; https://law.justia.com/codes/washington/2005/title9a/9a.88.030.html

Robinson, J. (2016, March 29). *Key O. J. Simpson witness reveals how those damning Mark Fuhrman tapes could have been destroyed.* Vanity Fair. https://www.vanityfair.com/hollywood/2016/03/people-v-oj-simpson-episode-9-fuhrman-tapes-laura-hart-mckinny-interview

*Robinson v. California*, 370 U.S. 660 (1962).

RSmo §§ 565.020, 565.021 (2021) https://law.justia.com/codes/missouri/2021/title-xxxviii/chapter-565/section-565-020/ https://law.justia.com/codes/missouri/2021/title-xxxviii/chapter-565/section-565-021/

Rumore, K. (2021, October 25). John Wayne Gacy: Timeline of the suburban Chicago serial killer's case and the efforts to recover, name his 33 victims. *Chicago Tribune.* https://www.chicagotribune.com/history/ct-john-wayne-gacy-timeline-htmlstory.html

Schemo, J. (1992, September 24). Amy Fisher pleads guilty to assault. The *New York Times.* https://www.nytimes.com/1992/09/24/nyregion/amy-fisher-pleads-guilty-to-assault.html

Schnuur, S. (2021, January 11). 25 years later, JonBenét Ramsey's dad is hopeful new documentary will "keep the case alive." *E! Online.* https://www.eonline.com/news/1226013/25-years-later-jonbenet-ramseys-dad-is-hopeful-new-documentary-will-keep-the-case-alive

Sederstrom, J. (2019, June 27). Daughter who was pulled into the family business robbing banks at 18 now wants fresh start. *Oxygen.* https://www.oxygen.com/crime-time/abby-catt-wants-fresh-start-after-joining-family-bank-robbery-business

Sepic, M. (2021, March 29). Televised Chauvin trial due to pandemic yields wide access—and concern. NPR. https://www.npr.org/sections/trial-over-killing-of-george-floyd/2021/03/29/982234571/televised-chauvin-trial-due-to-pandemic-yields-wide-access-and-concern

Shapiro, E. (2020, October 3). *25 years ago, OJ Simpson was found not guilty of double murder: The key moments in his life.* ABC News. https://abcnews.go.com/US/key-moments-oj-simpsons-life/story?id=48724637

Sheerin, J. (2018, October 26). *Matthew Shepard: The murder that changed America.* BBC. https://www.bbc.com/news/world-us-canada-45968606

*Sherman v. United States*, 356 U.S. 369 (1958).

Shiffer, E. (2019, July 9). *Michelle Carter's texts to Conrad Roy the day he committed suicide are devastating.* Women's Health. https://www.womenshealthmag.com/life/a28284327/michelle-carter-text-messages-conrad-roy/

Singleton, D., & Gentle, D. (2013, April 9). *Wolf pack's prey.* Daily News. https://www.nydailynews.com/services/female-jogger-death-savage-attack-roving-gang-article-1.1304506

Small, G. (2020, May 11). *"Subway Vigilante" Bernhard Goetz from "Trial by Media" was arrested again in 2013.* Bustle. https://www.bustle.com/entertainment/where-is-bernhard-goetz-now-the-trial-by-media-subject-still-lives-in-nyc-22885091

Smith, R. (2020, May 13). *The horrific true story of the "gay panic" talk show murder that shocked America.* PinkNews. https://www.pinknews.co.uk/2020/05/13/jenny-jones-show-gay-panic-murder-trial-by-media-netflix/

Sneed, M. (2021, October 29). *John Wayne Gacy story reaches out from the past again, with another victim identified.* Chicago Sun-Times. https://chicago.suntimes.com/2021/10/29/22753212/john-wayne-gacy-victim-identified-terry-sullivan-francis-wayne-alexander-crawlspace-killer-clown

Sokmensuer, H. (2019, February 25). *Man gets life for killing girlfriend's Munchausen mom after she "talked him into it" to stop abuse.* People. https://people.com/crime/gypsy-rose-blanchard-boyfriend-sentenced-life-in-prison/

*Sorrells v. United States*, 287 U.S. 435, 451 (1932).

Sorkin, D. (2014, June 23). *Donald Trump and the Central Park Five*. The New Yorker. https://www.newyorker.com/news/amy-davidson/donald-trump-and-the-central-park-five

Sorrentino, R., Musselman, M., & Broderick, L. (2019, July 24). *Battered woman syndrome: Is it enough for a not guilty by reason of insanity plea?* Psychiatric Times. https://www.psychiatrictimes.com/view/battered-woman-syndrome-it-enough-not-guilty-reason-insanity-plea

Srikanth, A. (2020, November 18). *Anti-trans hate crimes soar—and true numbers may be worse*. The Hill. https://thehill.com/changing-america/respect/equality/526609-anti-trans-hate-crimes-soar-and-true-numbers-may-be-worse

Staples, B. (2012, October 27). *When mass hysteria convicted 5 teenagers*. The New York Times. https://www.nytimes.com/2012/10/28/opinion/sunday/when-mass-hysteria-convicted-5-teenagers.html

*State v. Kelly*, 97 N.J. 178 (N.J. 1984).

*State v. Nations*, 764 F.2d 1073, 1080 (5th Cir. 1985).

*State v. Walden*, 306 N.C. 466, 293 (1982).

*State v. Yusuf*, 800 A.2d 590 (Conn. App. Ct. 2002)

Sterbenz, C. (2015, May 16). *Here's a surprising look at the average serial killer*. Insider. https://www.businessinsider.com/a-surprising-look-at-the-average-serial-killer-2015-5

Stockton, R. (2021, June 10). *How Aileen Wuornos became history's most terrifying female serial killer*. All That's Interesting. https://allthatsinteresting.com/aileen-wuornos

Stuelp, V. (2017, October 25). *Security guard called 911 about Palmdale boy abuse, was told case wasn't an emergency*. Eyewitness News. https://abc7.com/guard-called-911-about-palmdale-boy-was-told-it-wasnt-emergency/2563246/

Suddler, C. (2019, June 12). *How the Central Park Five expose the fundamental injustice in our legal system*. The Washington Post. https://www.washingtonpost.com/outlook/2019/06/12/how-central-park-five-expose-fundamental-injustice-our-legal-system/

Sylte, A. (2016, October 27). *Read the JonBenet Ramsey ransom note*. 9 News. https://www.9news.com/article/news/investigations/jonbenet-ramsey/read-the-jonbenet-ramsey-ransom-note/73-339934405

Tarmy, J. (2020, May 14). *A Netflix documentary series explores whether legal outcomes have any real connection to the court of public opinion*. Bloomberg. https://www.bloomberg.com/news/articles/2020-05-14/trial-by-media-review-court-tv-founder-investigates-his-role

Taylor, K. (2019, July 9). *What we know about the Michelle Carter suicide texting case*. The New York Times. https://www.nytimes.com/2019/07/09/us/michelle-carter-i-love-you-now-die.html

T.C.A. § 39-11-503 (2020). https://law.justia.com/codes/tennessee/2020/title-39/chapter-11/part-5/section-39-11-503/

*Tennessee v. Garner*, 471 U.S. 1 (1985)

Tex. Penal Code Ann. §§ 7.02(a)(2), 8.01, 8.06, 9.31, 15.01, 19.03, 29.02, 29.03 (1994). https://statutes.capitol.texas.gov/Docs/PE/htm/PE.7.htm; https://statutes.capitol.texas.gov/Docs/PE/htm/PE.9.htm; https://statutes.capitol.texas.gov/Docs/PE/htm/PE.15.htm; https://codes.findlaw.com/tx/penal-code/penal-sect-29-02.html; https://codes.findlaw.com/tx/penal-code/penal-sect-29-03.html https://statutes.capitol.texas.gov/Docs/PE/htm/PE.8.htm; https://statutes.capitol.texas.gov/Docs/PE/htm/PE.19.htm

*Texas v. Johnson*, 491 U.S. 397 (1989).

The Associated Press (2001, May 12). *Governor of Texas signs a hate crime bill*. New York Times. https://www.nytimes.com/2001/05/12/us/governor-of-texas-signs-a-hate-crimes-bill.html

Tron, G. (2019, May 14). *"I put my hands over my ears and then it all went quiet": Gypsy Rose describes mother's murder.* Oxygen. https://www.oxygen.com/martinis-murder/gypsy-rose-blanchard-describes-mother-dee-dee-blanchard-murder

Truesdall, J. (2021, August 30). *Man convicted of killing transgender teen after date in case that inspired mom to create change.* People. https://people.com/crime/washington-man-convicted-murdering-transgender-teen-after-date-case-inspired-mom-to-create-change/

*United States v. Bailey*, 444 U.S. 394 (1980)

*United States v. Bryan*, 591 F.2d 1161, 1163 (5th Cir. 1979)

*United States v. Johnson*, 872 F.2d 612, 620 (5th Cir. 1989)

*United States v. Michelson*, 559 F.2d 567, 569 (9th Cir. 1977)

*United States v. Nix*, 501 F.2d 516, 519 (7th Cir. 1974)

*United States v. Torres*, 604 F.3d 58 (2d Cir. 2010)

*United States v. Tran*, 568 F.3d 1156 (9th Cir. 2009)

7 U.S.C. § 2131 (1996). https://www.govinfo.gov/content/pkg/USCODE-2015-title7/html/USCODE-2015-title7-chap54.htm

15 U.S.C. § 78a (1934). https://www.law.cornell.edu/uscode/text/15/78a

16 U.S.C § 1531 (1970). https://www.fws.gov/endangered/esa-library/pdf/ESAall.pdf

16 U.S.C. §§ 3371–3378 (2003). https://www.animallaw.info/statute/us-lacey-act-chapter-53-control-illegally-taken-fish-and-wildlife

18 U.S.C § 17 (1984). https://www.law.cornell.edu/uscode/text/18/17

18 U.S.C. § 245 (1970). https://www.law.cornell.edu/uscode/text/18/245

18 U.S.C. § 249 (2009). https://www.justice.gov/crt/matthew-shepard-and-james-byrd-jr-hate-crimes-prevention-act-2009-0

18 U.S.C. § 373 (1984). https://www.law.cornell.edu/uscode/text/18/373

18 U.S.C. § 666(a)(1)(A) (2012). https://www.law.cornell.edu/uscode/text/18/666

18 U.S.C. §§ 1111 (2003), 1112 (2008) https://www.law.cornell.edu/uscode/text/18/1111; https://www.law.cornell.edu/uscode/text/18/1112

18 U.S.C. § 1591 (2018). https://www.law.cornell.edu/uscode/text/18/1591

18 U.S.C. §§ 1961–1968. https://www.law.cornell.edu/uscode/text/18/part-I/chapter-96

21 U.S.C. §§ 812 (2012), 841 (2018). https://www.law.cornell.edu/uscode/text/21/812; https://www.law.cornell.edu/uscode/text/21/841

42 U.S.C. § 2000 (1964). https://www.eeoc.gov/statutes/title-vii-civil-rights-act-1964

42 U.S.C. § 3631 (2012). https://www.law.cornell.edu/uscode/text/42/3631

52 U.S.C § 10101 (2015). https://www.govinfo.gov/app/details/USCODE-2014-title52/USCODE-2014-title52-subtitleI-chap101-sec10101/context

U.S. Const. amend. V. https://constitution.congress.gov/constitution/amendment-5/

U.S. Const. amend. XIV. https://constitution.congress.gov/browse/amendment-14/

U.S. Const. art. VI, clause 2. https://www.law.cornell.edu/wex/supremacy_clause

U.S. Department of Justice (2012, January). *An updated definition of rape.* https://www.justice.gov/archives/opa/blog/updated-definition-rape

Va. Code § 46.2-852 (2006). https://law.justia.com/codes/virginia/2006/toc4602000/46.2-852.html

Venkatraman, (2021, October 25). *Anti-Asian hate crimes rose 73% last year, updated FBI data says.* NBC News. https://www.nbcnews.com/news/asian-america/anti-asian-hate-crimes-rose-73-last-year-updated-fbi-data-says-rcna3741

Wade, B. (2021, August 10). *Why the sad tale of female serial killer Aileen Wuornos still shocks us.* Film Daily. https://filmdaily.co/obsessions/true-crime/aileen-wuornos-killer/

Walker, L. E. (2016). *The battered woman syndrome.* Springer Publishing Company.

Walsh, E. (1992, February 16). *Jury finds Dahmer was sane.* The Washington Post. https://www.washingtonpost.com/archive/politics/1992/02/16/jury-finds-dahmer-was-sane-7ba3ebb0-ec67-4e84-8e02-a75ee4da29bf/

Wikström, P. O. H. (2020). Explaining crime and criminal careers: The DEA model of situational action theory. *Journal of Developmental and Life-Course Criminology, 6*(2), 188–203.

Wiley, K. (2021, May 11). *Men plead not guilty to hate crimes in Ahmaud Arbery death.* News4Jax. https://www.news4jax.com/news/georgia/2021/05/11/men-who-chased-killed-ahmaud-arbery-due-in-federal-court/

Winter, T., Ortiz, E., & Fitzpatrick, S. (2021, December 30). *Ghislaine Maxwell convicted of federal sex trafficking charges for role in Jeffrey Epstein's abuses.* NBC News. https://www.nbcnews.com/news/us-news/ghislaine-maxwell-trial-verdict-reached-ghislaine-maxwell-sex-traffick-rcna9479

*Wisconsin v. Mitchell,* 508 U.S. 476 (1993)

Wis. Stat. §§ 971.15 (2013), § 939.48 (2014); 939.645 (2021). https://docs.legis.wisconsin.gov/statutes/statutes/971/15; https://docs.legis.wisconsin.gov/statutes/statutes/939/iv/645; https://docs.legis.wisconsin.gov/statutes/statutes/939/iii/48

Wright, W. (2021, February 26). *The true story of serial killer Aileen Wuornos.* Grunge. https://www.grunge.com/342800/the-true-story-of-serial-killer-aileen-wuornos/

WY Stat. § 7-11-304 (1997). https://law.justia.com/codes/wyoming/2011/title7/chapter11/section7-11-304/

Yan, H. (2015, July 8). *Bill Cosby's 'public moralist' stance backfired, led to document release.* CNN. https://www.cnn.com/2015/07/08/us/bill-cosby-sexual-assault-allegations/index.html.

Yang, A., Gowen, G., Taudte, J., Deutsch, G., & Lopez, E. (2019). *Timeline of many of Ted Bundy's brutal crimes.* ABC News. https://abcnews.go.com/US/timeline-ted-bundys-brutal-crimes/story?id=61077236

Yang, S., & Kay, G. (2021, April 14). *Bernie Madoff died in prison after carrying out the largest Ponzi scheme in history—here's how it worked. Insider.* https://www.businessinsider.com/how-bernie-madoffs-ponzi-scheme-worked-2014-7

Zacharin, J. (2020, July 16). *Why the Menendez brothers killed their parents—a look inside their murder case.* Biography. https://www.biography.com/news/menendez-brothers-murder-case-facts